DIMENSIONS OF W
MILITARY INTERVENTION

Books of Related Interest

Explaining NATO Enlargement
edited by Robert W. Rauchhaus

*Stability and Security in the Baltic Sea Region:
Russian, Nordic and European Aspects*
edited by Olaf F. Knudsen

NATO Enters the 21st Century
edited by Ted Galen Carpenter

*US National Defense for the Twenty-First Century:
And the Grand Exit Strategy*
by Edward Olsen

*International Security in a Global Age:
Securing the Twenty-First Century*
edited by Clive Jones and Caroline Kennedy-Pipe

Dilemmas of International Intervention
edited by Donald A. Sylvan and Michael Keren

DIMENSIONS OF WESTERN MILITARY INTERVENTION

Editors
COLIN McINNES and
NICHOLAS J. WHEELER
University of Wales, Aberystwyth

FRANK CASS
LONDON • PORTLAND, OR

First published in 2002 in Great Britain by
FRANK CASS PUBLISHERS
Crown House, 47 Chase Side,
Southgate, London N14 5BP, England

and in the United States of America by
FRANK CASS PUBLISHERS
c/o ISBS, 5824 N.E. Hassalo Street
Portland, Oregon 97213-3644

Website: www.frankcass.com

British Library Cataloguing in Publication Data

Dimensions of Western military intervention
  1. International relations 2. Intervention (International law)
  3. Humanitarian intervention 4. Europe – Politics and government
  – 1989– 5. United States – Politics and government – 1989–
  I. McInnes, Colin, 1960– II. Wheeler, Nicholas J.
  327.1'17

ISBN 0-7146-5276 8 (cloth)
ISBN 0-7146-8248 9 (paper)

Library of Congress Cataloging-in-Publication Data

Dimensions of Western military intervention / editors, Colin McInnes and
Nicholas J. Wheeler.
    p. cm.
Includes bibliographical references and index.
  ISBN 0-7146-5276-8 (hardback) — ISBN 0-7146-8248-9 (paperback)
  1. Intervention (International law) I. McInnes, Colin. II. Wheeler,
Nicholas J. III. Title.
  KZ6368 .D56 2002
  341.5'84—dc21
              2001007716

This group of studies first appeared as a special issue of *Contemporary Security Policy*,
ISSN 1352-3260, Vol.22, No.3 (December 2001) published by Frank Cass and Co. Ltd.

Printed in Great Britain by
Antony Rowe Ltd., Chippenham, Wilts

Contents

Preface   ix

Introduction: The Political and Moral Limits of
Western Military Intervention to Protect Civilians
in Danger   **Nicholas J. Wheeler**   1

Fatal Attraction? Air Power and the West   **Colin McInnes**   28

The RMA and Intervention: A Sceptical View   **Colin S. Gray**   52

Implications of the Weinberger Doctrine for
American Military Intervention in a Post-Desert
Storm Age   **Cori E. Dauber**   66

Missing the Story: The Media and the
Rwandan Genocide   **Linda Melvern**   91

The Doctrine Gap: The Enduring Problem of
Contemporary Peace Support Operations
Thinking   **Dominick Donald**   107

Fighting For Freetown: British Military
Intervention in Sierra Leone   **Paul Williams**   140

The Role of Monitoring and Verification   **Trevor Findlay**   169

Bosnia and Kosovo: Interpreting the Gender
Dimensions of International Intervention   **Jayne Rodgers**   183

Abstracts   196

Notes on Contributors   200

Index   201

Preface

This volume is the product of a series of meetings of the Security Research Group in the Department of International Politics at Aberystwyth. The meetings were held in 1999 and the first half of 2000 under successive convenors of the Group, Colin McInnes and Nicholas J. Wheeler, the editors of this volume. The programme culminated in a day-long seminar in May 2000, funded by the ESRC as part of its 'Politics of Emergencies' series. The editors would like to thank all members of the Security Research Group for their various contributions. In particular they would like to thank Eli Stamnes and Patricia Owens for their help in organizing the seminar, Jenny Edkins as convenor of the ESRC 'Politics of Emergencies' series, and Cliona Saidlear for her editorial assistance.

Introduction: The Political and Moral Limits of Western Military Intervention to Protect Civilians in Danger

NICHOLAS J. WHEELER[1]

The decade of the 1990s witnessed a fundamental transformation in the demands placed upon the United Nations' (UN) capacity to maintain international peace and security. The UN was set up in 1945 to manage inter-state violence on the model of the aggression of the Axis powers. But with the exception of the Chapter VII policing action against North Korea in 1950, and against Iraq in 1991, the UN Security Council has not mobilized its collective security powers under the UN Charter against this form of aggression. It might be argued that it should have done so to reverse Israel's illegal occupation of the West Bank and the Gaza Strip, or to evict Indonesia after its illegal annexation of East Timor in 1975. But in these cases, the patronage of the US protected Indonesia, and especially Israel, from any remedial UN action. But if inter-state violence was generally absent from the UN agenda during the Cold War, then the same could not be said of intra-state violence: the era of de-colonization in Africa and Asia ushered into existence newly independent states, many of which lacked any effective claim to political authority. As governments tried through a variety of rewards and punishments to foster a sense of national identity, legitimate political authority was frequently contested through violence. Ethnic and tribal groups resisted centralization and fought for greater autonomy, or even independent statehood. The Security Council's response to such conflicts was to argue that it had no mandate to intervene in the internal affairs of a Member State unless intervention was requested by it, or the parties to an internal armed conflict. Article 2(7) of the Charter served to protect even the most barbaric regime from external intervention. Thus, when thousands of Bengali civilians were slaughtered by Pakistani soldiers in 1971, the Council was united in arguing that whilst deplorable, this was a matter that fell within Pakistan's internal affairs.

The UN's position that it would only act if there was consent from the warring parties led it to create a new instrument of conflict management termed 'peacekeeping'. This was a third party military force comprising volunteer soldiers from Member States which would deploy under UN command with the consent of the belligerents. In addition to consent, the key characteristics of traditional peacekeeping were neutrality and the use of force only in self-defence. There was no question of UN forces imposing a peace on the parties. Peacekeeping was a brilliant doctrinal innovation of the then UN Secretary-General, Dag Hammarskjold, and Canadian Foreign Minister, Lester B. Pearson, to defuse the 1956 Suez crisis. Peacekeeping worked best where it could be insulated from superpower conflict, and after Suez there were successes in Cyprus and the Lebanon. But this fact limited its role because few conflicts could be de-coupled from the central geopolitical relationship in this way.

In most cases of intra-state violence, the normal response of Washington and Moscow was to pick sides, and arm their chosen ideological faction in the hope of bringing them to power. In the case of the Congo, the one instance where the US and Soviet Union initially agreed to pursue a concerted approach through the UN, the mission ended in disaster. In a salutary warning of what might lie ahead for the UN if it embarked on this kind of operation in the future, an 18,000-strong peacekeeping force was deployed in a political context where the consent of the Congolese parties could not be relied upon to hold. As the UN force in the Congo (known by its French initials ONUC) became embroiled ever deeper in the politics of the warring factions, the consent that it relied upon to operate broke down. Faced with this deteriorating situation, Hammarskjold took the fateful decision to break with the principles of traditional peacekeeping: he instructed the UN forces under his direct command to use force against those who were frustrating the implementation of ONUC's mandate. He could not carry the Security Council with him on this decision, and the fragile political consensus holding the operation together in New York collapsed. The force suffered mounting casualties as it tried to impose UN authority on the ground, and with its greatest supporter gone after Hammarskjold was killed in an air crash en route to the Congo, the UN ended its first disastrous experiment in peace enforcement.[2]

The importance of locating the contemporary debate over UN peace enforcement in this historical context is that it alerts us to the fact that the wars of the 1990s are not as new as is sometimes suggested. An identity-based politics in which civilians of one ethnic or minority group are the primary target of state authorities, or inter-ethnic violence, is not an arrival of the post-Cold War era.[3] What is new is the complete breakdown of traditional state structures, especially in sub-Saharan Africa. Where superpower patronage once propped up these failing states, the end of the Cold War has rendered many of these former prizes peripheral to the global political and economic map. These cases of state breakdown are labelled 'complex [humanitarian] emergencies' (CEs) and they exhibit some or all of the following characteristics: a collapse of the civil government; an absence of law and order; gross and systematic human rights abuses; massive violations of international humanitarian law; and private militias and factions controlling the means of violence.[4]

The other new element that moves in the opposite direction to the forces producing complex emergencies is the growing recognition that Article 2(7) can no longer serve as a barrier to international intervention. It is simply unthinkable today that the Security Council would define, as it did in the case of Pakistan's slaughter of the Bengalis in 1971, the mass killing of an ethnic minority as a matter falling within a state's 'domestic jurisdiction'. Instead, even states such as China, Russia, India, and the non-aligned group at the UN, are beginning to accept, however grudgingly, that there are limits to the exercise of sovereign rights: if a state breaches internationally agreed minimum standards of common humanity, there is growing acceptance of the notion that this justifies Security Council enforcement action under Chapter VII. During the 1990s, the language of a threat to 'international peace and security', the crucial enabling condition of UN enforcement action, was stretched from its traditional inter-state referent to encompass the protection of civilians.[5] Nevertheless, there are two crucial caveats. First, there is no case where the Security Council has expressly authorized the use of force against another sovereign state to defend humanitarian values (with the exception of the resolution authorizing a US-led force to restore the democratically elected government to power in Haiti).[6] Secondly, the developing normative consensus on UN intervention to protect civilians in danger does not extend to legitimating unilateral acts taken outside of Council authorization, as with NATO's intervention in Kosovo. The Milosevic regime's ethnic cleansing of the Kosovar

Albanians was condemned by the Council in three successive resolutions
adopted under Chapter VII of the Charter. However, NATO's efforts to
secure a UN mandate to back up its threats of force against the Federal
Republic of Yugoslavia (FRY) were derailed by Russia and China's
insistence that they would veto any resolution tabled by the Alliance.
They were not persuaded that NATO had exhausted all diplomatic
options, and Russia was particularly critical of what it viewed as NATO's
partisan support for the Kosovo Liberation Army (KLA).

Faced with an impasse in the Council, NATO decided to bypass its
authority to sanction the use of force. In justifying its unilateral action in
expressly humanitarian terms, NATO challenged existing norms on the
use of force. Given this, it is surprising to record that the Council did not
condemn the action, and a Russian draft resolution demanding a
cessation of the NATO air strikes was defeated by 12 votes to three.
NATO was quick to read into this vote collective legitimation of its
action, but the voting pattern has to be understood in the particular
context of the Kosovo case. The Council split three ways: firstly, there
was the minority (Russia, China and Namibia) who opposed the action
as a dangerous breach of the Charter's rules governing the use of force.
The worry here is that if individual states or groups of states are given
the right to decide when humanitarian intervention is given, this will
lead to the powerful imposing their values and interests on the weaker
states. From the point of view of states such as Russia, China and India,
it is the Security Council which must have the final authority on
determining when intervention should take place. Secondly, the four
non-aligned Muslim states were prepared in the exceptional moral
circumstances of the Kosovo case (one where memories of the
consequences for Muslims of the international inaction over Bosnia ran
deep among Muslim states) to tolerate or even excuse NATO's breach of
the rules of the Charter. But there was nothing in their public statements
in the Council to indicate that they welcomed NATO's action as setting
a precedent for a new norm of unilateral humanitarian intervention.
Finally, there were five NATO states that implicitly suggested that were
the same set of factors to arise again, they would be forced to act in a
similar way.[7]

The lesson that UN Secretary-General Kofi Annan and the Council
itself drew from the divisions over Kosovo was the importance of
maintaining the unity of the Council in future cases of humanitarian
disaster. This was reflected in the common position it took over the crisis

in East Timor, but this was an easier case for the UN to handle because President Habibie consented to the deployment of the UN-authorized Australian-led force. In the case of NATO's use of force against the Milosevic regime, there was no equivalent level of consent.

A key factor promoting the developing norm of Security Council action to prevent and stop gross and systematic human rights violations is the growth of an 'international community' that will not allow governments to ignore such violations. Governments are frequently reluctant to expend resources to end violence in areas of the world where they have peripheral interests. This reluctance stands in sharp contrast to the activities of the global human rights movement: through non-governmental organizations (NGOs) such as the Red Cross, Médecins sans Frontières and Oxfam, thousands of aid workers risk their lives every day helping to protect civilians trapped in war-torn societies. Speaking to the investigative journalist William Shawcross, the UN Secretary-General Kofi Annan defined the international community in terms of a 'public consensus ... to fight on matters of international concern', considering that leaders 'cannot ignore it'.[8] Annan readily acknowledged that a public opinion which is often guided by nothing deeper than the latest horror story on television is a fickle entity whose humanitarian gaze will always be a selective one. But without the relentless pressure of the world's media and public opinion, governments would find it easier to walk away from their commitments and responsibilities to the universally agreed standards enshrined in the UN Charter and international humanitarian law.

One leader who can argue with some justification to have responded to these humanitarian sentiments is the UK Prime Minister Tony Blair. His government, and especially his first Foreign Secretary, Robin Cook, championed the cause of elevating human rights concerns in the list of foreign policy priorities.[9] Yet within two years, New Labour confronted the fundamental question as to whether it should protect these values through the use of force. Defending his decision to go to war against the Federal Republic of Yugoslavia (FRY) to save Kosovar Albanians from Serbian repression, Blair argued in what has become known as his Chicago speech that: 'The most pressing foreign policy problem we face is to identify the circumstances in which we should get actively involved in other people's conflicts.'[10] In answering this question, he suggested five key tests that should inform ethical and strategic judgments. First, 'are we sure of our cause?'; second, have we exhausted all our diplomatic options?, third, are there military options we can sensibly and prudently undertake? Fourth, are we prepared for the long term? ... and finally, do we have national interests involved?' The Prime Minister argued that NATO's intervention in Kosovo met these five tests.[11] Even if there is agreement that this should be the framework for judging the legitimacy of military intervention, it still leaves open the question as to whether Blair was right to argue that Kosovo met these criteria.[12]

Two fundamental issues are eclipsed by Blair's criteria. First, he was silent on the question of whether Security Council authorization should be a vital prerequisite for military intervention. This issue created bitter divisions among the permanent members over Kosovo, and the question of what the UN should do if the Council is unable or unwilling to act in future emergencies continues to lack a satisfactory answer. The articles in this collection do not take a direct position on the issue of authorization, but several of the contributors raise issues that bear on this question. For example, the articles by Linda Melvern and Dominick Donald highlight the issue of whether the Rwandan genocide could have been prevented by using force in a preventive role. Even if the political will had existed in January 1994 to take enforcement action against the Hutu forces preparing the genocide, would the Council have authorized such an operation? Or would it have argued that there was insufficient evidence of genocide to justify a peace enforcement operation that risked UN soldiers and infringed Rwanda's sovereignty? And in the absence of UN authority, would any of the Western states capable of launching such an operation have embarked upon such an anticipatory intervention?

The second issue that Blair addresses only implicitly is whether the use of force is compatible with the protection of human rights. Even the most restrained use of force will involve harming enemy combatants, and crucially, the inadvertent killing of civilians. This leads Michael Ignatieff to ask: 'How can you have a human rights doctrine that puts the right to life at the centre of that doctrine but simultaneously legitimises violence to right human rights abuses either internally or externally?'[13] The pacifist answer to this question is that since violence always involves harming others, it cannot be justified. Others, not always pacifists, argue that using force to save strangers in peril should be avoided because it leads to a spiral of increasing violence and destructiveness. None of the articles that follow adopts either of these positions. Instead, what unites the authors is the conviction shared by Blair in his Chicago speech that whilst 'war is an imperfect instrument for righting humanitarian disasters',[14] it is sometimes the only means of ending terrible cruelty and suffering.

Some of the contributors are highly critical of the response of Western states and the UN to the humanitarian emergencies in Bosnia, Somalia and Rwanda: either for having unrealistic and dangerous moral ambitions, or for abdicating their global responsibilities to protect the victims of crimes against humanity. Others examine how the demand that interventions be casualty-free has structured where and how the West intervenes. Several of the articles shed important light on why the machinery of UN peacekeeping and enforcement failed to live up to expectations in the crises of the 1990s, and how this might be made to work better in future crises. Two of the contributors argue that the peace and security agenda has been defined too narrowly. The pursuit of human security on a global scale has to be located in the wider context of development issues and gender relations.

A common theme in the articles by Colin McInnes, Cori Dauber, Linda Melvern and Dominick Donald is the strong reluctance of Western governments and publics to place their soldiers in harm's way. In the opening article, Colin McInnes explores how this led to air power becoming the central instrument of Western military intervention in the 1990s. He argues that the new technology of precision-guided munitions has transformed the terms of the debate. Hitherto, the claims for air power have rested on its alleged strategic potential to break the enemy's will to resist by mass targeting of its civilian population: the bombing of Dresden, Hamburg and Tokyo are examples of this theory being put to the test in war. With the advent of precision weapons, air power can be used in a discriminating manner against strategic and tactical targets, and this opens up new possibilities for the coercive application of force that were not available to previous generations of air strategists. There are two aspects to this transformation of the nature of military intervention by the West. The first is that the precision allows the West to limit the harm it inflicts on civilians in the target state, so that the regime and its forces in the field become the target for air strikes. The requirement to avoid civilian casualties was a key element in the Kosovo campaign, and McInnes points out that certain key targets were not hit because of concerns about 'collateral damage'. Having justified the use of force on humanitarian grounds, it was incumbent upon the Alliance to ensure that its means of intervention were commensurate with this humanitarian goal. The second key point about the change in style of military intervention concerns the requirement of Western governments and publics to conduct casualty-free intervention, especially in cases where vital interests are not believed to be at stake. McInnes argues that the West is attracted to air power because against less technologically sophisticated rivals, it allows air crews to operate with minimal risk of being shot down or killed.

During 'Operation Allied Force', NATO pilots flew for 78 days against the Federal Republic of Yugoslavia (FRY) without one pilot being wounded or killed. McInnes quotes Eliot Cohen's quip that air power promises 'the fantasy of near bloodless use of force'.[15] Why is the West so preoccupied with not putting its forces in harm's way? The answer is that Western governments have been heavily influenced by the 'body bag' syndrome; the claim that Western publics are not prepared to accept the loss of members of the armed forces unless it is believed that vital national interests are at stake. McInnes argues that the 'body bag' problem is a lesson of Vietnam, and that it was reinforced by the loss of 239 US Marines in Lebanon in 1983, and by the loss of the 18 US Rangers in a Somali fire-fight in October 1993. This leads him to argue that this factor is a basic constraint on Western humanitarian interventions, considering that 'Those in the West may sympathise as they look on at those suffering, but they do not expect to suffer unduly themselves. Nor do they expect substantial numbers of their representatives in the armed forces to either.'[16] The great advantage of air power is that it enables the West to project power into theatres where it lacks the interests to sustain the costs of a protracted ground campaign.

McInnes is no ardent enthusiast for the new air power doctrine. He argues that a fundamental limitation revealed during Operation Allied Force is that it proved singularly ineffective in attacking the light infantry and militia forces carrying out ethnic cleansing in Kosovo. The irony of this is that the West's preferred military tool – air power – may do little directly to stop those acts which most concern the West.[17] In the case of Kosovo, NATO's response was to escalate by striking civilian targets in the FRY that were claimed to have military-related applications. Striking Serbian power plants, oil refineries, political targets and other infrastructural targets was highly controversial, raising concerns that NATO was allowing its preferred means of humanitarian intervention to undermine the Alliance's professed humanitarian ends.[18] McInnes does not enter into this controversy, but one can agree with

Adam Roberts that 'the disturbing lesson of the air campaign may be that its most effective aspect involved hurting Serbia proper (including its population and government) rather than directly attacking Serb forces in Kosovo and protecting the Kosovars'.[19]

In addition to his worries as to whether air power is an effective instrument of humanitarian rescue, McInnes argues that Milosevic was able to effectively counter Western superiority in air power by escalating the ethnic cleansing on the ground in Kosovo. His concern is that future enemies will employ such 'asymmetric strategies', perhaps including the use of weapons of mass destruction. On the other hand, he suggests that the knowledge that this would lead to massive Western retaliation should act as a deterrent to states employing such a strategy. A more pessimistic view of the dangers of this form of asymmetric warfare is proffered by Colin Gray in his contribution. Focusing on the information-led revolution in military affairs (RMA), Gray challenges its advocates who promise a new era in which Western states will be able to employ force with virtual impunity against the enemies of Western values. He identifies two fundamental objections: firstly, he argues that in their enthusiasm for the latest battle management technologies to lift the Clausewitzian 'fog of war', the exponents of the RMA have forgotten 'that frequently overlooked dimension of strategy, the enemy'.[20] Sun Tzu in his classic, *The Art of War*, stated that the iron law of strategy is to 'know thine enemy'. The US forgot this lesson to its great cost in Vietnam. The guerrilla forces of the North Vietnamese were able to avoid a decisive confrontation with US military prowess, and able to inflict sufficient casualties on American GIs that the US public lost the stomach for war. Similarly, it is foolish to expect future adversaries to play on ground where the West will be able to employ the 'speedy, precise use of information-led air power'.[21] Here, Gray worries that the spread of weapons of mass destruction will provide future enemies with the capacity to strike at the soft underbelly of liberal societies.

The second reason Gray cites as to why faith in the promise of the RMA is dangerously misplaced is that it overlooks how far future enemies are likely to enjoy a significant strategic advantage over their Western counterparts. At the heart of this concern is his fear that the West's strong desire to avoid casualties will leave it exposed to foes who 'are unlikely to be strongly casualty-averse'.[22] Consequently, he worries that the West will over-reach itself and pick a fight against an enemy that is able to employ asymmetric warfare in such a way as to impose devastating costs on Western societies.

The concern animating Gray's contribution is that the road to this military hell is being paved with the good intentions of interventions launched in the name of defending human rights. He reserves particular scorn for Robin Cook and Prime Minister Blair's humanitarian justifications for participating in NATO's use of force against the Federal Republic of Yugoslavia in March 1999. The belief that the costs of using force will be low (for the intervening side) is no reason for employing force when important interests are not at stake. Gray accepts that a doctrine of human rights interventionism will do 'little damage'[23] provided that 'Mr Cook is only a "cheap hawk" for doing good in the world'.[24] His worry is that if moral sentiment is allowed to become the driver of foreign policy, the West will be lulled into thinking that its technology can protect it from the human costs of war. He writes that 'the puffed up pride in moral judgment which produced the hubris which embroiled us foolishly in the Balkans in the 1990s may yet seduce us into much more perilous interventions'.[25]

The conviction that interests, not ethics, should be the key motivation behind Western intervention underpinned the doctrine enunciated in 1984 by then US Secretary of Defence, Caspar Weinberger. As Cori E. Dauber shows in her contribution, the doctrine continues to set the parameters governing the employment of US military forces. Indeed, given the close role played by Colin Powell (now Secretary of State) in drafting the document when working with Weinberger at the Pentagon, it is often referred to as the Weinberger–Powell doctrine. The cardinal tenets of this approach to US force employment are: (1) the existence of specific national interests; (2) the objective is to win; (3) clear political and military objectives; (4) an exit strategy; (5) overwhelming the enemy with superior firepower; (6) the support of the American people and Congress. Dauber argues that the primary function of the doctrine is to legitimate US actions, and that any President contemplating the use of force has to satisfy himself that he will be able to defend the action in terms of these publicly articulated criteria. And if missions cannot be defended in terms of these principles, then Congress and public opinion will not be prepared to support any casualties. As she puts it, 'if casualties are possible, but the rationale for support is something less than a vital national interest, then senior leadership will not believe that it will be possible to sustain support'.[26] President Clinton's decision to withdraw from Somalia after the loss of the 18 US Rangers in October 1993 is a classic example of an administration changing policy because of concerns about a backlash among public opinion. The intervention could not meet what Dauber calls 'the threshold test … of vital interest or of zero casualties'.[27]

The category of the national interest remains an elusive concept in both theory and practice. Realism tells us that statecraft should be guided by the compass of national interest, but realists can be found arguing different positions in particular cases. For example, Hans J. Morgenthau and Henry Kissinger disagreed over whether US national interests were engaged by the war in Vietnam. In the case of Kosovo, Kissinger lined up with Gray and those Congressmen cited by Dauber, who argued that the US had no national interests at stake in the Balkans. However, as Dauber shows, this interpretation was strongly contested by the President, who argued that the intra-state violence in Kosovo had the potential to escalate into a wider regional conflagration, and that preventing this was important to America's national interest.[28] To persuade public opinion that US national interests were engaged in the Balkans, Clinton invoked the analogies of US intervention in World War I and World War II, reminding his audience that had the US 'acted wisely and early enough, how many lives could have been saved, how many Americans would not have had to die'.[29] Clinton's national-interest-based justification for US intervention in Kosovo did not satisfy critics like Kissinger, but it struck a responsive chord among US public opinion. By appealing primarily to the national interest, Clinton showed that he appreciated the constraints established by the Weinberger–Powell doctrine. But in defining the national interest as requiring the ending of ethnic cleansing in Kosovo, the President stretched the doctrine to justify actions that were not previously legitimated under it.

The controversy in the US public debate over whether Kosovo satisfied the national interest requirement did not get out of hand because everyone could unite around the imperative that the operation be casualty-free. Clinton announced from the outset of the operation that the administration was not planning a ground invasion of Kosovo, and this ensured that public support for 'Operation Allied Force' remained high. Indeed, when respondents were asked whether they would support the war if it required the deployment of US ground forces, public support sharply declined.[30] Imagine, then, a case where there was no interest-based justification, and a strong conviction on the part of the political authorities that intervention would lead to

significant casualties. This is the story of the US response to the
Rwandan genocide in 1994.

During the 2000 US election campaign, as Dauber notes, the leading
contenders for the presidency both agreed that the Clinton
administration was right not to have intervened because no US national
interests were at stake. A very different judgment on US action was
offered by Clinton when he visited Rwanda for the first time in 1998. He
apologized to the people of Rwanda for the world's failure to stop the
genocide, and argued that the lesson of Rwanda was that 'each
bloodletting hastens the next, and as the value of human life is degraded
and violence becomes tolerated, the unimaginable becomes more
conceivable'.[31] Although the President did not put it in these terms, he
could be interpreted as saying that the global interest in preventing and
stopping genocide is also a US national interest. Far from human rights
protection being in Colin Gray's words a 'third or even fourth order
interest',[32] it was in the US's interest to defend justice in Rwanda because
to do otherwise risked creating a contagion that would eventually come
to undermine the values that Americans cherish.

It is fascinating to speculate whether Clinton would have acted
differently had the Rwandan genocide been his first test in Africa. As it
was, the administration was haunted by the ghost of Somalia and the loss
of the 18 Rangers. It was the fear of more 'body bags' that inhibited
Clinton from taking the lead to stop the genocide. The President should
have argued that whatever the mistakes made in Somalia, this was no
excuse for not sending American soldiers to risk their lives to end the
20th century's third genocide (the other two being the extermination of
the Armenians in 1916 and the Jews during World War II). As Dauber
shows, Clinton would have encountered domestic opposition, but it is
the responsibility of presidents to lead public opinion in such cases.
Instead of accepting the core premise of the US political discourse over
Rwanda that national interests and human rights were opposed values,
the President should have pressed the claim that the US had both an
interest and a moral responsibility to end the genocide.

In the absence of presidential leadership, the best hope lay in the
media mobilizing public opinion to produce a change in policy. The
failure of the Western television and print-based media to rise to this
moral challenge is well documented by Linda Melvern in her
contribution, which all too vividly recounts the horrors of the Rwandan
genocide. She charges the media with complicity due to their

representation of the killings. Instead of identifying the killings as the result of a planned and well-organized campaign of extermination against the Tutsis, most journalists interpreted the violence as the latest bloody chapter in an age-old ethnic conflict between the Hutus and Tutsis. As a result, the option of military intervention was presented in terms of ending a civil war, a proposal for which little enthusiasm could be expected among Western publics.

In terms of allocating responsibility for the genocide, Melvern is also highly critical of the role played by UN officials. A key moment here concerns the response of members of the Department of Peacekeeping Operations (DPKO) to the UN Force Commander in Rwanda's cable of 11 January warning that preparations for killing Tutsis were being set in motion by Hutu extremists. General Dallaire informed New York that he planned to seize weapons stockpiled by the Hutu militias. He was instructed in a cable from DPKO that this course of action was not acceptable, and to report the matter to the Belgian, French and US embassies, before taking up the issue with the Rwandan government. DPKO's position was that any searches would have to be undertaken in support of action taken by the gendarmerie and army. Since the Hutu extremists inside the government controlled the security services, no effective action could be taken against the militias.[33] When asked to justify this decision on BBC's *Panorama* programme in December 1998, Iqbal Riza, an Assistant Secretary-General in DPKO (now serving as Kofi Annan's Chef de Cabinet), stated that, although the warning from Dallaire was 'alarming', the DPKO view was 'not Somalia again'.[34] What Riza did not elaborate was that the UN Secretary-General, Boutros Boutros-Ghali, was particularly wary of involving the UN in disarmament again, given that he was personally associated with pushing for disarmament in Somalia with such disastrous results.[35]

After the genocide had started on 7 April 1994, General Dallaire asked for reinforcements to protect civilians in Kigali. In a letter to President Clinton dated 13 May 1994, senators Paul Simon and James Jeffords of the Senate Committee on Foreign Relations cite the UN force commander as believing that a force of '5,000 to 8,000 troops ... [could] stop the senseless slaughter...[and]...effectively achieve the desired result'.[36] By the time the senators were writing to Clinton, stopping the genocide would have required a much larger force since it had spread to the countryside by mid-May. However, Dallaire's request for a force of five to eight thousand was made around mid-April, and a report four years later by Scot Feil based on the assessments of a panel of experts concluded that: a force of 5,000 operating with air support, logistics and effective command and control, and deployed with a Chapter VII mandate, 'could have averted the slaughter of a half-million people'.[37] The report concluded that 'US participation would have been essential – to lead in supplying resources, carrying out critical functions, and achieving mission goals'.[38]

Melvern criticizes UN officials for failing to bring Dallaire's request for reinforcements and a change of mandate before the Security Council. The options presented to the Council by the Secretariat were to reduce the force to a token presence, withdraw it totally, or massively reinforce it so that it could end the violence. By representing the violence as a tribal conflict, the reinforcement option was framed in terms of an intervention to stop the warring parties. Dallaire, of course, had never presented the issue in these terms, and this invites the question why the intervention option was not framed in terms of protecting civilians in Kigali. In her compelling book-length study of the genocide, Melvern points out that the Permanent Representative for Nigeria, Ambassador Gambari, had argued in the informal Security Council discussions that none of the proposed options would protect the several thousand Rwandan civilians sheltering under UN protection, or those that were desperately in need of such rescue.[39] Protecting civilians required responding positively to Dallaire's request for reinforcements, but no state came forward with offers of troops in those crucial weeks in April, including Nigeria. The latter was prepared to speak behind closed doors in support of intervention, but it did not accompany this with any offer of additional forces for the United Nations Assistance Force in Rwanda (UNAMIR). The Secretariat is responsible for not properly briefing the Security Council about Dallaire's cables in January and April. But even if Council members had been fully aware of these, it is by no means clear that states would have volunteered the forces for enforcement action against the Hutu extremists. Once the Belgian contingent had been withdrawn after the killing of ten of their peacekeepers on 7 April, the UNAMIR force began to disintegrate. The United Kingdom's Permanent Representative, Sir David Hannay, reflected five years later that 'the situation the Security Council was facing … was the complete collapse of the peacekeeping force; it wasn't the Council that cut it back, they marched with their feet'.[40]

What emerges from Melvern's analysis is a strong faith in the moral convictions of ordinary men and women. She believes that if only the media and UN officials had named the violence as a genocide and not a tribal war, public opinion would have supported risking soldiers' lives to save Rwandans. Even if this judgment is accurate, she underestimates the fickle character of public opinion: it was media representation of starving Somalis on US television networks that pushed Bush into launching 'Operation Restore Hope'. And it was the same networks carrying pictures of Somalis dragging a dead and mutilated American through the streets of Mogadishu that ended the mission. Would public opinion in Western states have supported intervention in Rwanda once the 'body bags' began arriving home? Reflecting in 1999 on the international response to the genocide, Kofi Annan, who had been head of DPKO during the genocide, stated:

> In the case of Rwanda, what was missing was the political willingness to use force in response to genocide. The key factors here were the reluctance of Member States to place their forces in harm's way in a conflict where no perceived vital interests were at stake, a concern over cost, and doubts – in the wake of Somalia – that intervention could succeed.[41]

In the first week of September 1999, the UN was confronted with a new challenge to its authority that raised the question once again of whether it could muster the political will to use force to stop massive and systematic violations of human rights. Pro-Indonesian militias were inflicting terror on East Timorese civilians who had just voted overwhelmingly for independence in a referendum organized by the UN. The problem was that the UN had no armed presence on the island, and so its election monitors had no effective means to combat the violence. Indonesia had consented to the referendum, but it would not accept any armed peacekeeping mission to oversee the election. Consequently, when the result went against the expectations and wishes of the pro-Jakarta forces on the island, they responded by engaging in looting and violence that led to hundreds being killed and tens of thousands being driven from their homes. President Habibie ordered Indonesian army units on the island to maintain order, but they stood by and let the militias run amok.

Faced with the mounting violence, the Security Council sent a mission to the island. The horrors that greeted the ambassadors had a shocking effect on them, and the United Kingdom's Permanent Representative, Sir Jeremy Greenstock, publicly described the level of human suffering in the East Timorese capital as a 'living hell'.[42] There was growing international pressure on the Indonesian government to stop the massacres and forced population expulsions. The Australian government, under considerable domestic political pressure to stop the atrocities, offered to lead a multinational force to end the violence. The Liberal government of John Howard established two key pre-conditions: first, there must be a Chapter VII resolution authorizing the use of force, and secondly, the Indonesian government must consent to the action. There was a general determination that East Timor would not be the next Rwanda or Srebrenica. According to William Shawcross, the US Permanent Representative, Richard Holbrooke, telephoned Annan to express his worries that a failure to contain the crisis could lead to the spread of violence to other parts of Indonesia, producing a humanitarian and security crisis on the scale of the Balkans.[43] In contrast to the UN's failure to mobilize effective pressure against the Rwandan government in response to Dallaire's cable of January 1994, enormous pressure was mobilized to secure Indonesia's consent to the Australian-led intervention force.

The Secretary-General was constantly on the phone to Habibie to coax him into accepting the UN's help.[44] This moral persuasion was reinforced by a Security Council debate over the weekend of 9–11 September that involved 51 states and called for Indonesia to restore law and order to East Timor. Kofi Annan ratcheted up the pressure on 10 September by going public with a statement that Indonesia had proved unable to protect the security of the people of East Timor, and 'the time has clearly come for [it] to seek help from the international community'.[45] Again in stark contrast to the case of Rwanda, the Western-dominated global media also played a key role in bringing pressure to bear on Habibie. According to Penny Wensley, the Australian Permanent Representative, in the days leading up to the Security Council debate, 'international media coverage of the events in East Timor had reached a crescendo'.[46] In addition to the considerable moral pressure that was exerted on the Indonesian government, coercion was also applied. The US, Japan and other Western states threatened to withdraw IMF and World Bank credits and this had a sobering effect in Jakarta. Indonesia had been badly damaged by the 1997 Asian financial crash, and it was particularly vulnerable to the application of this kind of economic pressure. Faced with being an international pariah cut off from the world's financial markets, the Indonesian president reluctantly agreed to the deployment of an intervention force for East Timor (Interfet). This consent was crucial to the passing of Resolution 1264, which provided UN authorization for the operation.

In one sense Interfet confirms the wisdom of the consent-based model of intervention. Given the overwhelming strength of Indonesia's armed forces, Australian political and military leaders would have been reckless to launch an opposed landing of the island. The cardinal test any intervention must satisfy is that it must do more good than harm, and it must not result in a failure that costs large numbers of lives of the intervening force: an intervention to save East Timor that was opposed by the Indonesian army would have failed this test. Viewed from a different vantage point, the Australian-led intervention operated in the 'grey area' between traditional peacekeeping and enforcement action. There are two aspects that are important here: firstly, the pro-independence militias had not consented to 'Operation Stabilize', and secondly, whilst Habibie had given assurances that the Indonesian army would not oppose Interfet, the Howard government could not be confident that the army would follow the president's instructions.[47] Indeed, a survey of the Australian press at the time shows that many commentators worried that Australian forces would find themselves in fire fights with the Indonesian armed forces. As it turned out, the army provided assistance to Interfet in its mission of restoring peace and security, and delivering humanitarian assistance, and there were few clashes with the militias.

Dominick Donald, a former army officer, argues in his contribution that Western militaries lack a robust doctrine for operating in the grey area, and that this has severely impaired UN operations in the post-Cold War era. Focusing on the evolution in British, French and US doctrine, he charts how their experiences in Bosnia and Somalia led to new doctrinal innovations, especially in the case of the United Kingdom. Traditionally, as Donald shows, peacekeeping had been defined in terms of consent at the strategic, operational and tactical levels, but the *Wider Peacekeeping* doctrine developed by the British Army views consent as a dynamic element operating at multiple levels. The crucial development was the contention that consent could be lost at the tactical level without this jeopardizing consent at the operational level.[48] As Donald contends, 'this meant that the pivotal factor in the use of force in peacekeeping was how it was perceived'.[49] Thus, force used against renegade elements with the general consent of faction leaders need not undermine consent, but the general use of force against one party alleged to be in breach of agreements would cross the Rubicon separating 'wider peacekeeping' from warfighting operations. It was this model of consent from which the UN had departed with such disastrous results in Somalia. US Quick Reaction Forces operating under the flag of UNOSOM II, engaged in a witch-hunt for General Aideed (in response to the latter's complicity in the killing of 24 Pakistani peacekeepers on 5 June 1993) which was so indiscriminate in its use of force that 1,500 civilians were killed and 6,000–8,000 wounded. The response of Aideed's forces was to begin killing American soldiers as the UN found itself crossing what Sir Michael Rose later dubbed the 'Mogadishu line' between peacekeeping and war.

To try and avoid the errors of UNOSOM II in Somalia, British doctrine writers have begun to distinguish between peace enforcement operations and traditional warfighting such as the Gulf War. *Joint Warfare Publication 3-50 Peace Support Operations* defines peace enforcement as 'coercive operations required in the absence of consent, or at least in the expectation of one, or all, of the parties failing to comply with agreed conditions'.[50] Donald argues that consent separates 'Peacekeeping' (PK), relying on consent promoting techniques and the use of force only in self-defence from 'peace enforcement' (PE), which couples enforcement and consent techniques with a combat prepared force. He goes on to say that impartiality separates PE from war – 'which involves combat forces, warfighting techniques, and a designated enemy'.[51] Traditional peacekeeping defined impartiality in terms of equal treatment of the parties (this is also referred to as neutrality). Donald supports the doctrinal shift in the 1990s to explicitly separate out impartiality and neutrality. Impartiality is now defined in active terms whereas the traditional notion of impartiality/neutrality was a passive one. If one party or parties are in breach of existing agreements, then a force can still be acting impartially if it employs force against those violating the mandate. Effective peace enforcement in such cases depends upon deploying a robust combat capability. But as Donald shows with reference to the disasters in Rwanda and Srebrenica, the problem arises when consent is nonexistent, or breaking down, at the operational level, but strategic level responses inhibit an effective response because of fears that this will lead to an escalation of the violence. For all its imaginative doctrinal innovation, JWP 3-50 leaves what Donald calls 'a substantial lingering grey area – the quarter of the

quadrant where there is insufficient consent for PK yet insufficient
combat capability for PE'.[52] JWP 3-50's injunction to commanders is
that 'this quadrant should be avoided'.[53] Due to lack of reinforcements
and a change of mandate, this is exactly the quadrant that UNAMIR
found itself in during the Rwandan genocide of 1994.

Avoiding this quadrant in future UN operations is a key conclusion
of the report prepared by the panel on future UN peace operations
chaired by Lakhdar Brahimi. The panel's report argued for a definition
of impartiality that encompassed the use of force against parties that
breach existing agreements, considering in a crucial paragraph that

> continued equal treatment of all parties by the United Nations can
> in the best case result in ineffectiveness and in the worst may
> amount to complicity with evil. No failure did more to damage the
> standing and credibility of United Nations peacekeeping in the
> 1990s than its reluctance to distinguish victim from aggressor.[54]

The problem is that the important recommendations made in the
report for improving UN early warning and rapid response capabilities
do not address the fundamental issue that Annan highlighted about the
lack of 'political willingness' to use force in situations where no vital
interests are at stake and there is a significant risk of casualties. The
Interfet operation should perhaps lead us to qualify this verdict, given
that the Howard government knew there was a risk of Australian soldiers
returning in body bags. On the other hand, Donald argues that the
Australian military were preoccupied with force protection, and that this
was detrimental to the humanitarian mission. He writes that 'Australian
troops followed the US emphasis on force protection, moving only in
platoon-sized groups, and refusing to patrol outside Dili until they had
established an extremely secure base'.[55] In highlighting the issue of force
protection in contemporary operations, Donald's analysis points to a
fundamental mismatch between the growing doctrinal emphasis on PE
and the demands of force protection. Operating without consent at the
strategic and/or operational level requires forces that are prepared to
incur casualties. How can this be reconciled with NATO's recent
doctrinal injunction that domestic publics in member states expect
intervention to 'involve minimum cost in ... human life ... above all else
the lives of their national contingents'?[56]

The perennial gap between UN mandates and the means to back
them up is illustrated yet again by the fate of the UN mission that was

deployed in Sierra Leone in late 1999. As Paul Williams shows in his contribution, the Lomé Accord that ended the conflict between the government of President Kabbah and the forces of the Revolutionary United Front (RUF) was morally flawed. Despite being responsible for terrible atrocities committed against the civilian population, Foday Sankoh was given an amnesty and a ministerial position that left him in control of the diamond-producing areas of the country. The reason for this perverse outcome is that there was no effective military force on the ground that could defeat the RUF, and no political will to deploy one on the part of those states that had the resources and capability to do so. Instead, the UN found itself deploying a traditional PK force (UNAMSIL) to monitor the Lomé Accord.

No sooner was the ink dry on the agreement than the RUF began defecting from it. The rebels refused to disarm and hand over their areas of control to the 6,000-strong UN force. And the RUF showed its contempt of the UN by seizing 500 of its troops as hostages, and by marching on the capital Freetown. Once again, the UN found itself drifting hopelessly into the 'no go' quadrant in JWP 3-50: insufficient consent for peacekeeping, but not enough combat capability for peace enforcement. Annan called for a rapid reinforcement of UNAMSIL, but this plea fell on deaf ears. In what Shawcross calls 'a surprising and welcome development',[57] the Blair government decided to intervene, but not as part of UNAMSIL.

According to Williams, there were five imperatives that led the British government to launch 'Operation Palliser' in May 2000: the rescue of nationals; the humanitarian impulse to save strangers; the defence of democracy; living up to its claim to put ethics at the heart of foreign policy; and supporting the credibility of future UN peacekeeping in Africa. He notes that this last rationale did not figure prominently in public justifications, a reflection of the UK decision to operate independently but in co-operation with UNAMSIL. He suggests that this reflected concerns about 'the operational efficiency and calibre'[58] of the UN force. Domestic critics of the intervention ask what interests Britain has at stake in a small West African state that few British people could identify on a map, let alone care enough about to risk the lives of the armed forces. But worries about adverse public reaction to possible casualties did not deter the government, which led public opinion over Sierra Leone. To those who castigate his government for not following the national interest in sending forces to

Sierra Leone, the Prime Minister would reply that national interest is not a fixed category, and that changing values constitute new interests. He articulated this position in his Chicago speech:

> No longer is our existence as states under threat. Now our actions are guided by a more subtle blend of mutual self-interest and moral purpose in defending the values we cherish. In the end values and interests merge. If we can establish and spread the values of liberty, the rule of law, human rights and an open society then that is in our national interests too.[59]

In standing up for these values, the Labour government has shown that it is prepared to make sacrifices. Operation Palliser was not without its human costs. On 25 August 2000, a group within the RUF known as the 'West Side Boys' took 12 British soldiers hostage and after failed attempts to secure their release, a rescue mission was launched on 10 September that led to one British soldier being killed and several others seriously injured. Williams praises the Blair government for not losing its nerve and abandoning Sierra Leone: he considers that 'Such a withdrawal would have been foolish, for it would have signalled to the world that the British army is as casualty-shy as its US counterpart and would simply encourage groups in other parts of the world to ensure they surpass the necessary casualty threshold'.[60] His contention that ministers and the public are not imprisoned by the 'body bag' syndrome raises the question of how far the aversion to taking casualties in such operations is particular to a US polity and society still living with the trauma of Vietnam.

Williams sees the use of force as a necessary tool of crisis management in complex humanitarian emergencies, but his deeper concern is that we recognize the underlying causes of these humanitarian disasters. He argues that it is global economic dependency, poverty, social exclusion and a patrimonial power structure that explains why the unemployed and disaffected youth of Sierra Leone was prepared to express its political grievances by killing and mutilating civilians. He is keen to point out that military intervention has been only one aspect of New Labour's engagement with the crisis, and that it deserves praise for its economic assistance, efforts to train an effective and disciplined army, and support of a truth commission. Where Williams is highly critical of New Labour is in its failure to effectively address global economic inequalities which he sees as the root cause of violent conflict in Africa. He concludes that 'Britain and the rest of the G-8 need to seriously consider how the global economy they manage increases the likelihood of violence in countries peripheral to their interests'.[61] This is a concern shared by Kofi Annan, who argues that the key to developing a global culture of conflict prevention is 'healthy and balanced development'.[62] This echoes the vision of the founders of the UN that the organization would help create a world free from the threat of fear and poverty. The West, with its power and privileged position, is in the best position to help the UN realize both of these global ambitions, but what has been lacking on the part of Western societies is a sustained moral commitment to global justice.

Building a global culture of non-violent conflict prevention is a fundamental priority, but this should not drive out efforts to ensure that future peace agreements do not break down as happened with the Lomé and Arusha Accords. In developing the UN's capacity for crisis management, Trevor Findlay, in his contribution, argues that more emphasis should be placed on the monitoring and verification of peace agreements. He defines the latter as 'the process by which compliance with an agreement is determined', and such a determination depends upon monitoring which is 'essentially the technical process of collecting information'.[63] Effective verification increases the risks and costs of defection; helps provide the parties with the reassurance that others are not cheating; provides early warning to counter any defections; and provides legitimacy for any coercive sanctions, including military action, that might be directed unilaterally or multilaterally against the parties. Findlay gives several examples of successful monitoring and verification, including the pressure that was mobilized against Thailand for its violation of the arms embargo imposed on the parties to the Cambodian conflict. He also shows how verification was crucial in dispelling the Khmer Rouge's claims that not all the Vietnamese forces had left Cambodia as required under the accords. Such successes presuppose a measure of commitment to a peace process by the parties, or at least a situation where 'a mix of incentives and disincentives'[64] can cajole them into accepting the terms of the agreement. Crucially, it also depends upon a willingness by states and the UN to react effectively to defections.

A good example of this failure to react concerns the UN mission in Cambodia. As Donald points out, UN authority was challenged when the Khmer Rouge attacked a convoy of the United Nations Transitional Authority to Cambodia (UNTAC) carrying civilian police that was being escorted by a Dutch armed escort. One Japanese policeman was killed and five Dutch soldiers were seriously wounded, but there was no effective response from UNTAC. Indeed, he argues that this encouraged the Khmer Rouge to believe that UNTAC was weak, effectively ending the Dutch battalion's 'aggressive disarmament programme in the Khmer Rouge's stronghold province'.[65]

A key role for future verification missions highlighted by Findlay concerns the deployment of UN monitors to ensure that regional peacekeeping operations fulfil their mandate. He gives the example of the UN Observer Mission (UNOMIL) which observed the actions of the ceasefire monitoring group (ECOMOG) established by the Economic Community of West African States (ECOWAS) that intervened to restore peace and security in Liberia in late 1990. This Nigerian-led force was not expressly authorized by the Security Council, and the establishment of a small UN monitoring mission enabled the Council to exercise some oversight of the ECOMOG operation. Indeed, the Council was sufficiently satisfied with the conduct of the operation two years after its commencement to give it a measure of retrospective authorization in Resolutions 788 and 866.[66] However, there were several incidents involving ECOMOG forces that raised questions as to whether the force was employing means that were commensurate with its humanitarian ends. One example is Nigeria's decision to attack Charles Taylor's faction in Monrovia by using air power to bomb the capital. In using force, ECOMOG certainly did harm. Nevertheless, this has to be weighed against the lives that would have been lost by a policy of non-intervention, and the good the intervention produced in terms of ending the civil war inside Liberia.

The question of how to choose between conflicting moral considerations is taken up by Jayne Rodgers in the final contribution. Rodgers opens up the missing dimension of gender in the discourse on intervention, and in so doing, reveals its moral ambiguities. Building on her earlier work on Bosnia, she explores the tensions that NATO's intervention in Kosovo creates for feminists committed to a universalism that is sensitive to the cultural particularities of local communities. She accepts the claim that NATO's action signalled a major shift in attitudes on the question of whether state sovereignty could be breached in defence of the principles of international humanitarian law. But her contention is that this shift does not extend to a recognition on the part of a masculinized international community that rape in war should be a legitimate criterion for intervention. Rogers would welcome such a development at the universal level, but at the same time, she is profoundly ambiguous about the consequences of such a move when consideration is given to how this would play out at the local level.

The problem Rodgers identifies is that the international legal framework 'within which such acts are prosecuted ... places the responsibility for dealing with the issue of rape squarely on the shoulders of women: provide testimony and (possibly) achieve justice'.[67] The moral dilemma that this generates for the victims of sexual violence is graphically illustrated by Rodgers when she turns to the case of Albanian women in Kosovo. NATO's intervention in Kosovo has opened up a space for the victims of rape to witness the violence inflicted upon them by Serbian males. But Rodgers argues that expecting women to provide such testimony ignores the local contexts of gender and nationalism within which women's identities are constituted. If Albanian women claim their universal human rights as victims of sexual violence, then they will undermine the patriarchal system. For some feminists this is the very stuff of resistance to dominant power structures that are oppressive and violent, but Rodgers wants to alert us to the moral consequences that flow from such resistance. She writes that for those who choose to exercise their universal human rights, there is 'the risk of divorce or exclusion from their community or family, and many others ... never discuss what has happened to them in order to protect themselves and their families'.[68] Rodgers' torment as a feminist struggling with conflicting ethical claims comes out strongly in her contribution. She concludes that 'feminists need to decide whether they wish to defend a broad conceptualisation of women's human rights or to accept that some cultural contexts will fall outside of Western feminist ideas on fairness and justice'.[69]

The agonizing clash that Rogers draws out so well, between human rights as a universal value and local cultural values, could be enlarged to encompass the fundamental moral issues raised by this collection: which agents – local, national, regional or global – have the responsibility to protect the victims of global human wrongs? Western governments have ensured through their limited aid budgets and contributions to the UN that the victims of war, famine and poverty do not entirely drop off the map of moral concern. But the reluctance of these governments to give the UN the human and material resources to deploy robust peace enforcement forces; to risk soldiers' lives for anything other than vital interests; or to seriously address how the growing global inequalities between rich and poor create humanitarian crises in the poorest states, is symptomatic of a lack of moral engagement with the suffering of others. The supreme challenge that confronts leaders and citizens committed to an ethic of common humanity is to persuade Western publics that they have a moral obligation, seconded by national interest, to make the necessary sacrifices to protect civilians in peril.

NOTES

1. I would like to thank Anne Harris and Colin McInnes for comments on an earlier version of this introduction.
2. For an authoritative history of the UN intervention in the Congo see Brian Urqhart, *Hammarskjold* (London: The Bodley Head, 1973), pp.389–429.
3. This is the thesis of Mary Kaldor. See her *New and Old Wars: Organized Violence in a Global Era* (Cambridge: Polity Press, 1999).
4. For a good analysis of the challenge posed by CEs, see the Ministry of Defence's *Peace Support Operations Joint Warfare Publication* (JWP 3-50), para 205.
5. For a comprehensive analysis of changing Council norms on intervention, see Nicholas J. Wheeler, *Saving Strangers* (Oxford: Oxford University Press, 2000).
6. For an authoritative assessment of the Haiti case, see David Malone, *Decision-Making in the UN Security Council: the case of Haiti* (Oxford: Oxford University Press, 1998).
7. For a detailed analysis of the Council vote, see Wheeler, *Saving Strangers*, pp.275–81, 290–99.
8. Quoted in William Shawcross, *Deliver Us From Evil: Warlords and Peacekeepers in a World of Endless Conflict* (London: Bloomsbury Press, 2000), p.30.
9. For a discussion of the theory and practice of New Labour's ethical foreign policy, see Nicholas J. Wheeler and Tim Dunne, 'Good International Citizenship: a Third Way for British Foreign Policy', *International Affairs*, Vol.74, No.4 (Oct. 1998), pp.847–70 and Richard Little and Mark Wickham Jones (eds.), *New Labour's Foreign Policy: A New Moral Crusade* (Manchester: Manchester University Press, 2000).
10. Tony Blair, 'Doctrine of the International Community', speech given to the Economic Club of Chicago, 22 April 1999, p.6, www.fco.gov.uk/text_only/news/speechtext.
11. Blair, 'Doctrine of the International Community', p.6.
12. For a selection of recent assessments on this question: see Tim Judah, *Kosovo: War and Revenge* (New Haven: Yale University Press, 2000); Noam Chomsky, *A New Generation Draws the Line: Kosovo, East Timor and the Standard of the West* (London: Verso, 2001); Michael Ignatieff, *Virtual War: Kosovo and Beyond* (London: Chatto and Windus, 2000); Albrecht Schnabel and Ramesh Thakur (eds.), *Kosovo and the Challenge of Humanitarian Intervention: Selective Indignation, Collective Action, and International Citizenship* (Tokyo: United Nations University, 2000); and Ken Booth (ed.), *The Kosovo Tragedy: The Human Rights Dimensions*, Special Issue of *The International Journal of Human Rights*, Vol.4, Nos.3/4 (Autumn/Winter 2000).
13. Michael Ignatieff, 'Human Rights, Sovereignty and Intervention' (lecture given as part of the 2001 Amnesty International lecture series, 2 Feb. 2001, copy in possession of the author).
14. Blair, 'Doctrine of the International Community', p.6.
15. Quoted in Colin McInnes, 'Fatal Attraction?', p.30.
16. McInnes, p.34.
17. McInnes, p.38.
18. The most prominent critics were Amnesty International and Human Rights Watch. 'NATO/Federal Republic of Yugoslavia: "Collateral Damage" or Unlawful Killings. Violations of the Laws of War by NATO during Operation Allied Force', *Amnesty International Report*, June 2000; and 'Civilian Deaths in the NATO air campaign', *Human Rights Watch report* at

http://www.hrw.org/reports/2000/nato/natbm200.htm
19. Adam Roberts, 'NATO's Humanitarian War over Kosovo', *Survival*, Vol.41, No.3 (1999), pp.117–18.
20. Colin S. Gray, 'The RMA and Intervention', p.60.
21. Gray, p.62.
22. Gray, p.61.
23. Gray, p.60.
24. Gray, p.60.
25. Gray, p.60.
26. Cori E. Dauber, 'Implications of the Weinberger Doctrine for American Military Intervention in a Post-Desert Storm age', p.79.
27. Dauber, p.79.
28. Statement by President William S. Clinton, quoted by Dauber, p.78.
29. 'Statement by President Clinton to the Nation' (Washington, DC: Office of the Press Secretary, 24 March 1999).
30. For an excellent discussion of the polling data on Kosovo, see Steven Livingston, 'Media Coverage of the War: An Empirical Assessment', in Schnabel and Thakur (eds.), *Kosovo and the Challenge of Humanitarian Intervention*, pp.360–85.
31. Quoted in Philip Gourevitch, *We Wish to Inform You that Tomorrow We Will be Killed with our Families* (London: Picador, 1998), p.351.
32. Gray, p.58.
33. For authoritative discussions of this incident, see Linda Melvern, *A People Betrayed: The Role of the West in Rwanda's Genocide* (London: Zed Books, 2000), pp.91–6 and Shawcross, *Deliver Us From Evil*, pp.109–13.
34. Quoted in 'When Good Men Do Nothing', *BBC Panorama* programme, Dec. 1998.
35. Author's interview with Sir David Hannay, Permanent Representative of the United Kingdom to the UN during the Somali and Rwandan crises, March 1999.
36. Letter from senators Simon and Jeffords to President Clinton, 13 May 1994. I am grateful to Linda Melvern for making this letter available to me.
37. Scot R. Feil, *Preventing Genocide: A Report to the Carnegie Commission on Preventing Deadly Conflict* (New York: Carnegie Corporation, 1998), p.27.
38. Feil, *Preventing Genocide*, p.27.
39. Melvern, *A People Betrayed*, p.159.
40. Interview with Sir David Hannay, March 1999.
41. Kofi A. Annan, *Preventing War and Disaster: A Growing Global Challenge* (New York: *Annual Report on the Work of the Organization*, 1999), p.12.
42. Philip Sherwell, 'Cook Halts Hawk Sale to Indonesia', *Electronic Telegraph*, 12 Sept. 1999, available at http://www.telegraph...999999&pg=/et/99/9/12/ntim12.html.
43. Shawcross, *Deliver Us From Evil*, p.137.
44. Shawcross, *Deliver Us From Evil*, p.356.
45. Shawcross, *Deliver Us From Evil*, p.359.
46. Penny Wensley, 'East Timor and the United Nations', speech by ambassador Wensley to the Australian Institute for International Affairs, Sydney, Australia, 23 Feb. 2000, p.10.
47. I owe this assessment of the different roles played by consent to Tim Dunne. For a further discussion see Tim Dunne, Cameron Hill and Marianne Hanson, 'The New Humanitarian Interventionism' in Marianne Hanson and William Tow (eds.), *International Relations in the New Century* (Oxford: Oxford University Press, 2000), pp.93–115.
48. See *Wider Peacekeeping* (London: HMSO, 1995).
49. Dominick Donald, 'The Doctrine Gap', p.116.
50. *Joint Warfare Publication 3-50 Peace Support Operations*, para 308.
51. Donald, p.120.
52. Donald, p.122.
53. Quoted in Donald, p.122.
54. Panel on United Nations Peace Operations to the Secretary-General, A/55/305 S/2000/809, 17 Aug. 2000, ix.
55. Donald, pp.127–8.

56. Quoted in Donald, p.125.
57. Shawcross, *Deliver Us From Evil*, p.379.
58. Paul Williams, 'Fighting for Freetown', p.162.
59. Blair, 'Doctrine of the International Community', p.6.
60. Williams, p.163.
61. Williams, p.164.
62. Kofi A. Annan, 'Development is the best form of Conflict Prevention', First United Nations Lecture, World Bank, 19 Oct. 1999 in Kofi A. Annan, *The Question of Intervention: Statements by the Secretary-General* (New York: United Nations Department of Public Information, 1999), p.55.
63. Trevor Findlay, 'The Role of Monitoring and Verification', p.170.
64. Findlay, p.169.
65. Donald, p.118.
66. For discussions of the ECOMOG operation, see David Wippman, 'Enforcing the Peace: ECOWAS and the Liberian Civil War' in Lori Fisler Damrosch (ed.), *Enforcing Restraint: Collective Intervention in Internal Conflicts* (New York: Council on Foreign Relations Press, 1993), pp.157–204; Jeremy Levitt, 'Humanitarian Intervention by Regional Actors in Internal Conflicts: The Cases of ECOWAS in Liberia and Sierra Leone', *Temple International and Comparative Law Journal*, pp.333–75.
67. Jayne Rodgers, 'Bosnia and Kosovo', p.191.
68. Rodgers, pp.188–91.
69. Rodgers, p.191.

Fatal Attraction? Air Power and the West

COLIN McINNES

There are certain dates in the history of warfare that mark real turning points. Now there is a new turning point to fix on the calendar: June 3, 1999, when the capitulation of president Milosevic proved that a war can be won by air power alone ... the air forces have won a triumph, are entitled to every plaudit they will receive and look forward to enjoying a transformed status in the strategic community, one they have earned by their single-handed efforts.[1]

Over the past decade air power has emerged as the preferred instrument of force by the West. In the 1990/1 Gulf War it established the conditions necessary for rapid coalition victory; 'no fly zones' have been established over both Iraq and parts of the former Yugoslavia; and air campaigns were used to finish the war in Bosnia (Operation Deliberate Force) and Kosovo (Operation Allied Force). Air power on its own may not be sufficient in most circumstances (a point discussed below). Indeed, in the Gulf War it required a ground offensive to eject Iraqi forces from Kuwait, Operation Deliberate Force coincided with Serb setbacks elsewhere, including losses on the ground,[2] and although John Keegan famously recanted his original position to declare that Kosovo represented a triumph for air power acting alone,[3] a host of other factors may have been as significant, and arguably more so, in influencing Serbia's decision to concede.[4] Nevertheless air power has become synonymous with the West's use of force. It may not be the only instrument used, but it is often the first and is usually seen as the key to establishing not only military superiority but eventual victory.

The significance of air power is nothing new. Since the inter-war period its advocates have argued consistently that air power is 'the dominant factor' in modern war.[5] By World War II even ground force commanders openly acknowledged its importance. The Germans showed the advantages of using air power to support ground operations in the early *blitzkrieg* campaigns. The Allies and the Soviets followed suit. By the end of the war, air superiority was a key factor in deciding the outcome of ground operations: whereas doubts remained during and after the war over the effectiveness of strategic bombing, few doubted the significance of air power in the ground support role. Indeed during the 1980s the US Army described its warfighting doctrine as the '*Air*Land Battle'.[6] Similarly at sea, World War II had seen the demise of the battleship in favour of the aircraft carrier and the vulnerability of both surface and sub-surface ships to aircraft. After the war, carrier battle groups became the main strike force of Western navies, not least in the US Navy's 1986 Maritime Strategy,[7] while even relatively small ships such as frigates relied increasingly on helicopters as their principal weapons platform. What is new, however, is that the significance and more importantly the *attraction* of air power has increased. In terms of its significance, air power no longer simply supports ground or sea operations; it is now preceding them, enabling them and even replacing them. Traditionally air power has only operated independent of land or sea power in terms of strategic bombardment – the Allied bombing campaigns against German and Japanese cities in World War II being the pre-eminent examples. But these were bludgeons rather than rapiers. Air power can now be used in a discriminating manner against key targets, both strategic *and* theatre, to bring coercive pressure on an enemy, and thereby transform the nature of military intervention by the West.

The attraction of air power is in part that it is an area of comparative advantage for the West, and particularly the United States. The United States is the pre-eminent – some might argue the only – air power. Throughout the 1990s and beyond Western aircraft, and most particularly US aircraft, have been able to roam the skies above enemies with relative impunity, bringing devastating force to bear with uncanny accuracy. As Eliot Cohen has put it, 'If the claims of air power advocates are correct, the United States has acquired a military edge over conventional opponents comparable to that exercised in 1898 by the soldiers of Lord Kitchener against the sword-wielding dervishes of the Sudan'.[8] But the attraction goes beyond the simple fact of it being an area of comparative advantage offering a 'military edge'. Rather the nature of modern air power suggests that force may be used without undue risk. In 78 days of operations during the Kosovan conflict, not one NATO airman or woman lost his or her life. For nations unwilling to shed blood in wars of choice, air power offers 'gratification without commitment'.[9] Success can now be achieved without having to engage the main body of enemy forces in a messy and protracted engagement. Further, air power can be used in a discriminating manner. The wholesale destruction of enemy cities is no longer the sole option available to strategic air power. Precision guidance coupled to high quality intelligence gathering enables individual buildings or even sections of buildings to be targeted with high confidence. As a result air power now offers 'the fantasy of near bloodless use of force'.[10] Further, air power can be deployed quickly to the theatre of operations, can be based outside the area of conflict, minimizing risk, or even used from bases in Western Europe or the continental United States (during Kosovo for example, RAF Tornadoes flew from Germany and USAF B2 bombers from bases in the United States). The expectations of low risk to Western pilots, of precision accuracy minimizing collateral damage, of ease of deployment, have all created an image of the potency of Western air power. This image is however in danger of creating a 'fatal attraction'. In failing to engage with the full range of issues surrounding air power, but instead being drawn by the allure of some of the possibilities, a misleading impression is created. This article attempts to address some of these issues, both in the sense of the traditional debate over the characteristics of air power and in how air power might be used. It attempts to examine more fully the advantages, limitations and uses of air power for the West.

THE ADVANTAGES OF AIR POWER

The advantages of air power – what are sometimes called its 'characteristics' or 'features' – are well documented and there is considerable consensus over them, not least amongst its proponents.[11] These are speed, range, ubiquity, flexibility, observation and precision. To these are sometimes added lethality and the opportunity for independent action. Aircraft are inherently faster than ships and ground forces. This allows them not only to project force more rapidly into a theatre of operations but also to attack targets promptly, thereby maintaining operational tempo. In the 1990/1 Gulf War aircraft and airlifted ground forces arrived in theatre in a matter of days, sometimes hours; in contrast forces moved by sea took weeks, even months, to arrive. In 1987 the rapid deployment of French aircraft to Chad was instrumental in repelling Libyan attacks. Similarly, with response times in tactical situations as low as a few minutes, air power can quickly be brought to bear upon targets of opportunity or to support forces under pressure. In contrast, manoeuvring or reinforcing ground forces can take much longer. Air power is therefore highly responsive at strategic, operational and tactical levels. Air power also has considerable 'reach' – in some cases global reach. It can use its range to hit targets beyond the reach of ground forces. It provides both an overhead flank and direct access to an enemy's centre of gravity. Indeed, as Colin Gray has remarked, whereas naval strategists are fond of pointing out that 70 per cent of the world is covered by water, the entire globe is covered by air.[12] With the enormous range of some modern aircraft such as the B2 bomber, no target is beyond attack. Aircraft can also use bases located away from danger. In 1982, an RAF Vulcan bomber based on Ascension Island attacked targets in the Falkland Islands, in 1986 US F111s from the UK bombed Libya, in 1991 B52s also based in Britain bombed Iraqi positions in the Gulf, while in 1999 B2 bombers based in the US and RAF Tornadoes based in Germany attacked targets in Yugoslavia. Indeed during the Kosovo operation, no NATO fixed wing aircraft were based in the Balkans, the bulk operating from Italy, Corsica or ships in the Adriatic.

Air power is also a very flexible instrument. Aircraft are often able to move at ease between the different levels of war – tactical, operational and strategic. Thus B52 bombers originally designed to attack strategic targets were used against Iraqi troops in Kuwait during the Gulf War, while tactical F117A stealth bombers were used for strategic missions over Baghdad. Air power can be used as an independent agent at both the theatre and strategic levels, or as an enabling agent for other forms of military power. It can be used with startling precision against key targets, or as a bludgeon, devastating large swathes of ground. The same aircraft may also engage in a variety of different missions during a campaign. American F16 aircraft, for example, are equally adept at the ground attack and counter-air roles, while the European Tornado aircraft was explicitly designed as a multi-role aircraft. Perhaps most important, though, is that air power can be tailored to meet the specifics of each crisis. Wars do not come as a single type or even as several different types, but invariably demonstrate unique or unusual features. The flexibility of air power allows it to be matched to the requirements of each crisis or war, whether it is for tactical ground support or long-range precision strike; establishing air superiority (or, more usually for the West, air supremacy) in a theatre of operations, such as in the Gulf, Bosnia and Kosovo; or executing a single or limited series of strikes against strategic targets, such as the 1998 and 2001 operations against Iraq.

Air power also has a superior ability to observe. From acting as artillery spotters in World War I, to radar-equipped J-STARS and AWACS in more recent conflicts, aircraft have used their height to observe and to provide information to other forces, including other aircraft. Some go as far as to include satellites as part of air power (or 'air-space power'), given their ability to observe from a great height.[13] Indeed, the US Air Force recently declared that 'we are now transitioning from an *air* force into and *air and space* force on an evolutionary path to a *space and air* force'.[14] This power of observation allows commanders to see what is happening on the ground with increasing accuracy and timeliness. When this is coupled to air supremacy, then the advantage is potentially decisive.

For Western intervention however, air power offers a number of distinct advantages beyond these more traditional features; advantages that have made it the weapon of choice. Most obviously the precision available to modern air power allows collateral damage to be minimized and even casualties to the enemy's armed forces to be reduced. This is often seen as vital in ensuring domestic and international support for a campaign. Indeed it has almost become a self-fulfilling prophecy, with air forces proclaiming their ability to strike with precision, fuelling expectations of a near-bloodless campaign where enemy civilians are successfully avoided and only the regime is targeted. Such expectations prove problematic when collateral damage does occur, from the destruction of an Iraqi air raid shelter in 1991 through to the accidental bombing of the Vavarin bridge and Chinese embassy during Operation Allied Force. These exceptions aside, the trend is clearly towards both a reduction in collateral damage and a perceived incentive by Western governments to reduce such damage. At the time of the Gulf War, only 10 per cent of US strike aircraft were capable of delivering precision weapons and less than 10 per cent of the overall number of bombs dropped were precision-guided.[15] By the mid-1990s and Operation Deliberate Force in Bosnia, the link between the precision guidance offered by air-launched munitions and minimizing collateral damage was explicit. USAF Chief of Staff General Michael Ryan stated that 'minimizing not only collateral damage but also carnage was first and foremost in my mind'.[16] Similarly US Secretary of Air Widnall commented, 'the NATO air operation was operationally robust but it was politically fragile. With the first report of civilian casualties, the entire operation would have been put at risk, but that report never came'.[17] The percentage of precision-guided weapons used had by now increased to 60 per cent. Paul Kaminski, a senior weapons official in the Department of Defense, commented that 'the bomb damage assessment photographs in Bosnia bear no resemblance to photos of the past, where the target, often undamaged, is surrounded by craters ... The photos from Bosnia usually showed one crater where the target used to be, with virtually no collateral damage.'[18] By the end of the decade, Operation Allied Force could be described by the US Department of Defense as 'the most precise and lowest-collateral-damage air operation ever conducted'.[19] Over 90 per cent of US strike aircraft were capable of delivering precision-guided munitions, these forming the bulk of NATO strike aircraft during Operation Allied Force.[20] The decision to avoid collateral damage was a crucial element in the campaign, even to the extent that certain key targets might not be hit due to fears of collateral damage. Driving this was the fear that alliance solidarity and popular support would be eroded by pictures of innocent Serb civilians being killed, wounded or even losing their property as a result of NATO's bombing campaign.[21]

Because it is an area of comparative Western advantage, air power also offers comparatively low risk. Air power is inherently sensitive to technology. The West's lead in aerospace technology means that its aircraft can operate if not without risk, then at least with much reduced risk. In contrast, no matter how capable ground forces might be, they are inherently more exposed to risk. During Kosovo, the West's technological lead, coupled with the decision to fly at a height where hand-held SAMs could not reach them, and the extensive use of stand-off weapons such as cruise missiles, meant that no allied lives were lost and only two aircraft downed in a campaign lasting 78 days and over 38,000 combat sorties.[22] Operation Allied Force may have been unusual in that no allied aircrew lost their lives, but very low casualties have been the norm since the 1986 US raid against Libya and Operation Desert Storm. In contrast, RAF Bomber Command suffered a death rate of 47.5 per cent amongst its aircrews during World War II,[23] while during the Vietnam War the 1972 Linebacker 2 campaign saw 16 B52 bombers lost in 11 days.[24] This recent phenomenon of an extremely low loss rate has, moreover, become the popular expectation. Weaned on a succession of campaigns where Western air power has operated with near impunity, the public now sees air power not only as a precise weapon which can (or more accurately perhaps, should) avoid causing collateral damage, but one which can be used at little or no cost to the West.

This is significant given the 'body bag' problem – the perception that Western domestic support would be eroded by large numbers of its armed forces returning in body bags. What constitutes 'large' is undefined and is probably a function of the interests at stake together with elite and popular consensus.[25] The body bag problem is usually seen as a 'lesson' of Vietnam. It was reaffirmed by the deaths of 239 US Marines in a car bomb explosion in Beirut, was actively played on by Saddam's talk of 'the mother of all battles' in 1990/1 and was instrumental in the pull-out of American forces from Somalia. Indeed, prior to Operation Allied Force, NATO's commander in Europe, the American General Wesley Clark, was widely reported as having ordered that there be no allied casualties and that commanders were to avoid losses at all costs. Though this was later denied, the very fact that such a story could be given credibility is a revealing insight into the body bag issue.[26] Those in the West may sympathize as they look on at those suffering, but they do not expect to suffer unduly themselves. Nor do they expect substantial numbers of their representatives in the armed forces to either. The pain of war is to be experienced at one remove, and even then to be minimized or even eradicated. Western air power, through its relative invulnerability, is much better suited to this than the more exposed ground forces and is therefore the preferred instrument for intervention where interests may be low and consensus fragile.

THE LIMITS OF AIR POWER

Although air power has become the preferred tool of military power for the West, this does not mean that it is without its limitations. Traditionally these have been related to technological factors, some of which are inherent while others can be mitigated as technology improves. These limitations include problems with range, payload, accuracy, operating in poor weather, the high cost of airframes, weapons and aircrew, limited loiter time over target and poor intelligence.[27] In the case of Western intervention however, four problems have come to dominate. These are the limitations placed on the use of air power by the requirement to minimize collateral damage, the sometimes limited and occasionally counter-productive impact of air power, the limited reach of air power, and its costs both financial and political. The imperative to minimize collateral damage, and the advantages of air power in this respect, have already been discussed. But this imperative also has a major impact on the efficiency and impact of air operations. In Bosnia, for example, NATO aircraft were unwilling to implement the no fly zone for fear that target aircraft, particularly helicopters, might be carrying wounded, politicians or civilians.[28] In Operation Allied Force, the rules of engagement were deliberately framed to avoid collateral damage. As a result pilots were authorized to release bombs only if they could see the target and be assured of no civilian casualties.[29] Unsurprisingly this meant that a substantial number of missions did not lead to weapons release, particularly when cloud cover made it difficult to identify targets definitively.[30] Further, NATO opted for a campaign which gradually increased pressure on Milosevic, again in order to minimize the damage caused and therefore to maintain alliance solidarity and public support. But these restrictions led to frustration that air power was not being used effectively. USAF General Michael Ryan commented that 'the campaign did not begin the way that America would apply air power – massively, striking at strategic centres of gravity that support Milosevic and his oppressive regime'. Instead political pressure, especially from other NATO allies, restricted the initial use of air power. As a result Ryan concluded that the first month's bombing, during which the Serbs engaged in ethnic cleansing in Kosovo, was ineffective and NATO was forced to expand its air campaign.[31] Similarly USAF General Michael Short, who commanded NATO air forces during Operation Allied Force, commented that 'I think we were constrained in this particular conflict to an extraordinary degree and were prevented from conducting an air campaign as professional airmen would have wanted to conduct it … we were restricted by enormous concern for collateral damage and unintended loss of civilian life'. Short's preference would have been for the Serb leadership to suffer an immediate and massive blow rather than a campaign of gradually increasing pressure, to wake up 'after the first night … to a city that was smoking. No power to the refrigerator … and no way to get to work.' Instead, Short wryly observed, 10 to 12 days into the campaign they were still holding rock concerts in downtown

Belgrade.[32] The argument therefore is that concerns over collateral damage and other political factors unduly limit the effectiveness of air power. But the danger of ignoring these concerns is all too apparent. The level of public expectation, and the political costs of collateral damage and other mistakes, is extreme. It is therefore unlikely that air power will be granted the unfettered role some of its senior commanders believe that it needs to maximize its effectiveness. Instead its use will in all likelihood remain constrained and its effectiveness thereby reduced.

A second series of concerns relates more directly to the impact of air power. The ability to attack targets, especially with precision strike, is highly dependent upon accurate and timely intelligence. But not even the United States currently possesses sufficient tactical and strategic intelligence-gathering capabilities for this.[33] Further, camouflage and deception can still prove remarkably effective. During the Gulf War for example, coalition aircraft were unable to distinguish between Scud missile launchers and decoys, buses and tankers.[34] More recently, during Operation Allied Force the Serbs used a variety of means to hide or protect both their military forces and fixed installations such as bridges and buildings. The means used by Serb forces ranged from exploiting natural cover and hiding military vehicles in buildings, through decoys and camouflage, to dispersing forces amongst civilian traffic. This latter tactic both hid forces and ensured that, even if they were detected, NATO would have a reduced ability to attack them due to fear of collateral damage. As the Department of Defense's After-Action Report acknowledged, 'future adversaries are likely to study Serbian denial and deception techniques and [this] could present more advanced threats to future operations'.[35] Operation Allied Force also demonstrated the difficulties in using air power against light infantry and militia targets, the very forces used for the ethnic cleansing of villages in Kosovo.[36] Finally, despite remarkable advances in technology and in particular in imaging, the continuing considerable difficulties in determining whether targets have been hit and destroyed by air attack (what is termed 'bomb damage assessment') means that the 'fog of war will persist'.[37]

The impact of air power is therefore limited by the (in)ability to identify targets and then confirm their destruction. But problems with intelligence do not end there. Even if targets can be successfully identified and their destruction confirmed, it is difficult to gauge the impact of this upon an enemy's decision-making. In a land campaign, territory gained can be measured and progress assessed accordingly, albeit rather crudely. In a naval blockade, the numbers of ships prevented from arriving or departing can give some indication of the economic impact of a campaign. But with a coercive air campaign, the relationship between destroying targets and changing enemy decision-making is much more difficult for intelligence analysts to gauge. Such a campaign also requires some intelligence insight into which targets are especially valuable to an enemy leadership. This is a difficult activity, and potentially controversial if attacking those targets risks an erosion of domestic support for a campaign. A coercive air campaign may successfully hit and destroy a particular target set which intelligence analysts believe the enemy values highly, only to be mistaken in this belief and the impact therefore much reduced. Identifying these levers correctly is the first problem. But even if these can be identified, it is then extremely difficult to gauge how much of an impact destroying these targets is having upon an enemy leadership. An enemy is unlikely to share its thoughts on the matter, indicating how much pressure it is feeling. As the campaign develops, therefore, planners will have little hard information on how it is affecting the enemy leadership. Even if it can accurately gauge the damage inflicted (something which the aftermath of both the Gulf War and Kosovo demonstrated is fraught with difficulties), assessing whether or not this is likely to be successful in coercing the enemy is a different and much more difficult calculation.

A major complication here is the extent to which an air campaign, rather than placing a regime under pressure, may actually solidify support for it. During the Kosovo campaign, NATO's bombing initially resulted in apparently spontaneous rallies in Serbia in support of Milosevic, although over time this support fell and both popular and elite dissatisfaction could be seen. Saddam remained in power throughout not only the Gulf War but the decade following, with no serious threat of a widespread popular uprising. In Somalia, air strikes by US helicopters may have helped both to provoke an anti-US mood and to legitimate Aideed as a local leader resisting the US, while Russian bombing in Chechnya helped to unite opposition.[38] Historically the ability of air power to produce a mood of dissatisfaction, resentment or even panic amongst the civilian population has been articulated regularly, beginning with H. G. Wells a century ago[39] and reaching its operational climax with Arthur 'Bomber' Harris's campaigns against German cities during World War II.[40] The success of such campaigns has been at best mixed, however. The reasons why some campaigns may be more effective than others are still not understood. Critical variables may be a regime's ability to suppress dissent through propaganda and other tools of state control, the stakes involved, and the length of a campaign (initially support for a regime may increase in the face of the common crisis of strategic bombardment, but over time it may fall). But these uncertainties at the very least serve to complicate assessments of the likely impact of an air campaign and at worst suggest that a campaign may prove counter-productive, at least initially. As a result the ability of air power to act as a coercive tool may be compromised.

Air power also has a limited ability to affect what happens on the ground. In part this is due to the brevity of its presence. Air power is an impermanent form of military force, entering and exiting a target area quickly both through technical factors (limited fuel constrains the ability to loiter) and the desire to limit exposure to possible attack from SAMs. Aircraft may also fly thousands of feet above the ground to avoid attack, particularly from the large numbers of hand-held SAMs readily available. Although this may give them an air of invulnerability that makes them appear formidable, it also distances them from what is happening on the ground. Only ground forces can occupy and control territory; the best air power can do is to deny its use to the enemy, and it is not always successful in this. During the first weeks of NATO's Kosovo campaign, for example, air strikes were unable to prevent Serb forces from engaging in ethnic cleansing or to prevent the exodus of Albanian refugees; in Bosnia, NATO air strikes in May 1995 were not only unable to protect safe areas but led to UN ground forces being taken hostage in Gorazde and elsewhere.

A third set of concerns relates to the reach of air power. Although this can be a major advantage as discussed above, it also reveals the limits of air power. Global reach may be possible, as demonstrated by an RAF Vulcan bomber attacking the Falkland Islands in 1982 and B2 stealth bombers attacking targets in Serbia from their bases in the US in 1999, but few aircraft are capable of these extreme ranges. Such missions also impose huge strains on aircrews. The round trip for a B2 bomber attacking targets in Serbia took 30 hours.[41] Even at a lesser distance, RAF Tornado crews were placed under considerable strain in flying from their base in Germany to Yugoslavia on a daily basis. These raids also revealed a problem in that the weather may change during a long flight so that, even though conditions above the target may have been perfect when the aircraft took off, by the time they reached the target several hours later the weather could have deteriorated causing the mission to be aborted. Such missions also require considerable tanker support as well as overflight rights. In the 1982 Falklands war, the one successful use of strategic bombers involved a single Vulcan bomber, with one more in reserve, but 11 tanker aircraft and six air-to-air refuellings.[42] Similarly, obtaining overflight rights proved to be a major problem for the US 1986 raid against Libya, and the failure to secure all those required greatly complicated the mission. In the most extreme circumstances, the failure to obtain overflight rights may even prevent missions. Basing aircraft nearer to or within the theatre of operations may of course alleviate some of these problems. But this is not always possible due to a lack of political support in nearby countries (particularly if intervention is controversial) or a lack of suitable bases. B2 bombers, for example, could have cut their flight time to Serbia dramatically if they were based in Europe rather than the United States, but due to their stealth design they require specialized shelters and facilities and the US lacked a deployable version of these in 1999.[43] Even less specialized aircraft may require considerable support when operating away from home bases, adding not only to the cost and complexity of a mission but placing a limit on the number of aircraft which can be deployed.[44]

A final limitation concerns the costs involved. This most obviously refers to the high financial costs of developing, purchasing, operating and maintaining modern combat aircraft. Capable aircraft are not cheap but are essential if casualties are to be kept low. Although Serb air defences were not considered 'state of the art', they still forced NATO aircraft to fly at 15,000 feet to avoid hand-held SAMs and prevented the use of low-flying aircraft such as AH64 Apache helicopters and, for a time, A10 ground attack aircraft.[45] Less capable aircraft and weapons may not only risk the loss of planes and aircrew but increase collateral damage, both of which may erode support for a campaign. But the high costs of capable aircraft means few are bought, risking overstretch. This is particularly so if campaigns are fought simultaneously or within a short time of each other, as happened in 1998/9 with Operations Desert Fox and Allied Force following quickly on each other. Indeed, General John P. Jumper, commander of US Air Forces in Europe, admitted that Operation Northern Watch over Iraq had to be virtually shut down to provide aircraft for Kosovo.[46] Precision weapons are also expensive so that few tend to be bought. This risks running out of munitions at a key moment. Cruise missile and JDAM stocks ran perilously low during

Operation Allied Force, while the RAF was only spared running out of laser-guided bombs because of poor weather preventing their use on all but a few days.[47] A modern air campaign also requires considerable support. In the air (and in space) this includes intelligence gathering, bomb damage assessment, electronic warfare support, air superiority fighters and air-to-air refuelling, while on the ground aircraft deployed from home bases require extensive support to be moved into theatre to maintain aircraft availability. Few can afford the full range of capabilities and even within NATO, Operation Allied Force revealed that real disparities existed between allies.[48] Indeed it may well be that only the United States can conduct anything other than a minor campaign against a poorly equipped adversary with high confidence.

The use of air power might not just be financially costly, however. Rather than compete directly against Western strength, enemies may use asymmetric strategies. The US Department of Defense argues that

> The campaign over Kosovo was not a traditional military conflict. There was no direct clash of massed military ground forces in Operation Allied Force. Milosevic was unable to challenge superior allied military capabilities directly … Therefore he chose to fight chiefly through asymmetric means: terror tactics and repression directed against Kosovar citizens; attempts to exploit the premium the alliance placed on minimizing civilian casualties and collateral damage; creation of enormous refugee flows to create a humanitarian crisis, including in neighboring countries; and the conduct of disinformation and propaganda campaigns.[49]

Almost a decade earlier, Saddam had pursued asymmetric strategies in the Gulf War, targeting Israel (a non-belligerent) with Scud missile attacks, using Western hostages as a 'human shield' to defend key sites, releasing oil into the Gulf, and implicitly threatening to use chemical weapons to offset coalition conventional strength. In the future, such strategies may not be limited to the theatre of operations. Rather, enemies may attack Western military bases outside the theatre of operations or even centres of population, either with terrorist attacks or ballistic missiles as that technology spreads. How realistic this possibility is remains unclear. Not only might such attacks be more difficult than imagined – despite raised concerns during the 1990s, the United States like most Western powers remains the victim of non-state rather than state-sponsored terrorism[50] – but the West's reaction may be to escalate or seek revenge rather than to give way. In such circumstances an asymmetric strategy may backfire dramatically. The concern is such, however, that during the 1990s international terrorism occupied the place vacated by the Soviet Union as the United States's arch enemy, while the distant threat of ballistic missile attack has been sufficient to reactivate the debate over missile defences in the United States.[51]

THE USES OF AIR POWER: BRUTE FORCE AND COERCION

As David Gates has commented, the strategic objective of any conflict is to break the enemy's will.[52] This may be done in a variety of ways, but the classic distinction is that of Thomas Schelling, between brute force and coercion.[53] The aim of brute force is to deny the enemy the use of certain assets by their destruction. Classically these assets would be its military forces, though other targets, such as communications facilities, may be hit. In contrast the aim of coercion is to compel the enemy to do your will either by the threat of force, or by the limited use of force with the threat of more to come. For Schelling, with coercion it is not the act of violence itself but the threat of more to come that is important. Coercion offers an inducement to comply and is therefore a form of negotiation – what Schelling called the diplomacy of violence.[54] Alexander George similarly talks of 'coercive diplomacy' as a strategy whereby threats are 'injected' into an enemy's calculations, persuading him to comply rather than resist. Like Schelling, George distinguishes not so much between force and diplomacy, but between different levels of force. The threat may be to use force, but equally it may be to use *increased* force. Importantly, the level of force required in a coercive campaign may be quite considerable, sufficient to hurt an enemy and thereby persuade them that the threat of more would be against their interests.[55] As Lawrence Freedman concludes, 'the study of coercion is concerned with the role of threats in international politics. The distinguishing feature of coercion is that the target is never denied choice, but must weigh the choices between the costs of compliance and of non-compliance.'[56]

It is this element of negotiation that is missing from strategies of brute force: in coercion there remains a way out for the enemy. Coercion is therefore a more obviously psychological strategy: the coercer must gauge what acts of force will affect an enemy's decision-making. But assessing this is far from easy and the mechanisms for successful coercion remain poorly understood.[57] Coercion is also a dynamic process.[58] As threats and the use of force escalate, so the enemy will in all probability respond with moves of his own. Coercion is therefore a two-sided game where the situation may change and with it calculations of costs and benefits.[59] This in turn makes it much more difficult to gauge an enemy's breaking point – that level of force which, with its implied escalation, will lead the enemy to give way. Once force is used, the resolve of an enemy leadership may stiffen, political balances within an enemy state may shift and domestic support for a coercer's actions may change.[60] Progress is therefore difficult to gauge – success is not a function of numbers of missions undertaken or targets destroyed, but of changes in political will which may not be obvious during a campaign.[61] Even once a campaign is over, a simple binary divide between success and failure may be inadequate.[62] The dynamic nature of the conflict may mean that goals change during the conflict, while the element of negotiation involved in coercive strategies suggests that the campaign may end not when all the stated goals are achieved but when sufficient goals are achieved. An enemy may accede to some demands and this may be deemed sufficient by the coercers. This may be particularly so if continuing the campaign would cause more harm than the good achieved in securing the additional objectives, or if domestic support is wavering in the face of a protracted campaign where concessions have already been offered. In these circumstances, what constitutes success? Coercion, therefore, is not an easy strategy to implement, requiring difficult judgments to be made over the level of force required in a changing, dynamic environment.

In contrast, the success of a strategy of brute force appears much easier to gauge: simply put, it is the military denial of an enemy's political objectives. This element of 'denial' in a strategy of brute force has led Michael Clark to suggest that it would be a better term, avoiding some of the latter's connotations of overwhelming violence.[63] Although in some respects Clark's use of the term 'denial' provides a useful distinction, it also suggests a reactive strategy. Force may however be used proactively, particularly in cases of aggression (Iraq's use of force against Kuwait and that by the Bosnian Serbs against the Bosnian government may only be considered 'reactive' through linguistic and political sleight of hand). Denial may also form part of a coercive strategy, whereby the ability to deny an enemy what he wants persuades him to desist.[64] The fact that denial can be seen as an element of both a strategy of brute force and one of coercion suggests that the distinction between the two is not always clear cut. Indeed campaigns such as Kosovo involve elements of both coercion and brute force – the strategic campaign was designed to coerce but the attacks against Serb forces in Kosovo were as much about the use of brute force to prevent ethnic cleansing as about coercing the Serb leadership.

Coercion has nevertheless become the favoured strategy for the West. It offers a more discriminatory use of force, the potential for violence to be limited and tailored to specific political objectives. As USAF Chief of Staff General Ronald R. Fogelman argued in 1996, a new American way of warfare was emerging. Whereas previously the US had relied 'on large forces employing mass, concentration, and firepower to attrit enemy forces and defeat them in what many times became costly but successful battles ... [force can now be used] to compel an adversary to do our will at the least cost to the United States in lives and treasure'.[65] This new 'way of warfare' was not limited to the United States. In the UK, a key Army paper on future war echoed Fogelman's sentiments by emphasizing that operations must achieve success 'for the minimum cost in blood and treasure',[66] while General Rupert Smith, commander of UNPROFOR in Bosnia, commented 'one [now] fights in such a way as to preserve one's force'.[67] The implication of what Fogelman was saying was that technology in general, and air power in particular, allowed the Americans to avoid attritional campaigns and therefore minimize costs to themselves. But a second trend was emerging, namely that the costs imposed on an enemy should also be limited. In particular Western governments attempt to avoid public protest over the use of force by minimizing collateral damage: from the Gulf War to Kosovo, Western governments have attempted to avoid unnecessary civilian casualties. What is important to note here is that in such a situation coercion, with its deliberately limited use of force, offers a more appealing strategy than that of brute force. Further, not only does coercion encourage a more discriminate use of force, but it is a strategy that can be presented as being targeted against the enemy leadership rather than against the people in general.

Paralleling the rise of coercion as the West's preferred strategy has been the view that air power is 'the ultimate instrument of military coercion'.[68] Air power offers an economy of violent effort through its ability to precisely target key assets. It can attack strategic targets directly without having to engage the main body of enemy forces, thereby focusing attacks on the enemy leadership. It is potentially a far more discriminatory tool than land power while at the same time minimizing exposure of friendly forces. In the wake of Western campaigns in the Gulf and the former Yugoslavia, it has also come to be seen as an image of potency, of the West's ability to strike wherever and whenever it chooses with impunity. In a coercive campaign when the threat of more to come is a critical element, this image of potency may prove a vital factor in persuading an enemy leadership to give way.[69] But air power is not always the ideal tool. Some circumstances may require ground to be taken and/or held; others may require an embargo implemented by naval forces stopping and searching ships. Air power can also make mistakes. When collateral damage occurs, as it has and probably will continue to do, domestic support may be weakened and enemy resolve stiffened. If the level of violence required is over-estimated, then by avoiding more traditional military targets air power will be unnecessarily destroying infrastructure and other targets (power grids, communications facilities, etc.) which may be important for the civilian population. Unlike ground forces which will generally be used to engage the main body of enemy forces, generally seen as a legitimate target in war, air power may be used against strategic targets whose legitimacy is more questionable, particularly if the level of violence is over-estimated. But equally if the required level of violence is under-estimated, then a campaign may become overly protracted, eroding domestic support and allowing an enemy to accustom itself to the state of war it finds itself in. Ground forces may be tasked to take and hold ground or to destroy certain enemy formations, and their progress can easily be gauged; coercive air power however is a much less certain activity and the progress of a campaign much more difficult to judge. If the level of violence is under-estimated, then a campaign may prove ineffective *without the coercer realizing this.*

AIR POWER ALONE?

The attraction of air power raises the question of whether it might be sufficient as a coercive instrument acting on its own, and that land and maritime forces might be relegated to support functions. Because air power can strike at key political and economic targets directly, its advocates argue that it can bring sufficient pressure upon an enemy leadership to coerce them into acceding to the West's demands without extensive recourse to sea and land power.[70] This coercive ability is in part a result of improved technology in the form of increased ordnance, greater precision and better intelligence gathering, which has transformed air power's capabilities. But it is also due to the transformed nature of war whereby the target is no longer the state or the people, but the enemy leadership – arguably a much easier target on which to bring coercive pressure to bear via air power.

Given the relative advantages of air power for the West – most especially its reach, its ability to minimize collateral damage and the reduced exposure of friendly forces – the question of whether air power can act as an independent coercive agent is of particular significance. If it can, then force may be used successfully at relatively low cost; if not, then the use of force will remain a risky and potentially expensive option. NATO's Kosovo campaign certainly seemed to suggest that air power might be able to act alone – after 78 days of bombing the Serb leadership gave way, without NATO having to use ground troops. This followed the success of Operation Deliberate Force, where air power was used to coerce the Serb leadership over Bosnia.[71] As Richard Hallion has argued, 'as a result of NATO's first sustained air campaign, all military and political objectives were attained: safe areas were no longer under attack or threatened, heavy weapons had been removed from designated areas, Sarajevo's airport opened (as did road access to the city), and a path to a peace agreement had been secured'.[72] As a result, it was not difficult to construct the case for air power on the basis of recent experience. But neither of these two cases is quite as straightforward as first appears. Operation Deliberate Force also included substantial artillery attacks from British and French forces on Mount Igman while the mounting Bosnian government and Croat ground offensive also placed considerable pressures on the Serbs. In Kosovo, air power was only one of a number of pressures being exerted on the Serb leadership: the threat of a NATO ground offensive was growing, the Russians offered no support to Belgrade, KLA operations in Kosovo were increasing and Milosevic had been indicted on war crimes charges.[73] Arguing that air power alone determined the successful outcome of both Operation Deliberate Force and Operation Allied Force therefore appears problematic, though its key role in both is suggestive.

Air power also suffers two major limitations in its ability to decide campaigns independently. First, for all of the advances in weight of ordnance carried and its accuracy, air power can still only deliver a

fraction of the firepower available to artillery. This means that pressure
has to be applied over time, particularly if military forces are being
targeted. Therefore NATO air strikes were unable to prevent Serb
ethnic cleansing in Kosovo in part because they lacked the firepower.
Second, air power is unable to take and hold disputed territory. Only
land power can do this. Although air power can do much of the work in
preparing the way for land power, and can perhaps deny the use of
territory to an enemy, if territory is to be (re)gained and then held,
ultimately land power will have to be used. Air power may therefore be
necessary, but on its own it may not be sufficient.

The limits of air power in holding and controlling territory raise a
separate question: to what extent is control of territory and the
destruction of an enemy's military forces, particularly their ground
forces, important in coercing an enemy? Admittedly in a campaign of
brute force this might be the case (though perhaps not always then). But
in a campaign of coercion, might not discrete strikes against strategic
targets prove more effective – strikes which do not require the
occupation of territory until the campaign is over? This question has
prompted a debate over the relative utility of strategic and theatre strikes
in which the US Air Force, the pre-eminent air power, has been a
staunch advocate of strategic attack. US Air Force General Michael
Short, for example, commented that the attacks on Serb forces in
Kosovo did little to help achieve NATO's war aims. It was only when the
emphasis shifted to attacking strategic targets that coercive pressure was
successfully applied. Attacking forces engaged in ethnic cleansing had
not prevented those atrocities, nor had it placed the Serb leadership
under sufficient pressure to persuade them to desist. Rather it was
attacks upon state control and infrastructure, and the threat of more
attacks to come, which Short argues finally persuaded the Serb
leadership to give way.[74] Similarly US Air Force Chief of Staff General
Michael Ryan commented 'Airpower could not stop the door-to-door …
thuggery and ethnic cleansing that [was] going on directly… The only
way you were going to be able to do that [was by] taking it to the heart
of the matter – in this case Belgrade.'[75]

From a study of the empirical evidence, however, Robert A. Pape has
argued that strategic bombing is only marginally effective as a coercive
tool and that attacks against theatre targets are likely to be more effective
in persuading an enemy that it cannot achieve its military objectives. For
Pape, strategic bombing is only likely to be effective in long wars of

attrition, when material and economic factors come into play, but not in short wars lasting a few weeks or months. In contrast theatre air power is effective in both long and short wars. Pape's thesis has yet to attain widespread acceptance[76] and the US Air Force for one has decided that strategic strikes remain the more effective option. What the debate does reveal however is that the case for strategic bombing has not been proven. In particular, doubts remain over the effectiveness of the decapitation strikes that would make war quick and easy for the West. Nor does the evidence convince that air power can guarantee success in war, particularly if air power is used on its own. Rather Pape's thesis suggests that air power remains more of a blunt instrument than a rapier, and that campaigns are likely to take longer than expected in order to be successful. Neither of these claims has been satisfactorily refuted. What is also clear is the degree of uncertainty which still surrounds the use of air power and how it can be used most effectively.

CONCLUSION

The attraction of air power for the West is clear. It enables the prompt use of force and is capable of being employed at long range. It offers minimum exposure of friendly forces, both because of the small numbers involved (many of which may be deployed adjacent to the zone of conflict rather than within it) and because of the West's lead in this most technologically sensitive of combat arenas. Air power can be deployed rapidly and is often based outside the theatre of operations. And air-launched precision-guided munitions are capable of extraordinary accuracy, thereby reducing the risk of collateral damage. In contrast both land and naval forces suffer from a variety of disadvantages which reduce their attraction. But this does not mean that air power is unproblematic. By its nature air power is impermanent. It cannot therefore hold or control ground. Despite advances in intelligence gathering and analysis, capabilities here still prove a major limitation both in the identification of targets and the assessment of damage done. Nor does precision guidance mean a 'bloodless war' – mistakes have been made and will continue to be made, with the result that collateral damage will always occur. Most importantly, there is still insufficient evidence to demonstrate that air power can act alone: it may be necessary in order to secure military victory, but it is not sufficient except in the most extreme circumstances of a limited campaign against targets vulnerable to attack. Even then the long-term benefits may be questionable. The Israeli raid against the Osirak nuclear reactor in Iraq, the 1986 US raid against Libya and British and US raids against Iraq in December 1998 and 2001 are all examples of air power being used on its own, but in all instances the campaign was limited in terms of targets and duration and produced limited long-term benefits. More significant air campaigns, such as Operation Desert Storm in the Gulf, Operation Deliberate Force in Bosnia and Operation Allied Force in Kosovo, are at best inconclusive in demonstrating the ability of air power to secure victory on its own. Finally, the manner in which air power is used is subject to debate. The debate between proponents of strategic and theatre strikes remains unresolved, although the preferences of the US Air Force, the most powerful air force in the world and the most influential air force in the West, remain clearly in favour of strategic strikes. In contrast the debate over coercion or brute force appears to have been resolved in favour of the former – although distinguishing between the two may not always prove to be as easy in practice as it is in theory. Nevertheless the issue of how best to use air power for coercion, and even the viability of coercion, remains subject to debate. Thus although air power has emerged as the preferred Western instrument of force, it is not the only instrument likely to be used and the manner of its use remains a subject of debate.

NOTES

1. John Keegan, 'Please, Mr Blair, Never Take Such a Risk Again', *Electronic Telegraph*, 6 June 1999. Available at: www.telegraph.co.uk:80/et

2. John Stone, 'Air-power, Land-power and the Challenge of Ethnic Conflict', *Civil Wars*, Vol.2, No.3 (1999), p.30.

3. Keegan, 'Please, Mr Blair, Never Take Such a Risk Again'.

4. Department of Defense, *Report to Congress: Kosovo After-Action Report* (Washington, DC: Department of Defense, 2000), pp.10–11.

5. Air Marshal M. J. Armitage and Air Commodore R. A. Mason, *Air Power in the Nuclear Age, 1945–82* (London: Macmillan, 1983); Colin S. Gray, *Explorations in Strategy* (Westport, CT: Greenwood, 1996), pp.121–34; Richard P. Hallion, 'Control of the Air: the Enduring Requirement', unpublished paper from Air Force History and Museums Program (Washington, DC: Bolling AFB, 1999).

6. Department of the Army, *FM 100-5 Operations* (Washington, DC: US Government Printing Office, 1982, 1986).

7. Admiral James D. Watkins, 'The Maritime Strategy', *US Naval Institute Proceedings*, special issue Jan. 1986, pp.2–17.

8. Eliot A. Cohen, 'The Mystique of US Air Power', *Foreign Affairs*, Vol.73, No.1 (1994), p.111.

9. Cohen, 'The Mystique of US Air Power', p.109.

10. Cohen, 'The Mystique of US Air Power', p.121.

11. Gray, *Explorations in Strategy*; RAF [Royal Air Force] *AP 3000: Air Power Doctrine* 2nd edition

(London: HMSO, 1996), pp.13–15; Philip Towle, 'The Distinctive Characteristics of Air Power', in Group Captain Andrew Lambert and Arthur C. Williamson (eds.), *The Dynamics of Air Power* (London: HMSO for Royal Air Force Staff College Bracknell, 1996), pp.3–17.

12. Gray, *Explorations in Strategy*, p.67.
13. Major General William E. Jones, 'Air Power in the Space Age', in Stuart Peach (ed.), *Perspectives on Air Power: Air Power in its Wider Context* (London: TSO, 1998), p.208.
14. United States Air Force, *Global Engagement: A Vision for the 21st Century Air Force*, 2000, available at: www.xp.hq.af.mil/xpx/21/global.pdf
15. Department of Defense, *Kosovo After-Action Report*, p.88.
16. Quoted in John A. Tirpak, 'Deliberate Force', *Air Force Magazine*, Vol.80, No.10 (1997), available at: www.afa.org/magazine/1097deli.html, p.8.
17. Quoted in John T. Correll, 'The New American Way of War', *Air Force Magazine*, Vol.79, No.4 (1996), available at: http://www.afa.org/magazine/0496newam.html, p.2.
18. Quoted in Tirpak, 'Deliberate Force', pp.2–3.
19. Department of Defense, *Kosovo After-Action Report*, pp. xvii and 84.
20. Department of Defense, *Kosovo After-Action Report*, p.88.
21. Department of Defense, *Kosovo After-Action Report*, p.86.
22. Department of Defense, *Kosovo After-Action Report*, pp.xvii, xviii and 91.
23. John Ellis, *Brute Force: Allied Strategy and Tactics in the Second World War* (London: Andre Deutsch, 1990), pp.xix, 552.
24. Armitage and Mason, *Air Power in the Nuclear Age*, pp.109–10.
25. James Burk, 'Public Support for Peacekeeping in Lebanon and Somalia: Assessing the Casualties Hypothesis', *Political Science Quarterly*, Vol.114, No.1 (1999), pp.53–78; see also Edward Luttwak, 'Towards Post-heroic Warfare', *Foreign Affairs*, Vol.74, No.3 (1995), pp.109–22; 'A Post-heroic Military Policy', *Foreign Affairs*, Vol.75, No.4 (1996), pp.33–44; John Mueller, *Policy and Opinion in the Gulf War* (Chicago: University of Chicago Press, 1994).
26. John A. Tirpak, 'Victory in Kosovo', *Air Force Magazine*, Vol.82, No.7 (1999), available at: http://www.afa.org/magazine/watch/0799watch.html, p.6.
27. RAF, *AP 3000: Air Power Doctrine* pp.14–16; Towle, 'The Distinctive Characteristics of Air Power', pp.9–13.
28. Michael Clarke, 'Air Power and Force in Peace Support Operations', in Group Captain Andrew Lambert and Arthur C. Williamson (eds.), *The Dynamics of Air Power* (London: HMSO for Royal Air Force Staff College Bracknell, 1996), p.178.
29. John A. Tirpak, 'The First Six Weeks', *Air Force Magazine*, Vol.82, No.6 (1999), available at: http://www.afa.org/magazine/0699watch.html, p.3.
30. The weather had a major impact on Operation Allied Force. Most precision-guided bombs rely on laser designators to illuminate the target. Lasers cannot penetrate cloud cover and, given the requirement to fly at 15,000 feet to avoid hand-held missiles, NATO aircraft were particularly constrained when the weather was cloudy. Sixth Report from the House of Commons Defence Committee, *Lessons of Kosovo*, HC347 (London: TSO, 2000), p.4.
31. John A. Tirpak, 'Lessons Learned and Re-learned', *Air Force Magazine*, Vol.82, No.8 (1999), available at: www.afa.org/magazine/watch/0899watch.html, p.2.
32. John A. Tirpak, 'Short's View of the Air Campaign', *Air Force Magazine*, Vol.82, No.9 (1999), available at: www.afa.org/magazine/watch/0999watch.html, p.3.
33. Department of Defense, *Kosovo After-Action Report*, p.59.
34. Lawrence Freedman and Efraim Karsh, *The Gulf Conflict 1990/1* (London: Faber, 1993), pp.308–9.
35. Department of Defense, *Kosovo After-Action Report*, pp.62–3.
36. Daniel L. Byman and Matthew C. Waxman, 'Kosovo and the Great Air Power Debate', *International Security*, Vol.24, No.4 (2000), p.25.
37. Cohen, 'The Mystique of US Air Power', p.119; *Lessons of Kosovo*, 2000: lv.
38. Byman and Waxman, 'Kosovo and the Great Air Power Debate', p.21.
39. H. G. Wells, *The War in the Air* (London: George Bell, 1908).
40. Max Hastings, *Bomber Command* (London: Michael Joseph, 1979).
41. Tirpak, 'The First Six Weeks', p.4.
42. Anthony H. Cordesman and Abraham R. Wagner, *The Lessons of Modern War Vol. III: The*

Afghan and Falklands Conflicts (Boulder, CO: Westview Press, 1990), p.314.
43. Tirpak, 'The First Six Weeks', p.4.
44. RAF, *AP 3000: Air Power Doctrine*, p.16.
45. Department of Defense, *Kosovo After-Action Report*, p. 70; Tirpak, 'The First Six Weeks', p.6.
46. Tirpak, 'Victory in Kosovo', p.7.
47. Tirpak, 'The First Six Weeks', p.4; Department of Defense, *Kosovo After-Action Report*, p.93; National Audit Office, *Kosovo: The Financial Management of Military Operations*, HC530 session 1999–2000 (London: TSO, 2000), p.31.
48. General Wesley Clark, Admiral James Ellis and Lieutenant General Michael Short, Combined Prepared Statement to Senate Armed Services Committee Hearing on Operations in Kosovo, 21 Oct. 1999. Available at: www.senate/gov~armed_services, p.8; William S. Cohen, Prepared Statement to Senate Armed Services Committee Hearing on Operations in Kosovo, 20 July 1999. Available at: , p.6; William S. Cohen and General Henry H. Shelton, Joint Statement to Senate Armed Services Committee Hearing on Operations in Kosovo, 14 Oct. 1999. Available at: www.senate/gov~armed_services, p.10; Department of Defense, 1999, p.24.
49. Department of Defense, *Kosovo After-Action Report*, p.6.
50. Thomas J. Badey, 'US Anti-terrorism Policy: The Clinton Administration', *Contemporary Security Policy*, Vol.19, No.2 (1998), pp.50–70.
51. Ivo H. Daalder, James M. Goldgeier and James M. Lindsay, 'Deploying NMD: Not Whether, But How', *Survival*, Vol.42, No.1 (2000), pp.6–28; Dean A. Wilkening, *Ballistic Missile Defence and Strategic Stability*, Adelphi Paper 334 (London: Oxford for IISS, 2000).
52. David Gates, 'Air Power and the Theory and Practice of Coercion', *Defense Analysis*, Vol.13, No.3 (1997), p.242.
53. Thomas Schelling, *The Strategy of Conflict* (Cambridge, MA: Harvard University Press, 1960), *Arms and Influence* (New Haven, CT: Yale University Press, 1966*)*.
54. Schelling, *Arms and Influence*, pp.2–3; Lawrence Freedman, *The Revolution in Strategic Affairs*, Adelphi Paper 318 (Oxford: OUP for IISS, 1998); Freedman, 'Strategic Coercion', in L. Freedman (ed.), *Strategic Coercion* (Oxford: OUP, 1998), pp.20–23.
55. Alexander L. George, 'Theory and Practice', in Alexander L. George and William E. Simons, *The Limits of Coercive Diplomacy* (Boulder, CO: Westview Press, 1994).
56. Freedman, 'Strategic Coercion', p.36.
57. Michael Clark, 'Air Power, Force and Coercion', in Group Captain Andrew Lambert and Arthur C. Williamson (eds.), *The Dynamics of Air Power* (London: HMSO for Royal Air Force Staff College Bracknell, 1996), p.84.
58. Freedman, 'Strategic Coercion', pp.33–6.
59. Byman and Waxman, 'Kosovo and the Great Air Power Debate', pp.10–11.
60. Clark, 'Air Power, Force and Coercion', p.74.
61. Robert A. Pape, 'The Limits of Precision-Guided Air Power', *Security Studies*, Vol.7, No.2 (1997), p.96.
62. Byman and Waxman, 'Kosovo and the Great Air Power Debate'.
63. Clark, 'Air Power, Force and Coercion'.
64. Robert A. Pape, *Bombing to Win: Air Power and Coercion in War* (Ithaca, NY: Cornell University Press, 1996); Robert A. Pape, 'The Limits of Precision-Guided Air Power', *Security Studies*, Vol.7, No.2 (1997), pp.93–114.
65. Quoted in Correll, 'The New American Way of War', p.1.
66. Army Doctrine Committee [UK], 'British Army 2000 – The Future Army', unpublished paper APRC/P(97)28, 31 July 1997, p.7.
67. Lieutenant General Rupert A. Smith, 'A personal perspective on the changing nature of warfare in both high and low intensity conflict', unpublished talk to AFNWEUR Study Day, archived at British Army Tactical Doctrine and Retrieval Centre, TDRC 12179, (1996).
68. Clark, 'Air Power, Force and Coercion', p.67.
69. Clark, 'Air Power, Force and Coercion', pp.74–83.
70. Daniel L. Byman, Matthew C. Waxman and Eric Larson, *Air Power as a Coercive Instrument* (Santa Monica, CA: RAND, 1999); John A. Warden, 'Employing air power in the twenty-first century', in Richard H. Schultz and Robert L. Pfaltzgraff (eds.), *The Future of Air Power in the Aftermath of the Gulf War* (Maxwell Air Force Base, AL: Air University Press, 1992).

71. Tirpak, 'Deliberate Force'.
72. Hallion, 'Control of the Air: the Enduring Requirement', p.47.
73. Fourth Report from the Foreign Affairs Committee, *Kosovo*, HC28 Session 1999–2000 (London: TSO, 2000). Also available at www.publications.parliament.uk/pa/cm/cmf.faff.htm; Byman and Waxman, 'Kosovo and the Great Air Power Debate'; Department of Defense, *Kosovo After-Action Report*, pp.10–11.
74. Tirpak, 'Short's View Of The Air Campaign', pp.1–2.
75. Tirpak, 'Lessons Learned and Re-learned', p.2.
76. See for example John A. Warden, 'Success in Modern War: A Response to Robert Pape's *Bombing to Win*', *Security Studies*, Vol.7, No.2 (1997), pp.172–90 and Barry D. Watts, 'Ignoring Reality: Problems of Theory and Evidence in Security Studies', *Security Studies*, Vol.7, No.2 (1997), pp.115–71.

The RMA and Intervention:
A Sceptical View

COLIN S. GRAY

The illusion persists that politics and even moral choice can be reduced to the more tractable, simpler, realm of military prowess. In this contribution I will expose and discuss critically the fact that much of the West's (and especially Britain and America's) contemporary willingness to intervene in foreign quarrels is highly contingent on a very demanding set of military expectations keyed to zero–low friendly casualties. Fundamentally, of course, that point is not at all remarkable. Statecraft and strategy must always be a process of means–ends calculation (or guesswork) and all foreign policy ethics are prudently consequentialist. So much is not in doubt and is not really worth debating beyond the confines of introductory textbooks on International Politics. What is well worth debating, though, is how these enduring general and structural relations between means and ends are playing out in the field of actual policy today, a decade into one of the great military debates of modern history, on '[the] Revolution in Military Affairs' (RMA). Because this essay is about the nexus between foreign policy and military power, I will trouble the less strategic reader with as little strategic studies jargon and arcana as the mission allows. The proposition debated here holds that an information (I)-led RMA enables advanced militaries (i.e., principally the US, at present) to wage war (including intervention in others' quarrels) far more cost-effectively than before. An RMA is defined with useful parsimony as a radical change in the character and conduct of war (e.g., edged weapons to gunpowder, mercenary armies to national armies, reinvention of combined-arms land warfare led by indirect artillery fire in 1917–18, nuclear weapons). But it is essential to remember that RMA is a heavily and essentially contested concept. References here to *the* RMA are made in full knowledge of the rich stew of relevant competing ideas.

The strategic history of the 1990s was 'bookended' by events which pointed to an I-led RMA as the only defence story worth thinking about for a cutting-edge modern force. Information-led warfare was to the US defence debate in the 1990s what nuclear weapons had been in the 1950s: the only game in town. From the severe mauling of an Iraqi armoured corps at Khafgi in January 1991,[1] to the 'victory through airpower (above 8,000 ft)' in Kosovo in 1999, a new era of near-bloodless (at least, to the victor) military advantage appeared to have dawned.[2] The 1990s showed yet again that by prudent innovation, and with some luck, states can secure a significant lead in military prowess over all foes, albeit only for a while.

The RMA literature relevant to the current debate has deep multinational roots which need not detain non-specialists. RMAs need prophet–advocates, and the I-led case is no exception. At some small risk of offending the editors of this distinctly scholarly journal, I recommend two American novelists whose 'techno-thrillers' capture best the spirit of the contemporary I-led RMA. For access to the I-led RMA mindset one can do no better than read the novels of Dale Brown and, of course, the legendary Tom Clancy.[3] The last quarter of Clancy's latest fantasy, *The Bear and the Dragon*, provides unparalleled amusement for those who want to see how technologically challenged armed forces (the Chinese People's Liberation Army (PLA), in this case) are taught the error of their ways when they mess with the best (trained at the US Army's National Training Centre at Ft. Irwin, California, and at the US Navy's Top Gun Fighter school at Miramar, California). Moving from explicit fiction to probable fiction, the most accessible sacred text of this alleged RMA is the new book by the revolution's foremost advocate, Admiral Bill Owens, USN (retd.), provocatively entitled *Lifting the Fog of War*.[4] As we shall see, Owens believes that RMAed armed forces can secure 'dominant battlespace knowledge' and exploit that inestimable advantage to achieve prompt victory through precision firepower and decisive manoeuvre, all at exceedingly low cost to friendly forces. In short, Owens has in mind a 21st-century variant of General Kitchener's triumphs at Omdurman in 1898, when an Anglo–Egyptian punitive expedition gave the Mahdi's courageous dervishes a tactical lesson in the effectiveness of modern firepower.

It is not hard to find variants of sceptical assessment of RMA theory, especially on theory of the kind just cited. The best places to begin are with Lawrence Freedman's Adelphi Paper on *The Revolution in Strategic*

Affairs and Williamson Murray's characteristically hard–hitting article, 'Thinking About Revolutions in Military Affairs'.[5] For more substantial fare, readers may care to consult one recent and two large forthcoming books: Michael O'Hanlon's *The RMA and the Future of Warfare* is a competent assessment by a first-rate technical journalist which casts a cumulatively deadly shadow of doubt over claims for swift technological progress; Williamson Murray and MacGregor Knox (eds.), *The Dynamics of Military Revolution*, offers a superb collection of historical case studies of RMAs; while my own *Strategy for Chaos: RMA Theory and the Evidence of History*, strives to bridge the great divide between theory and history.[6] The debate over RMA and the literature of that debate is now maturing rapidly.

It may be useful at this stage to provide a brief checklist of principal sources of scepticism about the promise in a much (and long) advertised information-led Revolution in Military Affairs.

1. Scholars are not agreed on the nature of this RMA. Is it a Military Revolution, after the fashion of the Industrial Revolution, which must change society? Is it a particular set of largely operational-level military challenges, to be met as an RMA with suitable programmes? Or is it merely a Military–Technical Revolution; yet another notable change in weapons, and weapons support, technologies?

2. RMA advocates have a disturbing habit of factoring out of contention the human element in war and strategy.[7] This charge has been denied vociferously, of course, but it has yet to be refuted convincingly. The RMA literature is abundantly seeded with the erroneous notion that 'weapons win wars' (as contrasted to the 'weapons with which wars are won').

3. As the reverse side of the coin just cited, technology is regularly overvalued. In the inimitable words of Admiral Bill Owens: 'I believe the technology that is available to the US military today and now in development can revolutionize the way we conduct military operations. That technology can give us the ability to see a 'battlefield' as large as Iraq or Korea – an area 200 miles on a side – with unprecedented fidelity, comprehension, and timeliness; by night or day, in any kind of weather, all the time.'[8] Should we laugh or should we cry at this hubris and general lack of respect for Clausewitz's master concept of friction?[9]

4. War is not bombardment. It is of course useful to be able to strike targets from a long distance, using means that do not expose friendly personnel. A systemic problem with this RMA is that it is narrowly focused at the sharp end upon the ability to conduct precise bombardment. If the bombardment should fail to hit the targets, or if the human players decline to be intimidated, inevitably the question arises, 'what next?' If anything, in its dominant air power variant this RMA augments the already severe problems of military and strategic effectiveness that tend to afflict the hammer-from-above.

5. I-led RMA advocates are so busy plotting their military prowess in the middle and far distance that they are apt to be dismissive of the large problems with operational performance now. To put it bluntly, the soldiers have to be good at fighting. Recall the embarrassment of the Apache helicopters that were supposed to terrify the Serbs in Kosovo?

6. A focus on high-tech RMAed armed forces, looking to use state of the art C4ISR to be able to deliver precision firepower, has a way of creating strategic tunnel vision. Dazzled by our own prospective military brilliance, we can forget that a well motivated and competent, if materially challenged, foe is going to be looking hard for asymmetrical sources of strategic leverage against us.

7. Heavy respect for the 'revolution' in RMA inevitably places history's continuities at a discount. History, even military history, is much more evolutionary than revolutionary. The RMA concept discourages careful thought about the variables that are truly slow to vary and, indeed, about the elements that are always true (importance of training, leadership, etc.).

8. Because RMA theory is radically future-oriented, with that future by definition promising superior returns to effort, a proper respect for careful historical evidence can be hard to locate. An advocate of the I-led RMA can be hard to persuade that all major RMAs have a comparable life-cycle, and that therefore there is much useful to learn from, say, 1917–18, and the 1950s and 1960s.[10]

9. It is not necessarily a criticism of the I-led RMA to note that because it is unfolding in real time, careful historical judgment upon its

emerging successes and failures is not possible. If there is much to argue about with respect to Desert Storm, how much greater is the uncertainty over the triumphs and disappointments of Allied Force 1999 in Kosovo? Analysis and judgment of an instant kind is merely journalism. History may or may not confirm that air power finally delivered in 1999. It is really much too soon to say.

THE TEMPTATION TO MEDDLE

Although our topic of the RMA and intervention has been promoted to scholarly notice by the mixed Realpolitik and Moralpolitik of the 'bookend' events of 1991 and 1999, it is important to understand that the RMA is a value-neutral concept/instrument. An I-led RMA can serve *any* genus of political urge in statecraft and strategy. To clarify, the RMA story can facilitate an internationally illegal Clintonite–Blairite humanitarian intervention in the Balkans, while it could just as well enable US intervention to thwart a PLA assault upon democratic Taiwan. Lest there be any misunderstanding, it is probably important to depersonalize the discussion. The officials and others criticized here are by and large both technically bright and politically and morally well-meaning people. The problem is that they are strategically ignorant. History shows as clearly as it can be shown that RMAs great and small do not cancel the holistic complex nature and functioning of strategy.[11] Even radical change in the conduct of war will prove to command only near-term advantage in a competitive context, while the performance of weaponry – *if* that is key to an RMA in question – is always hostage to the ability and willingness of people to use it, and to the wisdom of the policy that it should support. The Nazi Wehrmacht was one of the greatest armies in all of history, but it was wasted waging (some of) the wrong war(s).[12]

Because much of this discussion will be critical of the RMA concept, I must protect myself pre-emptively against any valid-seeming charges of advanced Luddism. Better weapons (for the jobs on hand) are preferable to worse weapons. Knowledge (rather than mere information) is preferable to ignorance. At least at a high level of ambition, the intention of US I-led RMAers is wholly admirable. There is nothing whatsoever wrong with the desire to build better informed, more securely yet flexibly commanded, armed forces able to strike over long distances both with high precision and in aid of dashing operational manoeuvre. The problem lies not in the vision, but rather in the items that the vision cannot encompass. Wise policy can be advanced by effective military power, but military power ceases to be *strategically* effective when in effect it is allowed into the driving seat of policy. The I-led RMA of concern here is dangerous exactly because it encourages a mindless equation of (nominal) military capability with desired political outcomes (i.e., intended strategic effect). What follows is a terse statement of the dilemma.

At least in consequentialist logic bearing on intervention, the much-advertised I-led RMA bids fair to enable circles to be squared and potential moral mazes to be evaded altogether. Classic moral and political tests for wise policy appear less and less relevant. The standard ways to probe rigorously for policy choices that would meet 'just war' criteria appear to be all but completely sidelined.[13] If our planned military action is certain to be highly discriminating and, if anything, disproportionately non-destructive, now we have the strategic rapier of the fencing master. We can and should question whether military power truly is as precise in its application, and especially in its consequences, as just suggested. But still it would be a mistake to permit this debate to descend strictly into the realm of the military tactical. If we allow that to happen, then we become vulnerable to persuasion by technical, rather than political or strategic, argument.

If the tests for just conduct in war are impacted by the evolving technical–tactical story of the I-led RMA, so also must be the criteria for potential action that we associate with the national interest discriminator. What just war and national interest have in common is a role as licensor of policy action, *ceteris paribus*. The RMA can unravel them both. National interest analysis is as essential a guide to statecraft as it is apt to be treated with disdain by scholars today.[14] Such analysis should tell us in roughly rank-ordered fashion what and how intense are our interests. Subject to higher political vision and determination of (probably shifting) policy goals, a firm grip on the concept of national interest enables the policy-maker to function strategically with some confidence and competence. Not to mince words, national interest analysis is in the pricing business. To support national interest ends, we have to be prepared to expend national asset means. This is what strategy is all about.

The I-led RMA does not and cannot threaten this logic of strategy, but by promising relatively cheap success it encourages an elevation of policy aspiration.[15] If means are cheap in our blood and treasure, let them be applied in pursuit of ambitious policy ends. In 1999, NATO undertook a protracted air campaign against Yugoslavia on behalf of what one would be hard pressed to identify as more than a third or even fourth order interest.[16] Of course, NATO had nearly talked itself into a diplomatic corner of commitment, in classic Schellingesque fashion,[17] but that sad fact does not alter the point that the alliance allowed itself to be held hostage to events which wiser policy might have chosen to ignore. Belief in the model of 'war' as precise and even stand–off bombardment enabled London and Washington to find moral and political justification essentially in the sword itself. The C4 (command, control, communications, computers), the ISR (surveillance and reconnaissance), and the strike assets all combine to help legitimate what this I-led RMA may accomplish as an instrument of policy. If the political and moral stakes are believed to be high, but the costs of action (to us and to them) are very low, deeper policy questions can be deflected by military answers. Traditional just war criteria require a more than fair prospect of success, as well as an intent to do a lot more good than evil. Our contemporary RMA is touted to provide inexpensive success, but with the proviso that even if a recalcitrant victim cannot be coerced from altitude, the costs of the war are going to be so low and controllable that strategic and political failure will not much matter. This is not Vietnam, after all! In the 21st century no RMAed US military machine is likely to be unleashed so as to destroy a country in order to save it from the error of its ways. All of which is very much to the good, except that as the costs of military action appear to drop off the chart so too does much of the strategic discipline which should be the governing element.

FROM HUBRIS TO NEMESIS

Much as errors in policy and strategy are wont to have temporally extensive consequences, while strictly tactical and operational mistakes can frequently be corrected in near real–time, so political folly at the highest level is apt to trump all other considerations. The truth of the matter about British foreign policy under New Labour is not that it has made a mistake here and there, but rather that it has rested upon an entirely fantastic world view. Some people would offer in partial mitigation the excusatory thought that Prime Minister Tony Blair and the Foreign Secretary during Labour's first term, Robin Cook, are but the latest exemplars of a long line of British and American politicians who simply did not understand that foreign policy has to be guided by the national interest, a concept which is not significantly capable of being expressed in moral terms. Mr Cook repeated the role and took the stance made painfully familiar in the 1880s by none other than William Ewart Gladstone. These portentous words by the great windbag bear directly upon the moral uplift the updraft of which New Labour was to celebrate 120 years later.

> Certain it is that a new law of nations is gradually taking hold of the mind, and coming to sway the practice of the world; a law which recognizes independence, which frowns upon aggression, which favours the pacific, not bloody settlement of disputes, which aims at permanent and not temporary adjustments, above all, which recognizes, as a tribunal of paramount authority, the general judgment of civilized mankind.[18]

The Blair–Cook doctrine for a moral foreign policy found it politically impracticable to try to appeal to any 'general judgment of civilized mankind', wherever such a treasure might be deemed to reside. Instead, military intervention was undertaken against Yugoslavia over Kosovo on the basis of what amounted to an *ad hoc* application of a test of moral outrage. Specifically, Cook was persuaded that the humanitarian crisis in Kosovo comprised 'extraordinary circumstances' which warranted an extraordinary and, we must add, illegal, military intervention.[19] One does not wish to be churlish or morally unempathetic, but there has to be something fundamentally unsound about a process leading to a decision rule for foreign policy which is allowed to descend to the level of moral indignation felt by key cabinet ministers. There may, or may not, be excellent reasons for Britain and the United States to lead a NATO coalition into militarily notable intervention. Those reasons, however, have to be rendered explicit in terms of interests, not simply sentiments. In outraged pride, or hubris, lurks the serious peril of nemesis by ambition. If Moralpolitik, for all its inappropriateness, translates strictly into policy urges to discipline and re-educate all but the most helpless among the world's failing polities, the course of events still may offer some unpleasant surprises; but the hubris of 'nation and state building' is pregnant with more dangerous possibilities. It is worth recalling that a later variant of the same school of prideful American social scientists who believed that they could build nations in South East Asia in the 1960s, was generating in the early 1990s a scarcely less absurd new literature on how post-Cold War America would reverse the course of history for 'failed or failing states'. The truly impressive continuity from the Vietnam to the Somali eras is the reappearance of overweening pride.

The Cook doctrine of intervention in 'exceptional circumstances' (judged to be such by Mr Cook, of course) wreaks little damage provided it is well led by hypocrisy. To explain, although the world is replete with cases of wrongdoing which might trigger executive action under the Cook doctrine, in practice Cook was only a 'cheap hawk' for doing good in the world. This is fortunate and prudent. British special operations forces are more than capable of spreading a little civilization at the expense of the West Side Boys in Sierra Leone, for example. From time to time, there will be a happy coincidence of very low costs both to ourselves and to truly despicable foes. One would like to know quite where the British interest lies in the stakes in such intervention, but no matter – if the price is low and the job is readily doable. We can regard such raids and active training missions as useful exercise for what otherwise tend to be underused elite soldiers.

It needs to be noted, though, that Sierra Leone lies on the spectrum of potential cases for intervention which contains also such actual challenges as Somalia, Bosnia, and Kosovo, not to mention Chechnya and Taiwan. Round two in Chechnya did not trip the alarm switch on Bill Clinton or Tony Blair's Moralpolitik meter, but it should have done so. As a guide for moral behaviour in foreign policy, plainly there is something rotten with outrage as the standard for offence against humane values. The problem, of course, is that scale of moral affront inherently is utterly disconnected from probability of strategic effectiveness. In short, our practical problem with Chechnya is that there is nothing useful that Britain or the United States could do to assist the Chechens. New Labour has had to learn what President Woodrow Wilson also had to learn, that crusaders for the good need large, sharp swords, and plenty of them.

This section is titled 'hubris to nemesis', because the puffed up pride in moral judgment which produced the hubris which embroiled us foolishly in the Balkans in the 1990s may yet seduce us into much more perilous interventions.[20] A large fraction of the difficulty lies with that frequently overlooked dimension of strategy, the enemy. Also important is the fact that bombardment, even precise bombardment, does not equal war, any more than military effectiveness necessarily equates narrowly to strategic effectiveness. Two aspects to the enemy dimension are worth emphasizing here. First, there may well be more to an enemy than meets our first glance. The easy mark, the apparently primitive foe, may be nothing of the kind when considered in his full context. Notwithstanding their numerous villainies and limitations, Saddam Hussein, Slobodan Milosevic and General Aideed were all of them more than capable of holding their own in cunning statecraft against the scions of Harvard, Yale, Oxford and West Point. Second, we need to venture a little Clausewitzian analysis and speculate to the effect that we may have to deal with 'adaptive enemies'.[21] Not only might our I-led, RMAed armed forces fail to bring home the coonskin with stand-off precise bombardment, but we might find ourselves confronting a regional or even just local foe (or coalition) who will elect, and be able, to join us in battle grand strategically and strategically. In other words, pride in our I-led modern RMAed armed forces might blind us to a nemesis lurking around the corner who has located a possibly effective answer to our whole way of war.[22] Contemporary strategic discourse has a somewhat unsatisfactory term for this phenomenon; it is called asymmetric warfare.[23]

In an outstanding analysis, the former Commandant of the US Army War College, Major General Robert H. Scales Jr., has shown how more and more non-Western countries are adapting to the American military hegemonic moment by declining to buy small versions of the full suite of Western military power.[24] From the People's Republic of China, through Iran, to Yugoslavia, and most way stations in between, polities can try to acquire particular military capabilities which could test the Western, especially the US, way of war quite severely. Many foes of the West should enjoy some truly significant systematic strategic advantages, for all their lack of the traditional major engines of war. Specifically, the West's enemies may well not be pushed for time – they will not be under domestic or international political pressure to go home for early tea; they are likely to be extraordinarily strongly committed to the stakes at issue (after all, the contest will be distinctly local for them); they are unlikely to be strongly casualty-averse; and they will probably enjoy home field advantage. The better fighting forces, even if they lose in war, adapt to their circumstances and seek to exploit their relative strengths in order to offset the effect of their relative weaknesses, as was the case with the Wehrmacht. As we consider Anglo–American (to flatter London) stewardship of the contemporary world order, it is all too easy to recognize just how narrow is the military base in intervention options which appears to license, and certainly enables, a supposedly righteous foreign policy.

Whatever the doctrine of justification – 'exceptional circumstances' or some other – Anglo–American military intervention will be led by manned and unmanned air power which works its effects via precision bombardment.[25] Serbs, and even Iraqis, have shown that they are more than capable of playing 'hiders and finders' with good success against a coalition unwilling to risk casualties among its fliers or among the probably innocent on the ground. At least the West was fortunate in 1999 in that Belgrade was prepared to confine the 'war' to traditional channels. In the future, Western theorists who believe that their RMA has provided an all-purpose rapier may well wake up to discover that 'war' is assuming a distinctly unfamiliar character. What if the 'war' has WMD (weapons of mass destruction) and terrorists as its leading edge? Or, how about a designer plague? More prosaically, what if a regional foe of the West declines to mass its military power in ways that must risk a Trafalgar or Desert Storm, but instead undertakes a patient programme of logistical harassment against access to the area in contention. Much as in Vietnam, definition of victory is key to strategic success. Western scholars of unconventional warfare should know that in an important sense guerrillas win by not losing and also that there are no decisive battles in guerrilla war.[26] No regional foe of Anglo–American I-led RMAed air power may hope to defeat that air power, but this would not be necessary. The US Army was not defeated in Vietnam, but by the time it had won most of what it could win on the ground – by late 1968, in other words – the strategic context had been transformed and there was no time for victory to be consolidated and exploited.

The name of the game for enemies of the West, therefore, must be to attack what passes for Western strategy. US and British armed forces most likely will be unbeatable in the field, so they will not be challenged there. Rather will the mission be to deny Anglo–American military power the ability to achieve swift political success via the speedy, precise use of information-led air power. Such a Western campaign could be contested tactically, operationally, militarily strategically, grand strategically, or at the highest level of policy legitimacy. Although the structures and caveats developed here may appear to be only idly speculative, in reality they are much more serious than that. I rest the scepticism in my argument upon the enduring nature of strategy and war and especially upon the fact that adaptive enemies are a structural item, not merely an occasional inconvenience.

It is not entirely obvious that Western military establishments trained for the operations of the 1990s will be at all ready for the asymmetrical challenges to which their masters may unexpectedly expose them in the years ahead. It was one thing to be outgeneralled by General Aideed, but what if the United States is outgeneralled yet again, only this time it is over the Taiwan Straits? A new struggle for mastery in Asia may well be beginning now.[27] China's PLA would be a very different enemy from the one for which all Western strategic thinkers over a certain age were trained. Asian geography, culture, politics, and history combine to produce a putative enemy all but designed by central casting to be misunderstood in Washington. It is scant consolation to register the parallel observation that we can repose little confidence in China's ability to understand US motivation and behaviour either. Suffice it to say for now that the hubris which encouraged NATO's Balkan follies in the 1990s is not at all unlikely to lead to a confrontation with what could be its nemesis in the form of China. Lest I am misunderstood, the problem as developed here is not so much with the need to discipline a would-be hegemonic China – that raises more fundamental issues, far beyond the scope of this discussion – but rather with the military confidence with which one approaches that formidable task. Ten years of some experience and a great deal of speculative debate suggests strongly that there is much less to the contemporary I-led RMA than appears to meet the eye.

This is unfortunate for Robin Cook and other like-minded moralists, because their preferred doctrine of military intervention rests on the assumption of a permissive military environment which allows immaculate bombardment from altitude. Whereas the Balkans were largely embarrassing to (low-level) Western interests, the 2000s and beyond could see Western military power bloodily repulsed – or even evaded by some 'doomsday terrorism'[28] – by a regional polity which had taken its asymmetrical warfare options seriously.

NOTES

1. See Lawrence Freedman and Efraim Karsh, *The Gulf Conflict, 1990/1: Diplomacy and War in the New World Order* (Princeton, NJ: Princeton University Press, 1992), pp.364–6; and Thomas A. Keaney and Eliot A. Cohen, *Gulf War Air Power Survey: Summary Report* (Washington, DC: US Government Printing Office, 1993), pp.109–11.

2. Daniel L. Byman and Matthew C. Waxman, 'Kosovo and the Great Air Power Debate', *International Security*, Vol.24, No.4 (Spring 2000), pp.5–38, sensibly places air power in its strategic context. In the 1990s, Edward N. Luttwak functioned as the prophet of casualty-averse warfare: 'Towards Post-heroic Warfare', *Foreign Affairs*,Vol.74, No.3 (May/June 1995), pp.109–21; 'A Post-heroic Military Policy', *Foreign Affairs*, Vol.75, No.4 (July/Aug. 1996), pp.33–44.

3. For representative products, see: Dale Brown, *Fatal Terrain* (New York: HarperCollins, 1998); and Tom Clancy, *The Bear and the Dragon* (London: Michael Joseph, 2000).

4. Admiral Bill Owens, *Lifting the Fog of War* (New York: Farrar, Straus & Giroux, 2000).

5. Lawrence Freedman, *The Revolution in Strategic Affairs*, Adelphi Paper 318 (London: International Institute for Strategic Studies, 1998); and Williamson Murray, 'Thinking About Revolutions in Military Affairs', *Joint Force Quarterly*, No.16 (Summer 1997), pp.69–76.

6. Michael O'Hanlon, *Technological Change and the Future of Warfare* (Washington, DC: Brookings Institution Press, 2000); Williamson Murray and MacGregor Knox (eds.), *The Dynamics of Military Revolution, 1300–2050* (Cambridge: Cambridge University Press, 2001); and Colin S. Gray, *Strategy for Chaos: RMA Theory and the Evidence of History* (London: Frank Cass, forthcoming).

7. This accusation figures prominently in a well-argued article by two marines. Paul K. Van Riper and F. Q. Hoffman, 'Pursuing the Real Revolution in Military Affairs: Exploring Knowledge-Based Warfare', *National Security Studies Quarterly*, Vol.4, No.3 (Summer 1998), pp.1–19.

8. Owens, *Lifting the Fog of War*, p.14.

9. Carl von Clausewitz, *On War*, Michael Howard and Peter Paret trans. (Princeton, NJ: Princeton University Press, 1976), pp.119–21.

10. As I argue at length in my *Strategy for Chaos*.

11. For an endeavour to explain what strategy is (and is not) and how it works, see Colin S. Gray, *Modern Strategy* (Oxford: Oxford University Press, 1999), especially chapters 1 and 3.

12. Unfortunately, one of the reasons why its fighting power and effectiveness was so high was that very strength of ideological commitment which reflected the political drive of a regime incapable of conducting statecraft and war with strategic prudence. See Omer Bartov, *Hitler's Army: Soldiers, Nazis, and War in the Third Reich* (Oxford: Oxford University Press, 1991); and Williamson Murray and Allan R. Millett, *A War To Be Won: Fighting the Second World War* (Cambridge, MA: Harvard University Press, 2000), esp. p.483.

13. The literature on just war is huge. On the medieval foundation and development of the concept see Frederick H. Russell, *The Just War in the Middle Ages* (Cambridge: Cambridge University Press, 1975). Excellent general treatments include James Turner Johnson, *Just War Tradition and the Restraint of War: A Moral and Historical Inquiry* (Princeton, NJ: Princeton University Press, 1981); Robert L. Holmes, *On War and Morality* (Princeton, NJ: Princeton University Press, 1989); and particularly A. J. Coates, *The Ethics of War* (Manchester: Manchester University Press, 1997).

14. Henry Kissinger, *Diplomacy* (New York: Simon and Schuster, 1994), is a fine corrective to such scholarly dismissal; while Condoleezza Rice, 'Promoting the National Interest', *Foreign Affairs*, Vol.79, No.1 (Jan./Feb. 2000), pp.45–62, illustrates admirably why Kissinger is correct.

15. For a literate overstatement of some of the dilemmas posed by information-led warfare, see Michael Ignatieff, *Virtual War: Kosovo and Beyond* (New York: Metropolitan Books, 2000).

16. In other words, our relevant interest(s) in, and relating closely to, 'the Balkans' (to use the familiar, if geographically inaccurate, expression), were neither 'vital' (meaning essential to fight for) nor 'major' (meaning plainly worth fighting for).

17. See Thomas C. Schelling, *Arms and Influence* (New Haven, CT: Yale University Press, 1966), ch. 2, 'The Art of Commitment'.

18. Quoted in Kissinger, *Diplomacy*, p.161. It would be difficult to compose a more erroneous characterization of the temper of statecraft in the very late 19th century than this.

19. Pre-Kosovo cases of intervention vs state sovereignty in the 1990s are well handled in Andrew Valls (ed.), *Ethics in International Affairs: Theories and Cases* (Lanham, MD: Rowman and Littlefield Publishers, 2000), Part IV.

20. Admittedly, there would seem to be much less danger of this happening now that the White House is occupied by George W. Bush.

21. For the fundamental point that belligerents are adaptive, see Clausewitz, *On War*, p.77.

22. Sun Tzu advises, 'Thus the highest realization of warfare is to attack the enemy's plans...' *Art of War*, Ralph D. Sawyer trans. (Boulder, CO: Westview Press, 1994), p.177. The Chinese master can be translated as attack the enemy's *strategy*.

23. For exceptional clarity on this generally rather murky subject, see Steven Metz and Douglas V. Johnson II, *Asymmetry and US Military Strategy: Definition, Background, and Strategic Concepts* (Carlisle Barracks, PA: US Army War College, The Strategic Studies Institute, Jan. 2001).

24. Robert H. Scales, Jr., 'Adaptive Enemies: Dealing with the Strategic Threat After 2010', *Strategic Review*, Vol.27, No.1 (Winter 1999), pp.5–14.

25. For reasons explained well in Benjamin S. Lambeth, 'The Technology Revolution in Air Warfare', *Survival*, Vol.39, No.4 (Spring 1997), pp.65–83; but note the caveats in O'Hanlon, *Technological Change and the Future of Warfare*, ch.4.

26. Mao Tse-Tung [attrib.], *On Guerilla Warfare*, Samuel B. Griffith trans. (New York: Frederick A. Praeger, 1961), p.52.

27. I thank Aaron L. Friedberg, who is of course indebted to A. J. P. Taylor, for the turn of phrase. See Friedberg, 'Will Europe's Past be Asia's Future?', *Survival*, Vol.42, No.3 (Autumn 2000), pp.147–59; and 'The Struggle for Mastery in Asia', *Commentary Magazine*, (Nov. 2000), (http://www.commentarymagazine.com/0011/friedberg.html).

28. See Martin Shubik, 'Terrorism, Technology, and the Socioeconomics of Death', *Comparative Strategy*, Vol.16, No.4 (Oct./Dec. 1997), pp.399–414; and Richard K. Betts, 'The New Threat of Mass Destruction', *Foreign Affairs*, Vol.77, No.1 (Jan./Feb. 1998), pp.26–41, for some blood-curdling possibilities.

Implications of the Weinberger Doctrine for American Military Intervention in a Post-Desert Storm Age

CORI E. DAUBER[1]

This article makes three key arguments. First, I argue that the Weinberger Doctrine, although it dates to 1984 and is seldom explicitly referred to any more (having given way to the preferred label the 'Powell Doctrine') is very much in play in the public debate over military intervention in the United States. Second, I argue that Argument Studies is an important form of analysis that has been neglected and can shed important light on the way the public debate influences decisions made in the United States over military intervention. Specifically it has a great deal to say about the way the Weinberger Doctrine influences these debates. Third I argue that understanding Weinberger requires first understanding the way history is marshalled as the basis for argument in the political sphere. This is of particular interest here because the dominance of the Weinberger Doctrine in public debate embeds a strong (but subtle) bias against humanitarian intervention. This arguably led to a strange distortion of mission structure in the 1990s as humanitarian missions were in a sense 'disguised' to look like Weinberger missions. And that matters because of a possibility that in response the Bush administration may hold to the Weinberger line in a way that will lead to a form of isolationism in outcome if not intent.

I will focus first on the role played by arguments over the meaning of Vietnam, and the way different interpretations of the Vietnam war have influenced public debates over potential American military deployments. I will then examine a specific argumentative structure generated from a particular interpretation of Vietnam – the Weinberger Doctrine. And finally I will explore the contributions an argument - centred study of Weinberger can make to our understanding of contemporary constraints on American decisions regarding interventions abroad.

HISTORICAL CONTEXT

Articulating military history (like any history) is an essentially rhetorical or argumentative process. History itself, meaning the actual events, what happened when, in what order, who did what, may be unchanging. Our understandings of history, the meanings we give it, are not. We accord meaning to history through the narratives we provide. Without a narrative, history is nothing more than a jumble of facts, figures and dates with no meaning – and no ability, therefore, to impact contemporary policy debates.[2] History is the raw material that generates lessons learned – itself a fundamentally argumentative process. Each set of lessons learned is a series of arguments in defence of a particular interpretation of events, and the meaning that interpretation has for the way we ought to proceed in the future.

Some interpretations achieve what might be called *hegemonic* status, reaching the point where they are widely seen as 'common sense'. These interpretations, understood as arguments in favour of a particular interpretation, require careful study. Seeing history in terms of its potential influence on policy debates means seeing historical interpretations as generative resources for arguments. Seeing them that way changes the focus of study from that normally associated with traditional historical inquiry.

Interpretations of historical events are never settled; they are fluid. History, or rather dominant interpretations of history, become an interpretive lens through which we see the choices that confront us now, and prior choices we have made.

This means, among other things, that the study of secondary texts and sources may actually be *more* relevant than the study of primary documents in some circumstances. Indeed, secondary texts are a vital resource, for it is in such texts that interpretative narratives are located. And it is such narratives that are the bedrock of arguments over contemporary policy based on argument from history.

From this perspective it is virtually impossible to discuss American military policy without discussing Vietnam. (It is not especially easy to discuss it from other points of view without a consideration of Vietnam, either.)

The Vietnam experience affected the US military so deeply and so broadly that it lurks behind most of what has been thought and done in military and security affairs since then, even when civilian or military officials specifically disavow a connection. Vietnam is so much a part of the foundation on which present behavior is premised that it forms part of the context of influence as a matter of fact, even when it is not accepted in this role as a matter of consciousness.[3]

For the military, Vietnam was a 'near death experience'.[4] In the immediate aftermath of the war, the services were silent, not even teaching it in their various academies and war colleges.[5] The implication was that Vietnam was an anomalous experience, one that could be bracketed out from the study of military history without cost. Only gradually did the services begin to come to grips with what had happened, and to search for explanations for what had gone wrong. This work, from the beginning, has been framed in the context of a desire to ensure that 'never again' would the American military find itself in similar circumstances. The issues that engaged civilian historians were not relevant. In that sense the Vietnam experience was completely decontextualized. All that mattered was the way Vietnam had been fought.

Early on in that process a study was produced by Colonel Harry Summers, Jr. This book has had a long history, moving from war college to war college, and finally being published by a civilian press.[6] It is easily one of the most influential studies of the Vietnam war. Its quality from the standpoint of academic historical work is irrelevant: it is compelling historical argumentation. It explicitly brackets out strategic considerations in order to focus on the 'operational' level, the connector between the strategic and tactical. Summers' argument is that there was no flaw in the performance of American forces. In fact, he argues that they were never defeated on the ground. He asserts that 'the sad tragedy of Vietnam was that at the tactical and operational levels ... [t]hey won every major battle ... The same was true in the air and on the sea.'[7] He quotes a historian as saying that the American forces did 'not lose a single important battle. It was a record unparalleled in the history of modern warfare.'[8]

How is it that an army (Summers' focus is on the US Army) never defeated in battle could lose a war? At the very beginning of the book

Summers notes that on 'the battlefield itself, the Army was unbeatable ... How could we have succeeded so well, yet failed so miserably? That disturbing question was the reason for this book.'[9] His position is that failure was the result of flawed connections between strategic and tactical performance. And suddenly the army is off the hook. They need not agonize over what they did wrong – because in point of fact they did nothing wrong. The real point of Vietnam, the real lesson to be learned if such a disaster is to be avoided in the future, from Summers' perspective, has nothing to do with the way the war was fought on the ground. The real point is that the relationship between the military and the civilian leadership then in place could not have produced a successful outcome.

The war, in essence, was lost because decisions which should have been left to professional military officers were made by civilians. These civilians, arrogant and overconfident, in point of fact lacked the appropriate expertise. They conceptualized war as an extension of diplomatic activity, as communication.[10] They did not produce militarily obtainable objectives.[11] They micro-managed, particularly with regard to bombing targets.[12] They hobbled the military with Rules of Engagement, sanctuaries for the enemy that were off limits, and periodic pauses (primarily an issue of concern for the Air Force). They did not, in short, permit the military to *fight*. And, perhaps above all, they made no effort whatsoever to ensure the support of the American people.[13] The intervention of civilian officials in these decisions was inappropriate, counterproductive, and ultimately cost the country a war it could easily have won. The central lessons to be learned from the Vietnam experience, therefore, have to do not with the specifics of military performance – which can hardly be evaluated negatively under such circumstances – but with the specifics of *civilian* performance, and the relationship between the civilians and the military.

From this point of view, contemporary academic analysts of the civil–military relationship thus miss the point.[14] Understanding the arguments surrounding public debate over military force does not involve an assessment of the solidity of civilian control over the military. This argumentative structure centres instead on the importance of civilians controlling *themselves*, making sure they do not interfere in matters best left to the military when taking the nation to war.

The Summers perspective slowly but surely attained hegemonic status within the military.[15] And, also as advocated by Summers, the services began to emphasize the importance of having the public's support before the nation was taken to war. Indeed, it was in roughly this period that the Army moved to the 'Total Force' concept, which involved moving several warfare communities and occupational specialities exclusively to the reserves. This would require that the President mobilize the reserves for any extended or extensive combat operation. It was quite clear at the time that this was done explicitly in response to Vietnam. (In that conflict the President had refused to mobilize the reserves, and both the President and the military saw that as an intentional move designed to detach the American public from the emotions of war.[16])

It was in this context that in 1984 the Weinberger Doctrine was announced. It reflected Summers' interpretation of what went wrong in Vietnam down the line, but inverted that analysis. While Summers' analysis is an assessment of what not to do, Weinberger instead produced a checklist of what *to* do in order to produce successful military operations.[17]

In a speech before the National Press Club, then Secretary of Defense Caspar Weinberger presented what are essentially conditions for the effective use of military power. The initial wording phrased the criteria as follows:

- Existence of a particular engagement or occasion deemed vital to our national interest or that of our allies.
- Wholehearted commitment with the clear intent of winning.
- Clear definition of political and military objectives.
- Forces capable of doing the job.
- Reassessment and adjustment of committed forces to meet combat requirements.
- Reasonable assurance of support of the American people and Congress.[18]

What is of interest for our purposes is the way various subsequent iterations of these conditions get articulated later. Each version simplifies and streamlines the checklist a little bit more than the previous one. Each compression enhances the ability of the Doctrine to function rhetorically as a 'common sense' argument structure. Weinberger paraphrases himself by translating these criteria into a formalized checklist. He begins with '1. Our vital interests must be at stake.'[19] That condition is rephrased in the literature in a fairly typical version as 'in defense of its vital interests'.[20] The second condition is paraphrased by Weinberger as '2. The issues involved are so important for the future of the United States and our allies that we are prepared to commit enough forces to win.' The version from the literature states that we should go 'with the clear intention of winning'. Weinberger then says in the paraphrase '3. We have clearly defined political and military objectives, which we must secure.' The later version says 'when the military objectives are clearly defined ...' Weinberger says '4. We have sized our forces to achieve our objectives', which seems to have simply disappeared as a discrete concern from the version taken from the literature. (Perhaps its intended parallel is the otherwise unmatched clause 'only when those objectives are worth the risk'.) Weinberger then paraphrases the original speech, '5. We have some reasonable assurance of the support of the American people.'(Note Congress is missing from this version.) The version from the literature reads, 'with the support of the American people and Congress' (Congress returns in this version, but support is here ranked second rather than Weinberger's fifth.) And '6. US forces are committed to combat only as a last resort', vs 'only as a last resort'. Thus Weinberger provides a paraphrase of himself that is in each clause simpler, tighter and less subtle than the original speech – and common versions in the literature are shorter and simpler still.

Today, this collective is often referred to as 'the Powell Doctrine' or 'Powellism'.[21] The Powell Doctrine itself is little more than an even more tightly compressed version of the Weinberger Doctrine:

> General Powell's approach has been that the military should be used only when there is a clear goal, a specific national interest at stake, popular support and an exit strategy – and when overwhelming numbers of troops and weapons can be marshaled for battle.[22]

The compressions and simplifications both function to make it easier for the Weinberger clauses to dominate public debate, and reflect the fact that they are already doing so.

The Doctrine has often been examined as military strategy. But it has not been explicitly studied as *argument strategy*. As argument, the Doctrine does two things. First, it demands that a President seeking to use American military power make a public and compelling case for the use of that power. His legal authority as Commander in Chief is not enough. The Doctrine presumes that the support of the public is essential, and that it is the President's job to rally that support. This can only be done through making the case publicly.

But the Doctrine goes further. It not only demands that the case for intervention be made by the President, in advance of any deployment, *it also lays out the criteria that should be used by the public to determine if the President has made a good enough case to justify their support*. How do we define a compelling argument in favour of intervention when we evaluate the case made by the President? By holding his arguments up against the standards set by the Doctrine; by evaluating the proposed intervention in the terms laid out by the Doctrine.

THE WEINBERGER DOCTRINE TODAY

The Weinberger Doctrine is certainly not *official* United States doctrine. The services began to back off from it in the early to mid 1990s, when it was quite clear that the Doctrine was placing them in an untenable rhetorical position. On the one hand, they were continuing to argue for the largest budgets they could obtain in a post-Cold War environment. On the other hand, they were also continuing to argue, on the basis of the Doctrine's tenets, that no possible deployment was quite right. The *sine qua non* of this problem was a now-famous exchange between then Chairman of the Joint Chiefs of Staff Colin Powell and then Ambassador to the United Nations Madeleine Albright. As he describes the story, the 'debate exploded at one session [regarding Bosnia] when Madeleine Albright ... asked me in frustration, "What's the point of having this superb military that you're always talking about if we can't use it?" I thought I would have an aneurysm.'[23] The story has been repeated so often it has virtually become a representative anecdote for the argument.

My point here is that, either way, its official status no longer matters. Rhetorically, argumentatively, it has achieved the status of *hegemonic discourse*. That is to say it so dominates *public* discourse that it is the controlling lens through which potential deployments are debated and justified. It is the Weinberger Doctrine which sets the terms of public debate in the United States, and which sets the grounds on which argument over intervention will take place. The Doctrine is so dominant that even deployments over the last ten years that have clearly not met the terms and criteria of the Doctrine have been justified in language suggesting that they have.

This was clearly the case in Bosnia, Haiti, and Kosovo. All were presented to the American people using language that made it sound as if troops would be used in situations more reminiscent of Desert Storm then the situation on the ground could possibly match.

Regarding the post-Dayton deployment of American troops to Bosnia, President Clinton said, the 'mission will be precisely defined with clear, realistic goals that can be achieved in a definite period of time',[24] meeting the standard of militarily obtainable objectives. He argued they would be making an 'overwhelming show of force' with the 'authority to respond immediately, and the training and the equipment to respond with overwhelming force to any threat to their own safety or any violations of the military provisions of the peace agreement',[25] meeting the standard of overwhelming force. He stated that in 'Bosnia we can and will succeed because our mission is clear and limited...' and that '[a]nyone – anyone – who takes on our troops will suffer the consequences. We will fight fire with fire – and then some',[26] again meeting the standard of overwhelming force.

Once the Kosovo bombing strikes began, President Clinton made it clear that the 'NATO allies have taken this action only after extensive and repeated efforts to obtain a peaceful solution to the crisis in Kosovo',[27] meeting the standard of using force only as a last resort. The objectives, as required, were specified in advance and were laid out as clear and militarily obtainable.

> Our strikes have three objectives: First, to demonstrate the seriousness of NATO's opposition to aggression and its support for peace. Second, to deter President Milosevic from continuing and escalating his attacks on helpless civilians by imposing a price for those attacks. And, third, if necessary, to damage Serbia's capacity to wage war against Kosovo in the future by seriously diminishing its military capabilities.[28]

Despite the lack of large-scale combat deployments easily designed to fit the Weinberger criteria, in other words, the Doctrine is still determinative in such debates. While it may no longer be the controlling argumentative structure of American military doctrinal statements,[29] it clearly continues to define American military preferences.[30] And there is no question it remains determinative in political debates. Weinberger sets the terms for debate, beginning with the rhetorical and argumentative justifications used by advocates of intervention, sustaining debates over proposed interventions and those on-going.

The Weinberger Doctrine as Argument Structure

The Weinberger Doctrine does more than dominate public debate in the United States. I would argue that it also functions as an argument structure itself, best understood as a template which establishes the terms under which political discourse over military intervention will be understood, assessed and evaluated.

Whenever the question arises as to whether or not the United States should deploy military forces in situations that might involve combat, there are actually three questions involved. Each triggers the other, in cascade fashion. Should we go in? If we go in, do we stay in? If we stay in, when is it time to leave? While it is useful to consider these questions as to some extent analytically distinct, they do not, of course, function quite that way in practice. The question of whether or not the United States should initiate intervention, for example, must involve predictive discussions to at least some extent. If my argument in the previous section is correct and the Weinberger Doctrine dominates public debates still, then there must be an accounting of cost and benefit up front. The Doctrine forces discussions of whether an intervention will be successful and how long it is likely to last. But in real debates the lines between the three questions can become very blurred.

It is nonetheless useful to keep them somewhat separate for purposes of analysis. In terms of public debate, the question of whether or not to intervene, and the role the other two questions play in that initial discussion, is fundamentally a debate over political viability. The kind of military deployment seen in Desert Storm – large-scale combat in response to one nation's invasion of another – is perhaps the least likely situation to be confronted by the US in today's world. Beyond the Persian Gulf and the Korean peninsula, it is difficult to imagine a context in which such a scenario might arise.[31] However, there are apparently failed states, ethnic conflicts and general carnage aplenty on every continent. Situations that would previously have been subsumed under the master narrative of Cold War containment, and thus essentially ignored as potential opportunities for US interventions, are suddenly on the table.[32]

In such a situation, given sufficient media attention, it may not take long before the perception is created, true or not, that there is, or will soon be, a demand from the American people that the United States 'do something.'[33] Indeed, this perception on the part of elites is often so taken for granted that it is not even questioned.[34] (This is closely linked with beliefs about the so-called 'CNN effect'.[35]) But the perception on the part of the 'punditocracy'[36] and other participants in the public debate that the public may demand action ironically does not necessarily eliminate the scepticism of the pundits themselves. Would an American intervention work? What would the disadvantages and costs be? Would we see it through? Thus participants in the media debate may simultaneously create the perception of a public demand for action (whether one exists or not) and argue strenuously against the wisdom of such action.

Weinberger in this context is best seen as a template used for debating the political viability of such missions. And the primary issue determining political viability is public support. This is not to say that there are not tensions and contradictions throughout the argument structure. It is, for example, to a large extent tautological. What else is political viability but the likelihood of continued public support? The question is why the likelihood of support is such a dominant issue when the initial impetus behind an intervention is the alleged demand from the American people that the United States 'do something'. An additional issue is, why, if the military exerts such extraordinary political control over which missions are chosen, public support matters at all. But despite these apparent[37] tensions and contradictions, the use of public support as something arguers appeal to in order to demonstrate the strength of their positions is real and must be explored.

First and foremost it must be understood that the Weinberger Doctrine, despite its six clauses, conditions or criteria, collapses into a demand for public support.[38] It is about support above and beyond any other issue. For while the Weinberger Doctrine as presented gives the impression that each of the criteria is of equal importance, close textual analysis makes clear that, in fact, public support as a requirement for successful military intervention is conceptually privileged – it functions as 'first among equals'.

It is, after all, the need for public support that drives the others. The others are conditions that define under what circumstances the public *should* give its support. The need for support is by definition what creates the need to determine when support is justified. It is also what functions as the trigger mechanism determining that the President must make a compelling argument to begin with. Indeed, the lack of a compelling argument is a central emphasis for opponents of American deployments. When President Clinton sent American soldiers to Kosovo in the aftermath of the NATO bombing campaign, Senator Bunning noted that the President 'has not given us any answers as to why sending these troops to Kosovo is so vital. President Clinton can tell us any time. But where is he? He has the bully pulpit ... I want to hear from President Clinton as to why this region is of a national security interest to the United States.'[39] Mr DeLay complained that 'before we get deeper embroiled into this Balkan quagmire, I think that an *assessment* has to be made of the Kosovo policy so far. President Clinton has never *explained* to the American people why he was involving the US military in a civil war in a sovereign nation...'[40] And the need for presidential argumentation links back to public support: 'Moreover, congressional and public support has been very weak because it has been unclear to most Americans how these interventions serve the national interest.'[41]

More fundamentally, the need for public support is the only condition that is not reducible. In other words, each of the other five conditions can be defended *either* on its own merits *or* because it will contribute to public support. Public support cannot be defended in terms of anything else, as something that translates into another desirable quality. Yet while each of the six conditions can be defended as intrinsic goods in and of themselves, they are not often defended *as* intrinsically good in public discussions. Instead, the other five are defended based on their capacity, if met as a condition, to ensure the continuation of public support. Why, then, do we go in only in support of vital national interests? We do so because the expenditure of blood and treasure will not be tolerated by the American people except insofar as that cost is balanced out by the vital nature of the stakes involved.[42] It is not that there is some intrinsic reason non-vital uses of force are unacceptable – they are assumed bad because it is assumed they would not receive or sustain public support. A 'purely' humanitarian intervention can be defended, but since public support will presumably be more fragile, it can only be defended successfully if the intervention can be presented as cost-free or very nearly so. Thus,

> the general reluctance to become involved in the actual fighting in Bosnia – despite years of the supposed 'CNN effect' – suggests that Americans reached the same conclusion regarding Bosnia as

they had over Somalia: The cost in American lives of policing a conflict like that should be virtually zero.[43]

The single determinant of public support that is assumed to matter more than any other is the number of casualties the US takes. And the link between casualties, public support and the public debate is made fairly explicitly.

> Ensuring that the war effort wins quick, wins big, and without casualties is the safest way to avoid the dangers of lengthy and indecisive conflict. Attaining these standards *denies critics the opportunities to mount an effective campaign against the war*. It also provides positive reinforcements for the home front.[44]

Given that Operation Allied Force in Kosovo resulted in zero casualties, this phenomenon is likely be exacerbated. This is all the more true in light of the fact that Kosovo occurred in the context, not just of Vietnam and Desert Storm, but of the American intervention in Somalia. After the American withdrawal from Somalia, in the wake of 18 casualties, the perception that every individual casualty may shake public opinion was only heightened.[45]

The notion that the acceptable level of casualties, particularly for humanitarian missions, is zero, seems somewhat overstated, until one looks at the public debates over the use of force. Thus the comment made by several opponents to particular interventions that all of (insert country name here) is 'not worth a single American life'. Regarding a range of military operations: 'It's not going to be a bloodbath or anything bad, but for one American to die for this dubious venture is too much.'[46] 'I don't think the President's made the case why a single American soldier put his life at risk there.'[47] 'Is it worth one more American funeral to be in Somalia for six more months? I say the answer is no.'[48] 'I have to tell you, in sincerity, that I don't believe the entire country of Somalia is worth one American soldier's life.'[49]

Thus public support, at least as manifested in polling data, is represented as brittle, fragile, subject to change very quickly. But these arguments are based on the assumption that while public support can change rapidly it can change in only one direction – down. Public debates over intervention, therefore, presume that public argument, in the form of case-making by advocates for intervention, will not work. Arguments may create support (hence the assumption that President

Johnson could have created support for Vietnam but chose not to) but cannot, apparently, be used to sustain support, at least not in the face of negative news. (And in this context negative news almost always means casualties taken.)

The argument goes that the only thing with even the potential to trump casualties is the existence of a vital national interest. And that has the potential to hold support steady, not to increase it. It is worth noting that in the places where the United States has chosen to intervene for humanitarian reasons, advocates of those interventions (Bosnia, Haiti and Kosovo) have defended each as justified for reasons of vital national interest. Thus both Bosnia and Kosovo were, at least initially, and at least intermittently, defended as being worthwhile because of the threat they posed of a larger conflict in Europe, a region of clear national interest to the United States. Haiti was defended in part due to the fear that a continued crisis in Haiti, a nation not only in the United States' sphere of influence but geographically quite close, would produce a refugee crisis in America. The Haiti example is an additional complication, in that it appears that President Clinton's decision to initiate an invasion of the island without support may have *itself* created support if overnight polls are to be believed, perhaps because doing so demonstrated leadership, perhaps because doing so was *in and of itself* an argument in favour of intervention.[50] Would a president invade a country without a good reason?

But Rwanda, a humanitarian crisis in a region not traditionally viewed as vital to American national interests, where there was no possibility of even a trumped-up argument for national interest, received no American intervention. It has since been reported that the White House exercised great caution in ensuring that the situation in Rwanda was never officially described as genocide, since the very use of the word would have triggered international obligations.[51] And it is widely believed that in the aftermath of events in Somalia, there was no support for a combat deployment to another African civil war. Noted one author, 'wealthier states are no longer interested in the African emergencies (except in parts of North Africa...) primarily because of the Somalia debacle'.[52] The *New York Times* noted in a retrospective of the Clinton years that 'two of Clinton's foreign policy advisors said the killings in Somalia had hung so heavily that the question of intervening in Rwanda never even reached Mr Clinton's desk'.[53] Another Clinton retrospective noted, '[h]aunted by memories of an ill-fated US mission in Somalia,

Clinton failed to support a US peacekeeping effort that might have prevented the genocide of more than half a million Tutsis'.[54]

Rwanda was presented to the American people, despite the press's best efforts, as a situation that could not meet the threshold test, either of vital interest or of zero casualties. Given the inability of an intervention in Rwanda to meet either test, the potential for casualties meant the potential for whatever support existed or could be generated to shatter. It could not be counted on to sustain. In other words, had events in Rwanda produced a vocal demand for action from the American people, it is unlikely American leadership would have wished to intervene militarily. Rwanda was viewed as a potentially open-ended deployment; a deployment that would have placed American troops at risk. The ability to create support, for whatever reason, or the pre-existence of support, will not be enough on its own to generate an intervention if casualties are possible. For if casualties are possible, but the rationale for support is something less than a vital national interest, then senior leadership will not believe that it will be possible to sustain support. Hence leadership may actually believe it necessary to tamp down demands for intervention present in the beginning if there is no faith that that support will hold if the going gets rough once troops are committed. Why, in the end, was Somalia a disaster? Because 'moral motivations never gave either President a sense of what the Somalia effort was worth to the American people. In the end, 18 American soldiers killed ... turned out to be too much for America. The result was a humiliating withdrawal because of a miscalculation over value and the threshold of national sacrifice.'[55]

It may seem contradictory, then, that once the genocide had for the most part exhausted itself in Rwanda the United States did intervene to provide humanitarian support for refugee camps in Zaire. Certainly it has been noted that there is a deep irony in America's refusing to intervene to stop a genocide while being willing to aid the perpetrators of genocide in the aftermath. But the difference is that, while the humanitarian cause may have been less, so was the risk to American troops. Both humanitarian crises fail to meet the threshold test of vital national interest. But only one intervention involved a risk of failing to meet the second threshold, of zero casualties. Therefore one was perceived to be politically viable and the other was not. Indeed, this characterization is fairly explicitly defended in the 2000 American Presidential debates. Vice President Gore argued in response to a

question as to whether he had second thoughts about the United States'
refusal to become engaged in Rwanda:

> One of my – one of the criteria that I think is important in deciding
> when and if we should ever get involved around the world is
> whether or not our national security is involved, if we can really
> make the difference with military force, if we've tried everything
> else, if we have allies. ... But because we had no allies and because
> it was very unclear that we could actually accomplish what we
> would want to accomplish by putting military forces there, I think
> it was the right thing not to jump in, as heartbreaking as it was, but
> I think we should have come in much quicker with the
> humanitarian mission.[56]

Note he is defending moving more quickly to participate in the camps,
not a move into Rwanda itself during the time of the actual genocide.
The ultimate winner of the presidential campaign, then-Governor
George W. Bush of Texas, noted that it would have been wise to use
influence to get other African countries to intervene in situations like
Rwanda, but concluded that bottom line, 'I thought they made the right
decision not to send US troops into Rwanda'.[57] Indeed, 'last January,
Bush said that if another Rwanda occurred on his watch, he would not
send American troops, though he would speak with the United Nations
and "encourage them to move".' This was not far from saying, 'It's none
of our business'.[58] As the same author noted, while President Clinton
ultimately apologized for America's inaction, 'Bush, presumably, would
not have apologized, because Rwanda, and Africa generally, do not make
the list of vital interests'.[59]

This is linked to the assumption that the public will only support
missions structured along the lines of the framework provided by
Weinberger. These assumptions impose certain circularities and
tensions on discussions of whether or not the United States should
intervene militarily in particular instances. Only the military can answer
questions regarding costs. How long is a given mission likely to take?
How many casualties can we expect? Only the military can provide
answers. But by monopolizing the cost side of the equation the military
controls the debate. In other words the question of cost is naturally one
for an expert. But the larger issue of whether the costs are *justified* by the
potential benefits is naturally one for the public. What are America's
vital interests? Are there missions that are not vital that are still

important enough to justify the costs of undertaking them? How much are we willing to pay? Those are not questions requiring a technical answer, for they are value-driven questions about the nature of the public good. Indeed, the Weinberger Doctrine implicitly recognizes this by the very act of demanding *public* support. But unspecified standards for levels of public support judged adequate to justify military actions leave open issues of balance between cost and benefit, and make the determination of when public support is adequate an issue for technical experts. Given these unanswered – indeed, unasked – questions, how does the need for public support impact public debates over humanitarian intervention?

Without a standard for what adequate support is, the military must answer the question as to whether that specific criterion has been met. Thus only the military can tell the public if they should support an operation, and only the military can determine if the public is supportive in adequate amounts. But without some understanding of what adequate support is, how it is to be determined? If it is deemed advisable to wait out a shortfall in support, criticism could in the interim bring about a free-fall of support, producing a self-fulfilling prophecy. The public should only support good interventions. But one of the ways it determines if an intervention is 'good' is if the proposed intervention has adequate public support. But only the military has the capacity, apparently, to determine when public support has met the threshold test of 'adequate'. And so it goes.

Additionally, 'public support' is presumed equivalent to 'public opinion'. But the idea that public opinion is obvious or self-evident is extremely problematic. There has been some discussion of the interrelationship between the press (especially the 'pundits') and public opinion.[60] It is clear that the press plays a role in shaping opinion as well as in reporting it. There is no reason not to believe that in some instances pundits are creating a self-fulfilling prophecy. If the pundits are on the air proclaiming that the public will no longer support a given mission inside the same news cycle (to the extent news cycles still exist) in which a particular event, say, heavy casualties taken in a fire fight, is initially reported, then is it really surprising when overnight polls show a drop in support? Polling data supports the importance of this question. The polling response to the failed Ranger raid in Mogadishu is suggestive:

A majority of Americans assumes that the public as a whole is more eager to withdraw in the face of troop fatalities than they themselves are. This suggests that the public is overestimating its own reaction. The present PIPA poll suggests that the public has begun to misinterpret itself through this widespread image ... When respondents were asked to estimate how many Americans, upon first receiving the news of the troop fatalities in Somalia, wanted the US to withdraw immediately, the average estimate was 62% – substantially more than the average 41% the polls found at the time.[61]

It is hard to see, therefore, what support is (how it should be defined, operationalized) how it should be measured, how often it should be measured, or how slippages in support should be dealt with. A lack of support (or a drop in support) is merely taken as a fait accompli.

The one question that is being begged here is perhaps analytically prior to all these others: why does public support matter? What happens if public support for a specific operation were to drop? Premised on Vietnam, where support for the war not so much dropped as imploded, where the country was torn apart by the passion of its feelings over Vietnam, it is taken for granted that support is necessary for successful combat operations. John Hillen, an analyst at the conservative Heritage Foundation, simply states: 'when intervention is required, the President should mobilize public support (as President Bush did during the Gulf War) so that American troops abroad will know that the nation and the Congress support not only the troops, but the actual goals of the operation'.[62] But that is a claim without a warrant: what is the rationale underlying the need for support?

There is an argument to be made that there is no more important decision then the deployment of American troops to a combat zone. If that is the case then it can be defended that it is wrong to initiate combat involvements, even in humanitarian situations, without public support because the people should have a say. (Summers edges towards this, with his evocation of the 'people's Army'.[63]) But that is not relevant to a discussion of Weinberger, which is ostensibly a discussion of what is necessary for *successful* deployments, not democratic ones. It is also important to note that the analytical distinction between creating and sustaining support collapses. They may be different things, but the Doctrine is now interpreted as requiring not just support at the time of intervention, but a predictive likelihood that support can be sustained. Both must now be demonstrated in advance. Again there is a circular quality: if the public does not believe there is adequate support or if the public believes support may collapse, then the public ought not to support the intervention even if it does. That is, an individual member of the public, believing an intervention is the right thing to do, should still withhold support if he or she does not believe other Americans support the intervention – or predicts other Americans' support for the intervention will falter before it is complete.

CONCLUSION

In argument theory, presumption is what tells someone evaluating competing claims which side has the burden of proof. In this instance, the Weinberger Doctrine is structured in such a way as to set presumption against intervention generally, and most especially against those interventions categorized as 'humanitarian'. The rhetor seeking to advocate intervention must prove that case; the opponent need only argue that the case has not been adequately proven.

The task will not be an easy one. Perhaps the most difficult argumentative burden will be that of demonstrating that a particular intervention satisfies the criterion of defending a 'vital national interest'. Neither Weinberger nor virtually any of the other advocates supporting the Doctrine have bothered to specify what, exactly, a vital national interest of the United States *is*. The concept has been left extremely ambiguous. And, of course, as used in the Doctrine this is a threshold test. In other words, all interests that fall below the standard of vital – be they important, central, helpful, useful, or merely of interest – still fall below the standard. There is no grounds for arguing that one interest came closer to meeting the threshold test than any other: failing to meet the test is failing to meet the test is failing to meet the test, period.

Further, the demands of Weinberger for an accounting of cost and benefit up front immediately shape and frame the debate over intervention into a discussion that quickly adopts the language and terms of cost–benefit analysis. In this type of debate, advocates for intervention on the grounds of humanitarian motivations are instantly disadvantaged in argumentative terms. Humanitarian impulses tend to be defended based on moral grounds, impossible to quantify. The Weinberger Doctrine criterion calling for 'precise military objectives' is a way to bias missions towards those that can be quantified in material terms. This criterion clearly and explicitly rules out a wide range of missions that have been clumped together under the pejorative rubric of 'nation building', which we are told are inappropriate missions for military forces. No doubt many of those missions are not missions requiring military force or military personnel. But humanitarian intervention *qua* humanitarian intervention does require military force and military personnel, and because so much of what is involved is closely intertwined with nation building and the work of civilian agencies engaged in such work, Weinberger makes it all too easy to taint all of it as nation building, inappropriate missions for the military, potentially throwing the baby out with the bathwater. This danger is enhanced when the criterion calling for 'constant reassessment' is used to block any change in ongoing missions, which are automatically tarred with the brush of 'mission creep', whether they make sense or not, whether they grow organically out of the deployed mission or not, and whether they are logically limitable or not.

All of this is in part a function of the Somalia mission following so shortly on the heels of what was presented at the time as the great success of Desert Storm. A decade on, with Saddam Hussein continuing to defy UN inspectors, more and more countries openly flouting the sanctions regime, and fewer and fewer nations supporting the United States in holding the line on what remains of the regime, it becomes more difficult to remember the euphoria of the end of that conflict. But at the time it seemed a total victory. The path chosen by the American military to return from the debacle of Vietnam seemed totally vindicated, as did their choice to plan, equip and train, based on the assumption that the Weinberger criteria would be in play. Soon after, the American military found itself in Somalia. Somalia seemed to vindicate those choices again. When Weinberger was put into play (in the early part of the mission, under American control, when the mission was tightly limited, and overwhelming force was used, during Operation Restore Hope) it was a great success. It was only in the later phase, when the Doctrine seemed absent (the mission was unclear or involved nation building, on-scene commanders were micro-managed, and so forth) that disaster ensued. Thus Somalia seemed to reinforce both the lessons learned from Desert Storm and those learned in Vietnam.

The result was an unspoken assumption that whenever military force is to be deployed, America confronts a *binary* choice. Military interventions will always be *either* another Desert Storm *or* another Vietnam: there are no other alternatives, no sense that a spectrum of options may be available. All of this raises two disturbing possibilities. First, if public support can only be judged adequate by the military (since whether or not support is adequate is in the process of being redefined as a technical issue) then since they are worried about support being sustained, the military will not trust advance polls because they believe support to be fundamentally brittle. The logic of this is that *the Weinberger criteria can never truly be met*. There will never be enough assurance for, or from, senior military leadership that any intervention, but most especially a humanitarian intervention, can sustain enough public support if casualties cannot be guaranteed to be zero. The Weinberger Doctrine is in this sense self-defeating.

Second, because of the concern with casualties at such low levels, and the link between casualties and public support, we have in a sense come full circle. Summers, and because of Summers, Weinberger, wrote out of a concern with what they saw as the extreme constrictions stemming from inappropriate levels of civilian control in Vietnam. Because of Weinberger there is also now a codified obsession with maintaining public support. But the result, at least in Kosovo, was a level of micro-management (at least as manifested in the decision to keep pilots above 15,000 feet) in order to avoid casualties that might erode support, that was at least equivalent to precisely the levels of civilian interference that animated the concerns that generated the Weinberger Doctrine to begin with. We have come full circle in the way missions are structured.

Rhetoric and argument have real power in the way events play out. In a recent book on the conflict in Kosovo, the authors note that when the president spoke to the nation on the night the air war began, he immediately ruled out the use of ground forces. This was done, they argue, because of fears that leaving open the possibility of ground force participation would sacrifice domestic public and Congressional (and allied) support for the air war. But 'publicly ruling out their use only helped to reduce Milosevic's uncertainty regarding the likely scope of NATO's military actions,'[64] and possibly lengthened the air war as a result. Yet, they report, National Security Advisor Sandy Berger 'who authored the critical passage in the president's speech, maintains that "we would not have won the war without this sentence"'.[65] It would be difficult to find more direct evident for the profound impact and influence that public rhetoric and debate have – and are understood to have – on policy, policy-making, and policy-makers at the highest level. Key policy-makers clearly attach great importance to rhetoric and argument. Rhetorical and argumentative analysis must be added to the methods normally used to assess the policies they produce.

NOTES

1. The author would like to thank Carol K. Winkler and V. William Balthrop for their help with earlier drafts and Donna Clodfelter for invaluable research assistance. The Air Force Historical Research Agency of the US Air Force provided critical research support, permitting research at the Agency archives, housed at Maxwell Air Force Base in Montgomery, Alabama.
2. For a theoretical analysis of the cultural uses of history, and the differences between history and memory, see Marita Sturken, *Tangled Memories: The Vietnam Wall, the AIDs Epidemic, and the Politics of Remembering* (Princeton, NJ: Princeton University Press, 1994).
3. David Mrozek, *The US Air Force After Vietnam* (Maxwell AFB, AL: Air University Press, 1988), p.1.
4. 'The American military has been profoundly reluctant to use force in the post-Cold War era. Somalia, Rwanda, Haiti, Bosnia, and eastern Zaire are cases in point. Whenever civilian leaders in the Bush and Clinton administrations have suggested applying military force to international crises, the Joint Chiefs have responded by stubbornly insisting that before US military forces be placed in harm's way, certain clear conditions for the proper use of force first be met. These military leaders pointed to costly failures and humiliating withdrawals from places such as Vietnam, Beirut, and Somalia as clear examples of the price to be paid for imprudent military interventions in ambiguous distant conflicts. Consequently, the Pentagon has become irrevocably committed to promulgating a doctrine of great caution in the use of military force.' Kenneth Campbell, 'Once Burned, Twice Cautious: Explaining the Weinberger–Powell Doctrine', *Armed Forces and Society*, Vol.24, No.3 (Spring 1998), p.357.
5. For a history of the introduction of Vietnam into the curriculum at the Air Force's institutions of Professional Military Education see Suzanne Bud Gehri, *Study War Once More: Teaching Vietnam at Air University* (Maxwell AFB, AL: Air University Press, CADRE Report AU–ARI–CP–85–7, Nov. 1985).
6. It was initially distributed through the Army War College, thence to the Air War College, then to a civilian press. See Harry Summers, Jr., *On Strategy: A Critical Analysis of the Vietnam War* (New York: Dell Publishing of Bantam Books, June 1984.) The book was first published by Presidio Press in 1982, but it was the Dell paperback that received widest distribution. It has recently been republished under the same title (Novato, CA: Presidio Press, 1995) and continues to be widely cited.
7. Harry Summers, Jr., *On Strategy II: A Critical Analysis of the Gulf War* (New York: Dell Books, 1992), p. 47. While ostensibly about the Persian Gulf War, this book essentially restates the author's arguments about Vietnam in the context of the claim that the lessons of South East Asia were applied appropriately to Desert Storm.
8. Summers, *On Strategy II*, p.47.
9. Summers, *On Strategy*, p.1.
10. Summers, *On Strategy II*, p.48
11. For a discussion of objectives see Summers, *On Strategy*, pp.78–9.
12. '…it would appear that our civilian leadership in the Pentagon, the White House, and in the Congress evidently believed the military professionals had no worthwhile advice to give', Summers, *On Strategy*, pp.42–3.
13. In Dean Rusk's formulation, they tried to do in 'cold blood' what could only be done in hot blood. Quoted, for example, in George C. Herring, *LBJ and Vietnam: A Different Kind of War* (Austin, TX: University of Texas Press, 1994), p.2.
14. I do not mean to suggest that the study of civil–military relations *per se* is not important, only that it does not focus on what matters when it comes to understanding the structure of public

debate on intervention. For an articulation of the importance of the traditional focus of the study of civil–military relations see Peter D. Feaver and Richard H. Kohn, 'The Gap', *The National Interest*, No.61 (Fall 2000).

15. There are points in this article where I use the term 'the military'. This is obviously a stylistic conceit. No organization with as many individuals (or communities) could possibly be monolithic in its interpretation of anything. The very point of labelling an argument 'hegemonic', however, is that it is dominant, 'common sense', and therefore difficult to dispute. I would argue that the doctrinal 'back to basics' movement that occurred roughly simultaneously is evidence of this. All of the services began to return to the study of Clausewitz. The Air Force rehabilitated the study of Douhet and Trenchard, their central canonical texts. The Navy returned to Mahan, and the Marine Corps to its roots as a truly amphibious force, rather than merely a smaller version of the Army, as it had been treated during Vietnam. This cannot be coincident given Summers' emphasis on the importance of Clausewitz. See Summers, *On Strategy*, starting with the explanation of the importance of Clausewitz on pp.3–7.

16. Summers, *On Strategy II*, p.73.

17. Weinberger clearly intended the Doctrine as a response to Vietnam. See Christopher Gacek, *The Logic of Force: The Dilemma of Limited War in American Foreign Policy* (New York: Columbia University Press, 1994), p.253.

18. Quoted in General Larry Welch, 'Air Power in Low- and Mid-Intensity Conflict', in Shultz and Pfaltzgraff (eds.), *Future of Air Power* (Maxwell AFB, AL: Air University Press, July 1992), p.149.

19. The Weinberger paraphrase comes from Caspar Weinberger, *Fighting for Peace: Seven Critical Years in the Pentagon* (New York: Warner Books, 1991), p.402. It reads:
    1. Our vital interests must be at stake.
    2. The issues involved are so important for the future of the United States and our allies that we are prepared to commit enough forces to win.
    3. We have clearly defined political and military objectives, which we must secure.
    4. We have sized our forces to achieve our objectives.
    5. We have some reasonable assurance of the support of the American people.
    6. US forces are committed to combat only as a last resort.

20. This version comes from C. Robert Zelnick, 'Public Opinion and the Emerging Military', in Robert Pfaltzgraff Jr. and Richard Schultz Jr. (eds.), *Naval Forward Presence and the National Military Strategy* (Annapolis, MD: Naval Institute Press, 1993), p.44. It reads:
    in defense of its vital interests;
    with the support of the American people and Congress;
    only as a last resort;
    with the clear intention of winning;
    when the military objectives are clearly defined; and
    only when those objectives are worth the risks.

21. Although, interestingly, it is more likely to be called that by people who disagree with it, so that 'Powellism' has come to mean advocacy of a large military combined with a reluctance to think the circumstances are ever quite right for using it. Powell was working directly for Weinberger at the time the speech was delivered, and it has been suggested both that he disagreed and that he himself wrote the relevant portions of the speech. Bob Woodward says they 'were good rules, in Powell's view, but he wasn't sure they should have been publicly declared'. *The Commanders* (New York: Pocket Star Books, 1991), p.90. Richard Kohn cites a *Washington Post* article (of 1 Oct. 1993) as claiming that Powell actually wrote the speech, but concludes, 'apparently the General only "facilitated" its production'. Dick Kohn, 'Out of Control: The Crisis in Civil–Military Relations', *The National Interest*, No.35 (Spring 1994), p.12.

22. Jane Perlez, 'For 8 Years, a Strained Relationship With the Military', *New York Times*, 28 Dec., A–13.

23. Colin Powell with Joseph E. Persico, *My American Journey* (New York: Random House, 1995), p.576.

24. William Jefferson Clinton, 'Statement to the Nation 27 November, 1995', (Washington, DC: Office of the Press Secretary, 27 Nov. 1995) www.whitehouse.gov

25. Clinton, 'Statement', 27 Nov. 1995.
26. Clinton, 'Statement', 27 Nov. 1995.
27. William Jefferson Clinton, 'Statement to the Nation 24 March 1999', (Washington, DC: Office of the Press Secretary, 24 March 1999) www.whitehouse.gov
28. Clinton, 'Statement', 24 March 1999.
29. The Marine Corps doctrinal statement, *Operational Maneuver From the Sea*, for example, states explicitly: 'In contrast to previous approaches to amphibious warfare, OMFTS is not limited to the high end of the spectrum of conflict. Indeed, in a world where war will be made in many different ways, the very notion of "conventional" warfare is likely to fall out of use. For that reason, the techniques of OMFTS must be of use in a wide variety of situations, ranging from humanitarian relief to a high-stakes struggle against a rising superpower.' United States Marine Corps, *Operational Maneuver From the Sea* (Washington, DC: Headquarters, US Marine Corps, n.d.), p.12.
30. Colin Powell was not shy about resisting a Bosnia mission publicly and I would argue that it was in large part the mismatch between the mission and the Doctrine that defined the problem. See Michael Gordon, 'Powell Delivers a Resounding No on Using Limited Force in Bosnia', *New York Times*, 28 Sept. 1992, A-1, Mead Data Central Lexis-Nexis.
31. See Richard N. Haas, *The Reluctant Sheriff: The United States After the Cold War* (Washington, DC: Brookings Institution Press for the Council on Foreign Relations, 1997), p.105.
32. A master narrative is an overarching story that can be used to explain virtually any political event, and, just as importantly, provide guidelines or templates for appropriate responses in light of those events. During the Cold War, the master narrative was one which posed two global 'camps' against each other, such that separate political events were always interpreted not as unrelated but according to a master narrative of global dominance and loss. Civil wars or ethnic strife were not individual acts requiring further American responses but were interwoven within the global demands of containment; seen as linked to Soviet moves designed to advance a goal of global dominance. American responses were designed accordingly. Only with the end of the Cold War and the collapse of the master narrative were events in other nations likely to be fully evaluated on their own terms, and the potential for American military intervention considered outside a framework of containment.
33. While this may initially be the perception of elites and pundits only, it is my argument that this may become self-fulfilling prophecy as time goes by, in large part because of the choices the press makes in covering such situations.
34. Noted one author, the 'presence of the above-mentioned factors [large refugee flows to developed states, the media spotlight on humanitarian suffering, continued defiance by nasty rulers, and increased sanctions], compounded by time, therefore, produces the *Do Something Effect*, and pushes the US government and other western countries into choosing the military option'. Karin Von Hippel, *Democracy by Force: US Military Intervention in the Post-Cold War World* (Cambridge: Cambridge University Press, 2000), p.169, italics in original. My point is that there is no evidence provided by the author for the claim, not even polling data: it is simply an assumption and assertion.
35. See Cori E. Dauber, 'Image as Argument: The Impact of Mogadishu on American Military Intervention', *Armed Forces and Society*, Vol.27, No.2 (Winter 2001), pp.205–30.
36. I take the phrase from Eric Alterman. See Eric Alterman, *Sound and Fury: The Washington Punditocracy and the Collapse of American Politics* (New York: Harper Perennial, 1992).
37. I say apparent because closer examination reveals the way the surface tensions are resolved in practice and in deeper structure.
38. Remember my focus is the way the Weinberger Doctrine functions in the public sphere as an argument structure, and further, I argue that it is properly read as being directed towards civilian leadership. Read that way this is not quite the radical statement it would be if Weinberger truly were a traditional military doctrine. It may generate beliefs about appropriate military planning and practice but it is not itself designed primarily for such practices.
39. Senator Bunning, 'President Clinton Sending American Soldiers to Kosovo', *Congressional Record*, Vol.19 (March 1999), S2987 http://thomas.loc.gov/
40. Mr DeLay, 'Removal of United States Armed Forces From the Federal Republic of Yugoslavia', *Congressional Record*, 28 April 1999, H2415 http://thomas.loc.gov/

41. John Hillen, *American Military Intervention: A User's Guide* (Washington DC: The Heritage Foundation, Backgrounder No. 1079, 2 May 1996). http://www.heritage.org/library/categories/natseg/bg1079.html

42. 'The effects of the casualty minimization imperative in situations not involving supreme US security interests are likely to be pervasive.' Jeffrey Record, 'Force Projection/Crisis Response', in L. Benjamin Ederington and Michael Mazarr (eds.), *Turning Point: The Gulf War and US Military Strategy* (Boulder, CO: Westview Press, 1984), p.158.

43. John Mueller, 'Policy Principles for Unthreatened Wealth Seekers', *Foreign Policy*, No.102 (Spring 1996), p.31.

44. Col. Ross Hieb, USMC, 'What Peace Dividend?', *Proceedings*, Vol.120, No.1 (Jan. 1994), p.162. My emphasis.

45. Part of this is an assumption regarding *imagery* and its impact on cost assessments that may or may not be correct. See Warren Strobel, *Late-Breaking Foreign Policy: The News Media's Influence on Peace Operations* (Washington, DC: United States Institute of Peace, 1997), p.47. In fact, polls indicate that support for the Somalia mission, which dropped in the wake of the widespread distribution of imagery of a US servicemembers' body being dragged through the streets of Mogadishu, quickly rebounded. See Steven Kull and Clay Ramsey, *US Public Attitudes on Involvement in Somalia* (College Park, MD: Program on International Policy Attitudes, 26 Oct. 1993). They argue that polls indicate that 22 per cent of those polled reported that they *had* supported withdrawal immediately after the Ranger raid but had since changed their minds, 'a striking number given that people generally resist appearing inconsistent', (p.4). Imagery does have powerful influences, but I suspect that they are not measurable in a strict cause–effect manner that can be captured easily by the assumptions of quantitative methodology. See Dauber, 'Image as Argument'. Nonetheless, the idea that it is the image from Mogadishu that changed American policy appears unshakeable. The media itself feeds this. Christiane Amanpour, for example, recently wrote, '[y]ou remember, for example, the image of the dead US solider being dragged through the streets of Mogadishu in October 1993. That picture, which we played over and over and over and over again, forced a new president ... to pull out of Somalia. The legacy of the photograph has affected US foreign policy ever since. Because of that enduring image, this country didn't intervene sooner in Bosnia ... It's the reason there was no intervention at all in Rwanda ...' Christiane Amanpour, 'Why do I do it?' *Brill's Content* (Jan. 2001), p.54.

46. Bob Novak, *Capital Gang*, 17 Sept. 1994. All citations from television transcripts were obtained from Mead Data's Lexis-Nexis News Service.

47. Pat Buchanan, *This Week with David Brinkley*, 3 Dec. 1995.

48. Senator Phil Gramm, quoted on *Capital Gang*, 16 Oct. 1993.

49. Larry Joyce, LTC USA (ret.), *Larry King Live*, 14 Oct. 1993. It should be noted that Mr Joyce was a guest that night not on account of his military expertise, but because his son had been killed in Somalia.

50. 'Unlike Clinton's overall approval rating [which had been hovering in the low to mid-40s at the time] his ratings for handling the situation have risen substantially – from 27 percent approval early this month to 48 percent today.' *St. Louis Post Dispatch*, 29 Sept. 1994, 7A. (From Academic Universe.) The polling numbers are provided by Gallup. The speech to the nation was given on the 24th: this is a phenomenal jump in such a short period of time if in fact it reflects a response to a single speech.

51. It was widely reported that White House officials were forbidden to use the word 'genocide' as that would trigger international treaty obligations under the 1948 Genocide Convention. See Nat Hentoff, 'Will Rice Remember Rwanda? Or Will Administration Turn Its Back Like Clinton's Did on Next "Unimaginable Terror"?' *The Denver Rocky Mountain News*, 14 Jan. 2001, 1-B from Academic Universe (Lexis-Nexis News Service). However, it was suddenly fine to use the word in reference to Bosnia, at least retroactively. See the President's announcement that air strikes had started in the Kosovo campaign. Clinton, 'Statement', 24 March, 1999.

52. Von Hippel, *Democracy by Force*, p.192.

53. Perlez, 'Strained Relationship', *New York Times*, A-13

54. 'Think Again: Clinton's Foreign Policy', *Foreign Policy*, (Nov./Dec. 2000), p.20.

55. Hillen, 'American Military Intervention', p.7.

56. 'Campaign 2000: Vice President Gore and Governor Bush Participate in Second Presidential Debate, October 11, 2000', provided by CNN.com.
57. George W. Bush, 'Campaign 2000: Vice President Gore and Governor Bush Participate in Second Presidential Debate, October 11, 2000', www.allpolitics.com provided by CNN.com
58. James Traub, 'W's World', *The New York Times Magazine*, 14 Jan. 2001, p.33.
59. Traub, 'W's World', p.33.
60. See Alterman, *Sound and Fury*. There is a long tradition of research on this relationship. See Ole Holsti, *Public Opinion and American Foreign Policy* (Ann Arbor, MI: The University of Michigan Press, 1996) for a truly comprehensive survey of this work.
61. Kull and Clay, *Public Attitudes*, pp.5–6. The same report also found (p.4) that the sentiment for withdrawal dropped very rapidly. The reliance on 'snap shot' polls taken an extremely short time after an event may also have the perverse effect of prompting interventions that might not otherwise have occurred. See Philip Taylor, *Global Communications, International Affairs and the Media Since 1945* (New York: Routledge, 1997), p.93.
62. Hillen, 'American Military Intervention', p.2.
63. He is quoting Army General Fred C. Weyand, Summers, *On Strategy II*, p.10.
64. Ivo H. Daalder and Michael E. O'Hanlon, *Winning Ugly: NATO's War to Save Kosovo* (Washington, DC: The Brookings Institution Press, 2000), p.97.
65. Daalder and O'Hanlon, *Winning Ugly*, p.97.

Missing the Story:
The Media and the Rwandan Genocide

LINDA MELVERN

In the course of a few terrible months in 1994, one million people were killed in Rwanda. It was slaughter on a scale not seen since the Nazi extermination programme. The killing rate in Rwanda was five times that achieved by the Nazis. Such a crime requires motives, means and opportunity. The motive of those responsible for the genocide was to continue to monopolize power and seek a 'final solution' to the political opposition. The means was the mobilization of militia and use of the civil administration to encourage people to take part. Both methods of mass killing had already been tried successfully in Rwanda and were well documented in human rights reports.[1]

The opportunity for genocide was provided by a conjunction of circumstances, allowing the hardliners to confuse the international community for long enough to be able to perpetrate the crime with extraordinarily little international response. These circumstances, contrived or fortuitous, included the almost immediate withdrawal of international groups when the killing began, the resumption of a civil war and an inaccurate portrayal of the killing by the international press as 'tribal violence'. It is the initial inaccurate reporting of the genocide by the Western press that is the subject of this essay. There is no doubt that the events in Rwanda in April 1994 took the British and the American media by surprise, but the message that the violence in Rwanda was the result of ancient tribal hatreds was quite simply wrong. The use of this cliché dominated the early reports on the genocide. The basic inference was that the killing represented uncontrollable tribal savagery about which nothing could be done. One British newspaper reported without question the view of a Western diplomat in the capital, Kigali, who told a journalist how 'various clans were murdering others'. Rwanda was described as a failed state. There was chaos and anarchy.[2] In reality a planned annihilation was taking place. This was not a sudden eruption of long-simmering hatreds. Genocide does not take place in a context of anarchy. What was happening was the deliberate slaughter of Hutu moderates and all the Tutsi, in carefully planned and clinically carried out massacres. There were daily deliveries of weapons to the roadblocks. There were dustcarts touring the capital into which prisoners who had been seconded to 'clean' the streets threw bodies. There were no sealed trains or secluded camps in Rwanda. The genocide took place in broad daylight and was broadcast on the radio. The vast majority of victims in Rwanda, it has since been ascertained, died in the first six weeks of genocide, in large-scale and organized massacres.[3]

The first large-scale massacre to be discovered by UN peacekeepers was at a parish called Gikondo in the heart of the capital city Kigali, and a stronghold of the Hutu Power faction. It was Saturday 9 April. A few weeks before, in March, a Major Podevijn had reported to the headquarters of the UN mission in Rwanda that weapons had been distributed to the members of the Interahamwe in Gikondo. On this particular Saturday the UN peacekeepers were answering a desperate call from two Polish military observers living in Gikondo. Setting out for the parish that day were two Polish Majors, Stefan Stec and Maric Pazik. They were experienced peacekeepers and they had served in the UN mission to Cambodia. With them went Major Brent Beardsley. Beardsley was the staff officer of the Force Commander, Major General Romeo Dallaire. The peacekeepers travelled to Gikondo in the one working Czech-made armoured personnel carrier (APC) with a three-man Bangladeshi crew. They were warned that the APC could break down at any moment. The APC had slowly made its way through the streets. A group of people had screamed at them to stop. They drove on. None of them spoke as they passed bodies that were littering the streets. The climb up the hill at Gikondo was laborious for the road was steep and there were deep ruts made by torrential downpours. At the top of the hill was a Catholic mission, a Pallotine order, which was operated by Polish priests and nuns, and set in terraced gardens surrounded by eucalyptus trees. It was a large mission, self-contained and dominated by a brick church. When they reached the church the peacekeepers had left the Bangladeshi crew with the APC, and walked into the garden. It was there they found the bodies. Whole families had been killed together, each person hacked to death with machetes. There were terrible wounds to the genitalia. Some people were not dead. There was a three-month-old baby, the mother raped and the baby killed with a terrible wound.

There were children, some with their legs or feet cut off, and their throats cut. Most of the victims had bled to death. Stec had returned to the APC. He wanted to get his camcorder to film it. There must be proof. They found the Polish UN observers huddled together in the church. Military observers (MILOBS) consisted of commissioned officers from the rank of captain to Lt.-Colonel, who were deployed around the country to monitor and ensure that all parties followed the peace agreement.

The peacekeepers in the UN Assistance Mission in Rwanda (UNAMIR) had come to Rwanda to monitor a peace agreement, the Arusha Accords, signed in 1993, ending a civil war between the mainly Tutsi rebels, the Rwandan Patriotic Front and the Hutu dictatorship that had ruled Rwanda for 20 years. The Arusha Accords provided for radical change, for political, military and constitutional reform. Rwanda was to have a broad-based transitional government until a democratically elected government was installed. The RPF and the Rwandan army would integrate; there would be disarmament and demobilization. Some 900,000 Tutsi refugees, expelled in the anti-Tutsi pogroms that had taken place since 1959, were to be allowed home. At first the job of the UN peacekeepers had seemed unambiguous: this was classic UN peacekeeping with the soldiers acting as a buffer between two former enemies. The peacekeepers observe, and they mediate. But it was not so simple. By April 1994 the peace agreement had stalled. There were delays in its implementation and the peacekeeping force was too weak to make any difference.

The UN military observers in Gikondo were part of a team of officers from 16 different countries under the command of Colonel Tikoca from Fiji, and supported by Operations Officer Lt.-Colonel Somalia Iliya from Nigeria. It was the Polish observers who reported that the Interahamwe militia had carried out the killing in Gikondo under the direction of the Presidential Guard. On Saturday morning, 9 April, at about 9 am the priests had organized a mass, and around 500 people, sheltering in the compound, turned up at the church. While they were holding the mass there were the sounds of shooting and grenades. There was a commotion. Then two Presidential Guards and two gendarmes burst into the church, followed by Interahamwe. The Interahamwe wore their distinctive clothing, the Kitenge, their multi-coloured pants and tunics. After the massacre was over the priests had tried to gather together the wounded in the porch. The priests said that the Rwandan army had cordoned off the parish. They said some of their parishioners did the killing. When the president's plane went down (Wednesday 6 April) there had been shooting all night long. The next day Tutsi had fled to the church for safety and some people were so afraid that they hid beneath floors, in cupboards or in the rafters. Another witness to the massacre recalled: 'The militia began slashing away … they were hacking at the arms, legs, genitals, breasts, faces and necks.' There was total panic. Some people were dragged outside and beaten to death. The killing lasted about two hours and then the killers had walked slowly among the bodies and looted them or finished off the wounded. One of the Polish military observers had watched the local police entering the buildings in the compound, followed by militia armed with machetes and clubs. One of the militia had what looked like a Kalashnikov. The Polish observer had seen militia climb over the fence and said he had tried to contact UNAMIR headquarters but the radio channels were jammed. He helped the wounded and had noticed how ears and mouths were slashed, clothes had been pulled off and the genitals of men and women mutilated. He took photographs. There was a pile of identification cards with the ethnic designation of Tutsi, burned in an attempt to eradicate all evidence that these people had existed. The next day the Interahamwe came back. They discovered that the survivors were hiding in a small chapel. When they failed to break down the door, the militia poured petrol in through the windows of the chapel followed by hand grenades.[4]

In the next three months massacres like this became commonplace. But at Gikondo there was film and proof. The Polish peacekeepers thought that Gikondo should alert the world, for they recognized what was happening as genocide.

Two days after the attack on the church in Gikondo, the story of what had happened there appeared in a French newspaper, *Liberation*, written by journalist Jean-Philippe Ceppi. Ceppi described seeing mutilated bodies, the men with their penises cut, and the women their breasts. Only a dozen people had survived the massacre and they were not expected to live. In the roads around Gikondo, and all over Kigali, there were murders taking place. Everywhere there were sounds of screams and gunfire. Presidential Guards toured the city in armoured personnel carriers, carrying lists of victims. The Interahamwe battered down doors, chasing Tutsi from house to house, and room to room. Nowhere was safe for Tutsi, not even the hospitals, where Rwandan soldiers were rampaging through the wards looking for them. So many bodies were delivered to the city morgue that they had to be stacked outside.[5]

The French daily *Le Monde* also carried a story about Gikondo, published on Tuesday 12 April by journalist Jean Helene.[6] Helene described how the victims of the killing in Kigali were mostly Tutsi. According to the Chief Delegate of the International Committee of the Red Cross, Philippe Gaillard, who had organized vehicles and delegates to go help the wounded of Gikondo, in the city of Kigali an estimated 10,000 people had already been murdered. Jean Helene speculated that by the time the RPF reached Kigali all the Tutsi would be dead. But in the Ceppi article in *Liberation* the word 'genocide' was used. Ceppi wrote that the RPF was advancing on Kigali, and according to some reports was only 15 km from the capital. 'But by the time they arrive', Ceppi speculated, 'a genocide of the Tutsi would already have taken place'. Ceppi told me recently that when he got to Kigali on 8 April, over land from Burundi, everyone was using the word genocide. He had met Gaillard, who told him that a genocide of the Tutsi had just begun. Ceppi's story in *Liberation* on 11 April, as far as can be ascertained, was the first mention of the word genocide in relation to what was happening. On that day in Britain a broadsheet published a report from Rwanda about the evacuation of a French woman's poodle as a 'veteran of African conflict', and the first paragraph described the evacuation taking place of foreigners from Rwanda. The headline ran: 'Foreigners flee bloody horrors of Rwanda', and the story explained that there was bloodletting between the majority Hutu and minority Tutsi groups.[7]

The word 'genocide' disappears from news reports after the mention in *Liberation*, and for the next few weeks a fog of misinformation shrouded what was happening. Roger Winter, the director of the US Committee for Refugees, who had known the problems of Rwanda since 1983, had just returned from Rwanda when the genocide started and he became quite desperate to change the perception in the press that this was tribal warfare. He wrote an article in order to explain how the violence in Rwanda was political in nature, and that what was happening was a plot by an extremist clique to cling to power. This clique was using ethnicity to achieve its aims. Winter's article was rejected by most American papers, including the *Washington Post* and the *New York Times*. It was eventually published in the *Toronto Globe and Mail* on 14 April. The next day in the *New York Times* there was an article describing Rwanda as small, poor and globally insignificant. Rwanda, the newspaper explained, was in an 'uncontrollable spasm of lawlessness and terror'. No member of the UN with an army strong enough to make a difference was willing to risk the lives of its troops for this 'failed central African nation-state with a centuries-old history of tribal warfare and deep distrust of outside intervention'. The newspaper explained that the American strategy was to keep expectations as low as possible. The headline on the story ran: 'For West, Rwanda is not worth the political candle.'[8]

In the first days of the genocide the Force Commander of UNAMIR, Maj.-General Roméo Dallaire from Canada, had thought that what was going on was a power grab by extremists, a military coup with the intention of eliminating all opposing politicians and ruining forever the possibility of reconciliation. But it soon became clear to him what the situation was. On 8 April Dallaire cabled UN headquarters in New York with his first detailed assessment of the situation. In this cable Dallaire described a campaign of terror that was well planned and organized. There must be no doubt, he told New York, that without the presence of UNAMIR the situation would be much worse. Dallaire wanted reinforcements. He wanted to take action to try to stop the bloodshed and he believed that with a minimum reinforcement of some 5,000 armed and trained troops a signal could be sent to those who were organizing the bloodshed. A show of force by the UN would intimidate the gangs of militia. Protected sites could be set up for civilians. Only a lack of means prevented him taking action. Dallaire argued that reinforcements could stop the terror spreading. Dallaire later explained that there was a window of opportunity when the political leaders of the genocide were susceptible to international influence. But there seemed little chance of any reinforcements. At the UN Secretariat in New York the focus was either on the evacuation of expats or the possibility of obtaining a ceasefire in the renewed civil war. In the Security Council there were similar concerns. On 12 April in a secret and informal meeting of the Council the British and American governments made it clear that the best course of action was to pull out all but a token force of the UN peacekeepers from Rwanda.

The issue of reinforcements was not discussed in any depth in the press, although there was a reference to it in an editorial in the *New York Times* on 23 April on the need to consider whether a mobile quick-response force under UN aegis was necessary to deal with such calamities. The editorial began with the words: 'What looks very much like genocide has been taking place in Rwanda ... The world has few ways of responding effectively when violence within a nation leads to massacres and the breakdown of civil order.' The Security Council had thrown in the bloodied towel when it decided unanimously to cut back the blue helmets. The editorial ended that without a rapid reaction force 'the world has little choice but to stand aside and hope for the best'.[9]

There remains to this day a lack of interest in the circumstances of the genocide. In the US there have been no Congressional hearings into the decision-making process within the US government. In Britain both the press and Parliament have failed to question the policies of the British government of John Major towards Rwanda. Britain is after all a permanent member of the Security Council with a special responsibility for UN policy. While the former President Bill Clinton later apologized for the international community's failure over Rwanda, the British government, a bystander to genocide, has yet to recognize its own role. Britain had voted for a peacekeeping mission for Rwanda in October 1993. Was there no subsequent monitoring of what was taking place in Rwanda? What did Britain know of the unfolding of the genocide? What was Britain's role in the decision-making in the Security Council?

The meetings held by the Security Council to discuss what to do about the peacekeeping mission and the crisis in Rwanda took place behind closed doors. Twenty years ago, when most Council meetings were held in public, it would have been possible to hear the options discussed, but nowadays most debates take place in a side room where the deals are concluded which make up 'UN policy'. This means that the policies of each member government are hidden from public scrutiny. Throughout the genocide the Security Council was in almost constant secret session, meeting sometimes twice daily and long into the night. These meetings would usually have remained secret forever were it not for the leak to me from within the Council of a remarkable 155-page document containing an account of them. This invaluable primary source gives a unique view of the Council's secret world, and without it an account of the international failure over Rwanda would be incomplete.[10] This document exposes some unpleasant truths – not the least of which is the fact that Dallaire's military estimate to try to prevent the spread of organized killings of civilians was not even put to the Council for discussion in the first crucial weeks. Just five days after the genocide began the British raised the issue of reinforcements, but then only to dismiss the idea. Sir David Hannay, the UK's ambassador to the

UN, had put forward four options. The first option was to reinforce the troops. But this, Hannay warned, could be a repetition of Somalia. Peacekeeping was not appropriate for civil war, for situations where there was no peace to keep and where fighting factions were unwilling to co-operate. Inadequate effort was worse than no effort at all. Second, UNAMIR could pull out completely but the negative signal that this would send to public opinion would be damaging. Third, the troops could stay on, although Hannay did query what they could effectively do for there was no evidence that UNAMIR was in any position to protect civilians. The fourth and last idea was to pull most of the peacekeepers out, leaving behind 'some elements'. Although this might initially attract public criticism, it seemed to be the safest course. There were no press reports about these choices. Whatever official briefing information that comes out of any closed-door session of the Council is censored, a culture of secrecy nowadays taken for granted.

In April 1994 the Council did not address the question of genocide in Rwanda until three weeks after it had begun. By this time the evidence was leaking from Rwanda with hundreds of bodies clogging the Kagera River flowing out of the country. The aid charity Oxfam had already determined that genocide was under way and on 28 April had issued a press release with the headline, 'Oxfam fears genocide is happening in Rwanda'. There was a flicker of interest in the press, but not a lot, for another story was now grabbing the headlines. Thousands of people were pouring out of Rwanda into Tanzania, the fastest exodus the world had ever seen. In Oxford the press officer for Oxfam, John Magrath, noted the huge numbers of journalists in South Africa covering elections for a new multi-racial parliament. Magrath dryly recorded in his diary: 'The South African elections were over and all the crews were diverted to Tanzania – the refugees became the story, not the genocide.' While the genocide took place in Rwanda, the number of reporters never rose above a maximum of 15. In South Africa, in early May, there had been 2,500 accredited press.

On the day after Oxfam produced its press release, 29 April, there was a long discussion about Rwanda in the Security Council. The President of the Council, the New Zealand ambassador Colin Keating, who had been given a briefing on the slaughter by Medecins sans Frontieres, had proposed a Presidential Statement to recognize that genocide was under way in Rwanda. Keating believed that if the Security Council was to admit that this was genocide, then under the terms of the

1948 Convention on the Prevention and Punishment of the Crime of Genocide, those states on the Council who had signed the convention were legally bound to act.[11] The ambassador for the Czech Republic, Karel Kovanda, had already confronted the Council with the fact of genocide at an informal meeting a day earlier, telling ambassadors that it was scandalous that so far 80 per cent of Council efforts had been spent discussing withdrawing the peacekeepers, and 20 per cent trying to get a ceasefire in the civil war. He told them: 'It was rather like wanting Hitler to reach a ceasefire with the Jews.' What was happening in Rwanda was genocide, conducted by the interim Hutu regime, he said. Yet the council had totally avoided the question of mass killing. There were objections to Kovanda's outburst and afterwards Kovanda says that British and American diplomats quietly told him on no account was he to use such inflammatory language outside the council. It was not helpful.

What Keating proposed in his Presidential Statement was to give the killing in Rwanda its rightful name – genocide. The statement included the paragraph: '...the horrors of Rwanda's killing fields has few precedents in the recent history of the world. The Security Council reaffirms that the systematic killing of any ethnic group, with intent to destroy it in whole or in part constitutes an act of genocide as defined by relevant provisions of international law ... the council further points out that an important body of international law exists that deals with perpetrators of genocide.' The draft warned the 'interim government of its responsibility for immediately reining in and disciplining those responsible for the brutality'. There were objections. Hannay did not want the word 'genocide' to appear in the Presidential Statement, and he argued that were the statement to be used in an official UN document, then the council would become a 'laughing stock'. To name this genocide and not to act on it would be ridiculous. Nor did America want the word used, and China argued against it. The Rwandan ambassador said that the civilian deaths were the result of civil war and he was ably supported in this by the French-influenced ally, Djibouti. The debate went round in circles. Keating, whose term as President of the Council would end the following day, tried the somewhat desperate measure of threatening a draft resolution, tabled in his national capacity. This would require a vote, and a vote was always taken in public. This would expose the positions of each country to public scrutiny. Only after this threat was a compromise reached. Thanks to the drafting ability of the British, known for resolutions with mind-numbing ambiguity, a watered-down statement was issued, and while the statement quoted directly from the Genocide Convention, it did not use the word genocide. 'The Security Council condemns all the breaches of international humanitarian law in Rwanda, particularly those perpetrated against the civilian population, and recalls that persons who instigate or participate in such acts are individually responsible. The Security Council recalls that the killing of members of an ethnic group with the intention of destroying such a group in whole or in part constitutes a crime punishable by international law.' The statement recognized that the massacres were systematic, although it did not identify the targets. It read: 'attacks on defenceless civilians have occurred throughout the country, especially in areas under the control of members of supporters of the armed forces of the "interim government" of Rwanda.' To satisfy French insistence that massacres had also been conducted by the RPF, the statement went on: 'The Security Council demands that the interim government of Rwanda and the Rwandese Patriotic Front take effective measures to prevent any attacks on civilians in areas under their control.' The statement appealed to all states to refrain from providing arms or any military assistance to the two sides in Rwanda and reiterated the call for a ceasefire. It provided that the Secretary General 'investigate serious violations of human rights law'. The statement was finally voted at 1.15 am on Saturday 30 April. 'We ended April exhausted but hopeful that the first few weeks of May would bring action to reinforce UNAMIR with a real force capable of doing what Dallaire had been urging', Keating said.

In an interview some years later, in December 1998, in a BBC Radio Four interview Hannay talked specifically about the genocide convention in relation to Rwanda: '...nobody ever started to say who will actually do the intervening and how will it be done'.[12] In an interview with me in December 1999 Hannay pointed out that the Council could not conjure up troops and although he believes that Dallaire did a fantastic job, Hannay remains deeply sceptical of Dallaire's belief that 5,500 troops could have prevented much of the slaughter. In any case, to have mounted an enforcement mission with so few troops was totally against American military doctrine. Hannay explained that the British were 'extremely unsighted' over Rwanda. There was no British embassy there. There were no British interests. Rwanda was a long way down the list of priorities and the telegrams about Rwanda, received from British embassies in Brussels, Paris and Washington were not treated as high grade. In April 1994 a lot of time and resources were being channelled into the problems of Bosnia, and in trying to disarm Iraq. The staff at the British mission in New York was overstretched. Hannay says the information coming from the Secretariat was insufficient; he complained about the inadequate briefings available to the Security Council. Secretary-General Dr Boutros Boutros-Ghali controlled the flow of information to the Council, Hannay said, allowing only those officials with his permission to brief ambassadors. In all the discussions held about Rwanda before the genocide began the focus had been on how to implement the Arusha Accords. 'Events proved', said Hannay, 'we were looking in the wrong direction, and that the Secretariat was telling us to look in that direction'. He had seen none of the Force Commander's cables from Rwanda because the Council was not meant to be involved in the day-to-day running of peacekeeping missions. Even so, Hannay is convinced that there was nothing the UN could have done to prevent the genocide in Rwanda, not with a Hutu-led government intent on it. Even had the Security Council recognized the killing as genocide it would not have saved any lives. Hannay said that he was not a lawyer and was therefore not in a position to decide whether or not what was happening was genocide. 'We knew a lot of Tutsi were being killed by a lot of Hutu', he said.

Another glimpse into British government thinking is afforded in a letter sent in July 1995 by the Foreign and Commonwealth Office (FCO), to an international enquiry. In this letter, written a year after the genocide ended, the FCO said it did not accept the term genocide. The FCO was inclined to regard a discussion of whether or not the massacres constituted genocide as 'sterile'. The Foreign Office approach was characterized from the outset by a determination to play the matter down, and, for a body that once regarded Africa as its area of special interest, an almost deliberate ignorance. For instance, on 9 May in the House of Commons, and in response to a question about Rwanda, Parliament was told: 'more than 200,000 may have perished in the recent fighting in Rwanda.' This was an extraordinary statement. The estimated death toll had reached 500,000 victims, whole families killed in organized massacres taking place nowhere near the renewed civil war.

The lack of Parliamentary scrutiny over British policy is evidenced in the fact that a debate on Rwanda was not held until 24 May 1994 – some six weeks after the genocide began – when Tony Worthington, MP (Lab. Clydebank and Milngavie) expressed shock that so little attention had been paid to Rwanda. Worthington had told an almost empty house at 11 pm: 'It is inconceivable that an atrocity in which half a million white people had died would not have been extensively debated in the House.' Worthington said that the press had a terrible tendency to dismiss the events as tribalism. 'Genocide is certainly involved', Worthington told the House. Britain was a signatory to the Genocide Convention. 'Has there ever been a clearer example of genocide?' he asked. The Labour Party had waited until May before putting pressure on the government to act, and only then because Oxfam telephoned the office of David Clark, Shadow Secretary of State for Defence. Clark called for the UN and the OAU to organize an immediate deployment of forces to try to end the mass killing of civilians and appealed to Malcolm Rifkind, the Secretary of State for Defence, so that the 'advice and expertise that our armed forces possess could be made available to the UN'. On 23 May Rifkind wrote back to say that troops for Rwanda would 'probably come from regional forces in Africa'. The UK, wrote Rifkind, 'has not been asked to provide any personnel for the operation'. It was an extraordinary sentence for Rifkind to write. Only a few days earlier Britain had voted in the Security Council to authorize more troops for Rwanda and at the time officials in the Secretariat were making desperate efforts to find soldiers. This was repeated in the House of Commons on 14 June when, in a written answer, Douglas Hogg claimed that the UK government had not been asked to contribute troops to the UN peacekeeping operation in Rwanda. In fact, the head of the UN's peacekeeping department, Kofi Annan, said that every UN member government with spare military capacity had received a fax with a list of urgently needed troops and equipment.

In July 1994 Britain's Minister for Overseas Development, Baroness Lynda Chalker, visited Kigali. She met Dallaire and she asked him what he needed. Dallaire had showed Chalker his list of basic requirements, which by then had been faxed around the world. 'I gave her my shopping list', he remembered. 'I was up to my knees in bodies by then.' Britain had previously promised Dallaire 50 4-ton four-wheel-drive trucks, but they had not materialized. On a BBC 2 *Newsnight* programme about Rwanda, Baroness Chalker later blamed Dallaire's lack of resources on 'the UN' which, she explained, ought to 'get its procurement right'. No one challenged this remark. Only after the genocide was over, and in response to another massive flight of people from Rwanda, this time into Zaire, did Britain become more generous. Chalker called the refugee tragedy the most ghastly in living memory, a replay of the Middle Ages, and on 28 July Britain offered military assistance in the form of 600 personnel from the Royal Electrical and Mechanical Engineers, (REME) to repair the large number of unroadworthy vehicles which belonged to Dallaire's mission, a field ambulance and a field squadron of Royal Engineers to repair roads and drill wells. Dallaire's only offers during the genocide, as a matter of record, were 50 trucks from Britain, a promise from Italy of one C130 aircraft plus crew, and six water trucks, a signals squadron plus aircraft from Canada, from the US 50 armoured personnel carriers, leasehold, and from Japan, US$3 million towards the cost of equipment. Nothing materialized.

In the years since the genocide, the shortage of accurate media coverage has been placed high on the list of reasons for Western inaction. One international report concluded that the Western media's failure to adequately report that genocide was taking place, and thereby generate public pressure for something to be done to stop it, had contributed to international indifference and inaction, and possibly to the crime itself. Although the coverage had been handicapped by danger on the ground, the press, in generally characterizing the genocide as tribal anarchy, was fundamentally irresponsible.[13] It was left to non-governmental organizations, – most notably Oxfam and Amnesty International – to lead a call for something to be done in Rwanda, to draw attention in those first crucial weeks to what was really happening. In a letter to the *Guardian* on 16 April 1994 Stewart Willis, the Overseas Director of Oxfam, had pleaded for the UN to immediately reinforce its peacekeepers in Rwanda: 'It is outrageous and despicable that at the same time as the UN Security Council is acting with vigour to protect civilians in Gorazde, French and Belgian troops have to look away while people are hacked to death.'[14] At the time the Serb bombing of the safe area of Gorazde was grabbing the headlines. On 20 April Jeri Laber, Executive Director, Human Rights Watch-Helsinki, wrote to the *New York Times* that the UN should find a means to protect the innocent. To describe ancient hatreds in Rwanda was deplorable, faulty and dangerous.[15] Another letter asked: 'One has to wonder why the atrocities in Bosnia receive the widespread attention they do while the massacres of tens of thousands in an African country is met with a collective denial of responsibility and a hasty retreat.' It was from William F. Schulz, executive director of Amnesty International, to the *Washington Post* on 1 May 1994.[16]

With no outcry about genocide in the press, no choices were given and no risks were taken. At the very least the genocide should have been condemned in the strongest possible terms by the press. Those responsible for the genocide, and their names were known, should have been publicly denounced. Even the story of Dallaire and the gallant contingent of the International Committee of the Red Cross (ICRC) under chief delegate Philippe Gaillard remained unreported. Indeed, there was later criticism of UNAMIR. One American journalist, Philip Gourevitch, wrote how in the summer of 1994 UN troops had killed dogs feeding off the corpses. Gourevitch noted: 'After months during which Rwandans had been left to wonder whether the UN troops knew how to shoot, because they never used their excellent weapons to stop the extermination of civilians, it turned out that the peacekeepers were very good shots.'[17]

While some 470 volunteer peacekeepers stayed on in Rwanda, the UN failed even to resupply them; at the same time the ICRC had managed to get tons of medical equipment into Rwanda. When Dr James Orbinksi of Medecins sans Frontieres arrived in Kigali in June 1994 he was shocked at the state of the peacekeepers, astonished that they were obliged to limit their rescue attempts for lack of petrol. Orbinski said of their commander: 'His tenacity and sheer drive to maximise the impact of UNAMIR was extraordinary.'

While diplomats and politicians were arguing that nothing could be done, these people were doing all they could to try to ease the suffering of the Rwandan people. Gaillard estimated that during the three months of genocide the ICRC looked after 9,000 injured people and a further 100,000 people were saved because of the work of ICRC delegates elsewhere in the country. In Kigali there had been 1,200 surgical operations and hundreds more treated from the back of ambulances. At the end of the genocide there were 2,500 people in the ICRC hospital compound in Kigali. Gaillard told me that this was 'no more than a drop of humanity in an ocean of blood'. It was the most extraordinary humanitarian operation since World War II, and my book told for the first time the amazing story of these people.

The international community could have publicly condemned the interim government in Rwanda for flagrantly failing to fulfil its obligations under international law, notably the Convention on Genocide, which it signed in 1975. Countries should have severed diplomatic ties with Rwanda and expelled Rwandan ambassadors.

Anyone who tried to represent a government that was presiding over genocide – in fact was perpetrating it – should have been refused a placed anywhere in the civilized world. Instead there was silence. For three months the British and US administrations played down the crisis and tried to impede effective intervention by UN forces. There was even reluctance to take the slightest action, such as jamming the hate radio, which could have saved lives. The lack of action over Rwanda should be the defining scandal of the presidency of Bill Clinton. Yet in the slew of articles on the Clinton years that followed Clinton's departure from power, there was barely a mention of the genocide. In the *Observer* of 7 January 2001 only Christopher Hitchens, one of several journalists interviewed about the Clinton legacy, mentioned how Clinton had 'vetoed the rescue of Rwanda'.[18]

If the media forget this story then it is the media that has failed. Why this pitiful lack of coverage in this great Age of Information? The lack of adequate reporting of the genocide in Rwanda raises some serious questions and most of them have yet to be adequately addressed. It is an unpalatable fact, but this story has a tragic contemporary resonance for the scars and the consequences of the genocide, and largely unreported, are with us today.

NOTES

1. Report by Mr B.W. Ndiaye, Special Rapporteur, on his mission to Rwanda from 8–17 April 1993. (E/CN.4/1994/7/add 1) 11 Aug. 1993. International Federation of Human Rights (FIDH), *Report of the International Commission of Investigation of Human Rights Violations in Rwanda since 1 Oct 1990*, 7–21 Jan. 1993.
2. Lindsey Hilsum, 'Rwandan PM Killed as Troops Wreak Carnage', 8 April 1994.
3. Human Rights Watch/Federation Internationale des Ligues des Droits de l'Homme, *Leave None to Tell the Story, Genocide in Rwanda*, 1999.
4. Linda Melvern, *A People Betrayed. The Role of the West in Rwanda's Genocide* (London: Zed Books, 2000).
5. Jean-Philippe Ceppi, 'Kigali livre a la fureur des tueurs Hutus', *Liberation*, 11 April 1994.
6. Jean Helene, 'Le Rwanda feet a sang', *Le Monde*, 12 April 1994.
7. Lindsey Hilsum, 'Foreigners Flee Bloody Horrors of Rwanda', *The Guardian*, 11 April 1994.
8. Elaine Sciolino, 'For West, Rwanda is Not Worth the Political Candle', *New York Times*, 15 April 1994.
9. 'Cold Choice in Rwanda', *The New York Times*, 23 April 1994.
10. Melvern, *A People Betrayed*, Chapter 14.
11. In April 1994 the non-permanent members of the Security Council were: Argentina, Brazil, Czech Republic, Djibouti, New Zealand, Nigeria, Oman, Pakistan, Rwanda, Spain. All but three of these states – Djibouti, Nigeria and Oman – had signed the Genocide Convention.
12. Misha Glenny, 'War Radio', *BBC Radio 4*, 10 Dec. 1998.
13. Joint Evaluation of Emergency Assistance to Rwanda, *The International Response to Conflict and Genocide: Lessons from the Rwandan Experience* (Copenhagen: March 1966), ch. 2, p.36.

14. Stewart Wallis, 'Looking the other way in Rwanda', *The Guardian,* Letters to the Editor, 16 April 1994.
15. Jeri Laber, 'Don't Write Off Rwandan Violence as Ethnic', *New York Times*, Letters to the Editor, 20 April 1994.
16. William F. Schulz, 'US Leadership in Rwanda's Crisis', *Washington Post*, Letters to the Editor, 1 May 1994.
17. Philip Gourevitch, *We Wish to Inform You that Tomorrow we Will be Killed with Our Families* (London: Picador, 1998), p.148.
18. 'The Clinton Years', *The Observer*, 7 Jan. 2001.

The Doctrine Gap:
The Enduring Problem of Contemporary
Peace Support Operations Thinking

DOMINICK DONALD[1]

Traditional peacekeeping[2] thinking evolved out of operational experience. It was shaped by peacekeeping's successes and glazed by its failures. It is hardly surprising that the thinking followed the practice, given that the term was only formalized within the United Nations (UN) 18 years after it invented the practice, and that it has never even had a generally accepted definition.[3] The three cardinal principles of peacekeeping thinking – consent, impartiality/neutrality and the minimum use of force – were the fruit of 48 hours of diplomatic efforts to find a solution to a single problem (the Suez crisis). Twenty years of operational experience, from Sinai to the Congo and Cyprus, seemed to confirm that these principles were broadly applicable; another 15 years demonstrated that they were essential for successful peacekeeping.

But the product was an operational lowest common denominator. This did not matter when peacekeeping's tasks were simple and the parties it assisted compliant. But the end of the Cold War shifted the world's political balance and launched peacekeepers into a complex environment they had ignored for 30 years. An already *ad hoc* and ill-defined activity became exponentially more confusing.

And peace support operations (PSO) doctrine has provided only limited clarity. Doctrine provides the foundation for military operations by establishing a framework for understanding how those operations should be approached. Given that commanders are supposed to train their men in accordance with the latest doctrine, it also provides the conceptual springboard for the preparation and conduct of operations.[4] But existing PSO doctrine is fundamentally flawed. In the new environment, tactical-level events have strategic-level consequences. Yet doctrine still denies tactical-level actors the freedom to make crucial decisions, both reflecting and contributing to political leaders' reluctance to loosen their grip. There is still no liberating tactical-level principle for the use of force in the wide 'grey area' between traditional peacekeeping and Desert Storm-style enforcement. Some doctrine acknowledges this, yet ducks the issue by suggesting that the murkiest reaches of the grey area – where the situation is confused, political will weak, and human rights abuses ever-present – can be ignored. They cannot.

It might be argued that the existence of a doctrine gap is of little relevance. After all, some armed forces' instinctive unease with doctrine means that they tend to use it only as the broad-brush starting point for the conduct of operations.[5] The importance of doctrine might also be discounted given that the slavish following of prescriptive principles is likely to hamstring operations in the extremely volatile environment of contemporary peacekeeping, where 'mission creep' and varyingly compliant parties to the conflict are a given.[6] But the fact of this volatility means that peacekeepers are constantly looking for conceptual guidance in situations where confusion often seems to be the only constant.[7] Doctrine can thus provide the hymn-sheet from which all actors in a peace operation – military, NGO, civilian, even the belligerents – can sing.[8]

As will be seen, the confusion inherent in the new environment extends beyond the field to those who would try to provide that guidance. Part of this confusion is about the nature of the grey area.[9] This is often characterized as the operational territory created when peacekeepers (*pace* UNPROFOR[10] in 1992–95) have to function with resources too small to execute their mandate. In reality it is wider. Grey area operations also include those where the means are sufficient (or even too great) for the mandate, but the mandate is not being executed;[11] those where a rapidly changing situation has made the mandate obsolete and left the force struggling to assert itself;[12] and those where either the intervention is separate from the political process, or there is no political process at all.[13] And as will be seen, the main characteristic of the grey area is confusion.

This article examines the principal trends in PSO doctrine since the early 1990s. It shows how the complexity of the new operational environment has confounded the doctrine-writers' efforts at simplification, created new problems where old ones seemed solved, and left peacekeepers grappling with the same conceptual void that confronted them a decade ago.

THE NEW OPERATIONAL ENVIRONMENT

To understand the difficulties with contemporary peacekeeping doctrine one first needs to understand that the ground-level operational environment has changed. For though the tasks required of grey area troops might be similar to those performed by one force or another in traditional peacekeeping's heyday, the operational environment is utterly different. Perhaps the analogy between training and operations is a fair one; mistakes made in training may result in little more than abuse and embarrassment; mistakes made on operations get people killed. The difference is that in the new environment, actions have real consequences. Yet no one suggests that training and operations are fundamentally the same, or even that operations do not exist.

The bulk of traditional peacekeeping's operational environments were utterly static. True, a force establishing a buffer zone between combatants would have an intense, volatile, initial stabilization phase. The parties' ceasefire would leave a battlefield occupied by exhausted, commingled, heavily armed state forces, still tense after the suspension of see-sawing, hard-fought hostilities, frequently grouped around their wreckage and their dead.[14] The job of the peacekeeper was to disengage them and fill the vacuum as they withdrew. Though the tactical situation might be a tinderbox, the chain of command still worked; the decision to suspend hostilities had been taken at the strategic level, and military units tried to do whatever they were told to achieve that.[15] But once the belligerents had been separated and the buffer zone established, the peacekeeper was king of an empty battlefield, frozen for decades, with crockery laid out in deserted houses and gun positions surrounded by uncased shells rusting in the sand. Almost all civilians would have been driven from their homes; the few civilians who returned did so on the UN's terms.[16] Though peacekeepers would occasionally mount patrols to check on reported infringements of the ceasefire agreements, they mostly manned observation posts or roadblocks overlooking emptiness. The peacekeepers were a garrison for a ghost zone, by and large psychologically and militarily unprepared for combat.[17] Little wonder that British troops rather scathingly called buffer zone duty 'cook and look'. This duty was so static and predictable that the British Army's 1988 *Field Manual for Peacekeeping* even set down on which side of an Observation Post dining table junior and senior observers should sit.[18]

Yet the 'kingdom''s existence was determined by the parties to the conflict. Exposed, outnumbered, and outgunned, the peacekeepers' only protection was provided at the tactical level by the parties' perception that they were utterly impartial, and at the operational and strategic levels by the state authorities' consent to the peacekeeping process. Throughout a traditional operation, peacekeepers themselves had no operational significance; their presence depended on consent, not their capabilities.[19] And if the situation deteriorated, the peacekeepers themselves could not effect a decision; that lay at strategic level.

Even a rare example of proactive traditional peacekeeping proves the point. In April 1979 an UNTSO observation post spotted an Israeli battalion advancing into the Demilitarized Zone (DMZ) in southern Lebanon and notified both UNIFIL HQ and the Irish detachment (Irbatt) in its path.[20] UNIFIL's commander, Maj.-Gen. Emanuel Erskine, ordered his mobile reserve to the Irbatt checkpoint and notified New York, where UN diplomats immediately launched protests. By the time the Israeli battalion reached the Irbatt checkpoint it found itself confronted by a substantial force equipped with anti-tank missiles and capable of offering some resistance, so it halted. A tense stand-off ensued as Erskine, who insisted on speaking only with the superiors of the Israeli battalion commander, refused the latter's request for a parley. Pressure applied in New York soon bore fruit; the Israeli commander was ordered to withdraw once the purported object of the incursion, the search of two houses where terrorists were supposed to be hiding, had been achieved – a task the Israelis were ready to permit UNIFIL to undertake on their behalf. The houses proved to be empty, so the Israelis withdrew.[21] The incident seemed to show the flexibility of the traditional principles of consent, impartiality and the minimum use of force in the face of a dangerous situation. But the Israelis were following orders throughout and could have overrun the UNIFIL units at any stage, and though the peacekeepers stopped Israeli progress, the critical decisions (to withdraw or to carry on) were being made at the strategic level. Effectively, the Israeli Defence Force (IDF) withdrew once they had demonstrated the limits of their consent to UNIFIL's presence, and UNIFIL had (by searching the houses) demonstrated its impartiality to Israeli satisfaction.[22]

So traditional peacekeeping was a military solution to a military problem. Armies had been used to pursue a policy; the policy had changed so third-party soldiers were used to prevent those armies from inadvertently scuppering the new political process. But the end of the Cold War rewrote peacekeeping's political rule book. Unprecedented unanimity in the UN Security Council committed peacekeepers to the kind of intra-state conflicts from which they had previously been barred by the zero-sum game of great power rivalry. These fluid intra-state conflicts faced by 'second generation' peacekeepers, particularly the Complex Emergencies (CEs), were 'essentially not military problems'.[23] And all of the old operational certainties had gone.

Typically, the political context was extraordinarily confused. Civil war would be raging; whereas traditional peacekeepers would deal with only two belligerents, their successors might be confronted with up to a dozen. Even coherent parties' grievances might be difficult to identify. More often, factions would have become little more than bandit groups camouflaged by acronyms, constantly fragmenting and reforming; their authority would be constructed on a village-by-village basis, and they might have apolitical interests, unreliable chains of command, and individual agendas for revenge and survival. Sometimes the only political certainty was that none of the parties wanted an agreement.[24] But the massive human deprivation and suffering in CEs created an overriding Security Council need to respond. Even if a host-country body existed to give consent, it might not be sought, particularly if that body's actions, intentional or not, had caused the crisis. Peacekeepers might be deployed without a thought-through mission, or a mission defined by higher authority;[25] if the mission had been defined, the force might be handicapped by having to operate without any civilian political control.[26] This lack of direction would be all the more damaging given that peacekeepers were serving in the midst of ongoing conflict, with ineffective or nonexistent ceasefires, and the ever-present danger of local armed opposition. This danger was heightened by the fact that the most common form of intervention, humanitarian relief, might directly affect a party's war aims by succouring the people it was trying to terrorize or kill.[27] Unlike their traditional predecessors, PSO troops would also be fully exposed to the play of politics. Every action could have a local political consequence, which the peacekeepers were ill-equipped to measure.[28]

At the same time, the peacekeeper was no longer the sole intervening authority. He might well be supported by air and sea power answering to organizations other than his own, with different political agendas. There might well be military officers from yet more

organizations, ostensibly present as observers.[29] The division of roles
and tasks might not be clear-cut. Crucially, there were also huge
numbers of non-governmental organizations (NGOs) and UN
agencies, ranging in size and professionalism from the International
Committee for the Red Cross/Crescent (ICRC) to a solitary driver
taking a week off from his day job to deliver food and clothing collected
by his local church. Many of these roles, too, would overlap, and even
co-operation between agencies within the same system – for instance,
UNHCR, WFP, UNICEF[30] – could not be guaranteed. Each agency or
NGO had its own agenda and chain of command, and some had
considerable political clout.[31] Many might have been in-theatre for
years, had developed their own *modus vivendi* with the belligerents, and
felt they had a far better understanding of the conflict than the military
latecomers.[32] Above all, their actions affected the peacekeepers'
mission, yet they were utterly independent of, and sometimes openly
antagonistic to, PSO troops.[33]

At ground level, the operational area was awash with people.
Warlords would avoid confronting each other, instead focusing their
violence on civilians, who were both prize and victim. The result was the
displacement of up to half the population. Civilians huddled in
temporary shelters, traumatized, ungovernable, and dependent on aid
perhaps for years on end. Any shift in violence could start a panic-
stricken exodus, depriving the already displaced of their latest refuge.
Family and clan structures would have broken down; the defenceless
would look to peacekeepers for protection they were frequently unable
or unauthorized to give.[34] The absence of law and order and the collapse
of civil infrastructure fostered an increase in crime, frequently fanned by
external organized crime syndicates, and often feeding off the tools of
third-party intervention – food, shelter, vehicles, and the need for
security.[35]

The operational area was also geographically undefined. This meant
that troops had to try to maintain freedom of movement in a war zone
where factions were indistinguishable from bandits or one another.
Drink and/or drugs might make fighters irrational or bellicose, or give
them the feeling of invulnerability – further complicating the process of
third party dealings with them.[36] A peacekeeper would probably be
unable to tell if the act of violence directed against him was random or
significant, yet he would have to make that judgment, and act
accordingly, on the spot.[37] The use of force would also have considerable

consequences on relations between contingents. Troops would be from different nations, of widely varying quality and ethos, and would have divergent approaches to, and competence in, dealings with the parties. Radically opposed notions of what would constitute an appropriate use of force could create a potential for inter-unit or -contingent schism which did not exist in the traditional buffer zone operation. One contingent's actions could rebound, fatally, on its neighbour.[38]

This in turn emphasized a basic peacekeeping command and control (C2) conundrum. The more likely the recourse to force, the more vital were unity of command and rapidity of execution; yet the likelier the use of force (and thus casualties), the greater the contributor-state interference in the C2 process – and the less likely the maintenance of force unity.[39] The command and control problem was exacerbated by the fact that hugely improved communications increased the scope for over-the-horizon micro-management of operations. Commanders could no longer rely on being able to react to events in their own time, calling on political or higher military authorities only when their support was required. Any number of actors could interfere with the commander's ability to do his job.[40]

Thus in a situation where the decision-making process had become infinitely more complex, the large number of players meant that every day troops in this new environment had to make a quantity of decisions at a level much lower, with consequences potentially far more dangerous, than ever confronted a traditional force. The 'strategic soldier' was born.[41] The fact that these decisions had to be made while large numbers of people were being maimed and killed also imbued the process with an overwhelming sense of urgency, while drastically shortening the time available for resolution or implementation.[42] And the need to nurse an increasing number of important civil–military relationships magnified the considerable inherent potential for treading on institutional toes.[43] Also, unlike traditional operations, peacekeepers' effectiveness (or, indeed, survival) in a violent and unpredictable environment depended on their operational capabilities; thus a higher calibre of soldier was required. This complexity, fluidity and danger meant that though the new environment exhibited characteristics of traditional peacekeeping and enforcement, it was something distinct from each. In effect, large numbers of varyingly capable troops had to make decisions the conflict made nigh-impossible, to attain long-term civil objectives they couldn't quantify, in situations the plethora of competing intervening bodies made difficult to remedy. Success was difficult to measure; the likelihood of casualties was ever-present.[44]

One soldier's experience can serve as an example of this shift. In August 1992 Lt. Justin Freeland 9/12 L was serving as a reconnaissance troop leader with UNFICYP in Cyprus.[45] His duties focused on policing the 18-year-old 'Green Line' buffer zone between Greeks and Turks. Tasks included removing illegally planted crops, reporting on the parties' military exercises, and acting as part of the quick reaction force at times of high tension. The job was 'highly static, quite mundane, and pretty predictable'; he did not once come under fire. Three months later he was serving in the same role with UNPROFOR. But central Bosnia 'couldn't have been more of a contrast'. No one knew what would happen next; the plan changed daily as the situation developed; there were so many incidents he couldn't keep track of them. The houses next to the officers' quarters in Vitez regularly came under heavy machinegun fire; the airport was shelled by Serb artillery twice a day; vehicles using the Kladanj–Tuzla road ('bomb alley') were often bracketed; and he was wounded by a mortar fragment while waiting to escort a Tuzla-bound United Nations High Commission for Refugees (UNHCR) convoy across the front lines. Later in the tour the battalion group found itself unable to control a descending spiral of violence. His troop would find deserted hamlets they had earlier seen being set alight; in one, Ahmici, they discovered a major war crime in which over 100 people had been murdered, and had to deal with its aftermath. Busloads of refugees, NGOs, UN agencies and the ICRC, the media, anti-sniper missions, regular small arms and heavy weapons fire, drunken belligerents with non-responsive chains of command, a battalion mission determined by its commander and not by higher authority – all set Lt. Freeland's UNPROFOR experience apart from his buffer zone duty in Cyprus.[46]

Yet it was an incident shortly after Ahmici which best demonstrates the huge shift between the old operational environment and the new. Lt. Freeland's troop was leading a party (including the battalion group commander, Lt.-Col. Bob Stewart) attempting to reopen a closed route into Vitez. His Scimitar light tanks had entered a deep sunken lane when they found their progress blocked by a booby-trapped bus, supported by Croats armed with at least eight rocket-propelled grenades (RPGs). Lt. Freeland reported the obstruction. Shortly afterwards Col. Stewart appeared with an entourage of nearly 50 people – interpreters, the RSM, other soldiers, and (crucially) the media.[47] Col. Stewart told the roadblock commander that he had ten minutes to remove the obstruction, or his troops would open fire. He and his entourage then withdrew a safe distance, leaving the recce troop to confront the roadblock. But the sunken lane was too deep and narrow to allow Lt. Freeland's Scimitars' guns to traverse; none of the other vehicles could bring their weapons to bear; and following Col. Stewart's public falling-out with the HVO after Ahmici, the Croats were in no mood to back down. So Lt. Freeland's two crews waited impotently for the expiry of the ultimatum. Eventually it was Col. Stewart who backed down and the party found a different route into Vitez. The play of local politics, the presence of the press, the level of the threat – all played a part in the creation and resolution of this confrontation. This was not 'cook and look'.

THE DOCTRINE GAP

All of this meant that the political and military situation was dictated by conditions at the tactical and operational levels. The response to the situation should therefore also have been decided at the same levels. But the development of PSO doctrine in the first half of the 1990s ensured that it was not.

The doctrine writers addressed the new environment by re-emphasizing old principles. The fact that armies rushed to put out new peacekeeping doctrines emphasized that the world had changed, yet in the letter of the doctrines they tried to minimize that change. '[T]he international community has failed, sometimes with catastrophic consequences, to distinguish adequately between peacekeeping and peace-enforcement – two activities that require radically different conceptual approaches.'[48] The doctrine debate was driven by the British Army's *Wider Peacekeeping*, and its US Army stablemate FM 100-23 'Peace Operations'. They were by no means identical. The British Army saw two intervention options, Wider Peacekeeping and Warfighting, with Enforcement as a subset of warfighting; while peacekeeping 'should be characterised by impartiality and minimum force [,][p]eace enforcement … dispenses with consent and is conducted, in the main, in accordance with standard military principles predicated on the identification of an enemy'.[49] FM 100-23, on the other hand, saw 'peace operations', subdivided into 'peacekeeping' (PK) and 'peace enforcement' (PE), as distinct from 'warfighting', and so allowed the use of force in PE to coerce or compel – but not defeat – when consent was not absolute. But the variables which determined the categories of operation in both manuals were the traditional trinity of consent, impartiality and the minimum use of force; and though the PK/Wider PK category was broader than its traditional predecessor, PK and PE had no common ground – 'the techniques of peacekeeping and peace enforcement cannot and should not be mixed'.[50]

The new spin in these doctrines was the emphasis on consent. Consent was the broad Rubicon separating PK and PE; tactical (or field operations) level consent formed the west bank and operational (or theatre) level the east. At the tactical level, the parties' consent was a nebulous, hard-to-measure quantity based on prevailing opinion, itself derived from local events and influences. At the operational level the parties' consent devolved mostly from formal agreements. A force could lose consent at the tactical level as long as it retained it at the operational; but once peacekeepers left the middle of the channel and set foot on the east bank – effectively, acted in such a way as to convince one or all of the parties that formal agreements had been broken – they had initiated uncontrolled escalation and thus an enforcement operation from which there could be no return.[51] The consequences of crossing the consent divide were so serious that the decision was to be a policy-level one; 'Commanders should avoid hasty or ill-conceived actions that unintentionally cause a degradation of the level and extent of consent.'[52] And the actions that were most likely to undermine consent involved the use of force; '[j]udgements concerning the use of force are therefore likely to be the most critical that a peacekeeping practitioner will make.'[53]

In operational terms, this meant that the pivotal factor in the use of force in peacekeeping was how it was perceived. Force used with general agreement (perhaps against crime or banditry), or with the consent of faction leaders (against units refusing to follow the party line, or those following faction orders in breaking agreements to test the limits of the peacekeepers' response), would not jeopardize the mission; but the unrestrained use of force, or its application to one party in the conflict, would make escalation to peace enforcement likely. The downing of three Serb aircraft violating the Bosnian no-fly zone was recognized as reasonable by faction leaders; in Somalia, the unrestrained use of force against civilians and one faction was not.[54] It was the Somali experience which gave the Rubicon of consent its pithiest tag: 'the Mogadishu line'.

The position of the doctrine-writers was actually not so surprising. The US and UK doctrine staffs were from NATO forces with limited peace operations experience; the experience that existed had been undermined by negligible institutional interest or memory and a paucity of organized thinking on the subject; and the staff themselves had no first-hand experience of their own. Thus they turned to the Nordic countries, which had made peacekeeping doctrine their own, to put the empirical evidence of the early 1990s in context. But traditional doctrine was based on shaky foundations. The armies which had monopolized it were second- or third-rate; little rigorous thinking had been applied.[55] In many cases, UN officials, staff officers and traditional doctrine writers had no experience of violence or active duty outside the narrow confines of peacekeeping, and so had no notion of the progressive escalation of the use of force; peacekeeping and general war were their only options.[56] They thus tended to ignore the UN's wider experiences and concentrate instead on the basic buffer zone model, in part because the institutional memory of those experiences – ONUC (United Nations force in the Congo) in particular – was so bad. Ironically enough, the very wider experiences these doctrines had rejected were used as a defence of the old. The fact that the civil conflict tasks of post-Cold War forces had been undertaken by traditional peacekeepers of the past encouraged the broad US/UK/Nordic conclusion that the reassuring verities of the Cold War still operated; no new approach was needed.[57]

Whereas *Wider Peacekeeping* and FM 100-23 represented attempts to grapple with the problem of the grey area by beefing up the traditional approach to peacekeeping, French efforts used enforcement as their starting point.[58] France's experience of unilateral intervention in *la Francophonie*, the humanitarian 'Right to Interfere' (*'Droit d'Ingérence'*), in defiance of Article 2 of the UN Charter, long promoted by MSF/MDM co-founder and Minister of Humanitarian Affairs Bernard Kouchner, and a traditionally assertive foreign policy, had combined to hew a characteristically individual French perspective on the new operational environment.[59] This acknowledged a middle ground between peacekeeping and enforcement, called 'peace restoration'. But this apparently three-option menu was in reality no such thing. The peacekeeping category rejected traditional peacekeeping's strictures on self-defence and insisted that a consensual, Chapter VI mission be equipped for combat and able to use force against non-compliance with the mandate. The guiding principle for this spin on traditional peacekeeping was to be 'active impartiality'; the mandate had the force of law, and belligerents were to be judged according to their compliance with it.[60] The peacekeepers' application of the principle of impartiality at a tactical level should not justify their inaction in the face of obstruction of the mission's mandate or objectives: '[O]nly passivity is dishonourable'.[61] But the emphasis on the consequences of the non–use of force and the importance of preparation for combat in a consensual process effectively removed what others recognized as traditional peacekeeping from an operational menu in which it still had a place.[62] After all, the passivity of traditional peacekeeping still had a role in buffer zone operations. And the kind of belligerents a buffer zone force would keep apart would be unlikely to agree to the presence of combat-capable peacekeepers, given that that would suggest they had every intention of breaking their word.

Three incidents serve to illustrate the ground-level consequences of the application of the doctrine writers' thinking. In May 1993, in Cambodia's Banteay Meanchay province, a Dutch marine company was refused permission to go to the rescue of a six-vehicle United Nations Transitional Authority in Cambodia (UNTAC) convoy (of unarmed Japanese policemen with a small Dutch escort) ambushed by the Khmer Rouge half a mile away, because the operation – an advance to contact – was deemed to be an enforcement one. This caused a complete breakdown in relations between the two contingents and the (Tokyo-approved) desertion of a third of the Japanese UNTAC police detachment; the lack of response encouraged Khmer Rouge perceptions of UNTAC powerlessness, and aborted the Dutch battalion's effective, aggressive disarmament programme in the Khmer Rouge's stronghold province.[63] In January 1994 the United Nations Assistance Mission in Rwanda (UNAMIR) obtained information about the Rwandan government's genocidal intentions and informed New York that it was to mount a cordon and search operation to obtain evidence, in the form of weapons and documents. But according to UNHQ this was 'an offensive operation for which permission would not be granted'.[64] Instead the SRSG[65] and force commander (Roméo Dallaire) were to inform the Rwandan president of New York's knowledge of these breaches of the Arusha Accords and remind him of his obligation to crack down on them.[66] It is likely that had the operation gone ahead, the mass murder of the spring might have been mitigated or even forestalled.[67] In July 1995, the commander of Srebrenica's hugely outnumbered UN garrison (Col. Karremans), aware that only air power could deter the Serb attackers, 'avoided armed confrontation and appealed... for support at the highest levels'.[68] His posts were under direct assault by Serb armour; the requests were in line with the mandate. But in a litany of command-level pusillanimity, up to five of these appeals were systematically deflected, sat upon or lost in UNPROFOR's tortuous bureaucracy. When close air support did finally come it was minimal (two bombs) and irrelevant (the Serbs had already captured the town).[69] Yet the Serbs' initially limited ambitions had only expanded to include seizure of the enclave when they assessed that UNPROFOR was unwilling or unable to stop them.[70]

In all three examples, strategic level inaction stemmed from the fear that any attempt by weak, widely dispersed peacekeepers to impose themselves on events in a volatile environment would put them at unacceptable risk; they might be seen to have 'entered the war' against a belligerent.[71] The cable denying Dallaire permission to act – which he had neither asked for, nor required – ended pointedly with 'the overriding consideration is the need to avoid entering into a course of action that might lead to the use of force and unanticipated repercussions'.[72] In all three instances, strategic-level responses to tactical or operational-level developments had disastrous effects. This was above all because of senior commanders' and officials' delusional attachment to the trinity of traditional peacekeeping principles. In the words of one, writing about Srebrenica, 'we tried to ... apply the rules of peacekeeping when there was no peace to keep. Knowing that any other course of action would jeopardise the lives of the troops, we tried to create – or imagine – an environment in which the tenets of peacekeeping – agreement between the parties, deployment by consent, and impartiality – could be upheld.'[73]

Yet stretching the traditional trinity to accommodate the new operational area was no more effective. 'Active impartiality' and 'wider peacekeeping' stretched the trinity from opposing poles, yet both failed to provide a way out of the quagmire. The basis of the French 'active impartiality' was the refusal to be passive in the face of low-level obstructions to the mandate, and it presupposed a military capability to implement the mandate and protect peacekeepers and civilians alike.[74] 'Wider peacekeeping', on the other hand, assumed that the emphasis on operational-level consent would allow a force slightly more heavily equipped than its trinitarian predecessor to assert itself against tactical-level obstructionists. But both approaches failed to allow for the grey area operational reality that these peacekeepers were widely dispersed, and so comparatively unsupported, in an extremely volatile environment. The practical consequences of the collision of environment and doctrine were demonstrated by the first Scandinavian battalion in the Bosnia element of UNPROFOR. Whereas most contingents would conduct extensive negotiations to get roadblocks removed, the well-armed Scanbatt 1 threatened immediate use of force if they weren't.[75] Initially they had considerable success and earned a reputation for robustness. Their approach lasted until vulnerable members of the widely dispersed contingent were taken hostage.[76] Tactical-level assertiveness could only complicate matters if coupled with a traditionally deployed, inherently vulnerable force. Like 'wider peacekeeping', 'active impartiality' was incompatible with a Chapter VI operation in the new environment.

The operational corollary of these new doctrines was a vicious circle of impotence. Troops dispersed throughout a fluid environment, with uncertain political support, and inappropriate conceptual body armour, were confronted with flagrant abuses which required responses other than those of enforcement or peacekeeping. But commanders then had to reconcile the irreconcilable – the traditional trinity and the need to use force – and so tended to fall back on 'wider peacekeeping''s operational perspective.[77] Governments, meanwhile, were terrified of having their troops inadvertently cross an invisible Rubicon, and thus being seen to be partial, or of simply putting their own people at risk; so when their approval was required for a forceful response, they insisted on doing nothing. This increased the perception of weakness, which prompted more forceful UN resolutions, which frightened governments would not provide the resources to implement; thus the impression of weakness was heightened once more. This vicious circle of impotence had become so undermining that by 30 May 1995 the UN Secretary-General was emphasizing the lowest common denominator of consent, suggesting in effect that 'the UN should only undertake those tasks which the most obstructive party ... will allow'.[78]

The most influential recent military manual for PSO, the UK's Joint Warfare Publication 3-50 *Peace Support Operations*, has built on this knowledge.[79] 'Peacekeeping' (PK), relying on consent-promoting techniques and the use of force only in self-defence, is separated from 'peace enforcement' (PE), which couples enforcement and consent techniques with a combat-prepared force, by consent; PE is separated from war, or Gulf-style enforcement (which involves combat forces, warfighting techniques and a designated enemy), by impartiality. The dependence of 'peacekeeping' (PK) operations on the parties' prior agreement to the terms of the mandate is restated, while the identification of a broad 'peace enforcement' (PE) category, separate from war, both acknowledges the volatility of the new operational environment and provides some conceptual safety within it. PE operations are coercive, necessitated by the absence of consent or the expectation of one or all parties failing to comply with agreements; their commanders need 'to be able to enforce compliance where there is opposition, to promote consent where there is indifference and to maintain and reward consent where it exists. In essence, this expands areas of consent at the expense of areas of opposition.'[80] A PE force is the most suitable PSO tool; it can stabilize a fluid operational area, so creating the consent vital for PK, restore stability if a PK force has had consent withdrawn, or threaten the use of force to ensure a process remains on track. Above all, as long as it remains impartial, it can operate in a constantly evolving environment with few (if any) changes to the force. The emphasis on PE is reflected in the fact that in the manual's diagrammatic representation of PSO as a quadrant, PE occupies a half to PK's quarter, while the 'Strategic Direction' arrow represents the '*desired* strategic direction' of all PSO; 'all commanders should be given the freedom of action to develop their operations accordingly'.[81]

JWP 3-50 thus helps to define the grey area between peacekeeping and war, and so offers policy-makers a wider range of more appropriate options.[82] But the significant clarification is provided at the more forceful end of the PSO spectrum. The divide between PE and warfighting provides a conceptual basis for avoiding UNOSOM II's unwanted descent into belligerency;[83] in effect, it maps out 'the Mogadishu line'. However, the emphasis on deploying a combat-ready PE force if consent is in doubt means that viable operations will never be launched, partly because contributors can afford fewer PE than PK missions, and partly because belligerents may accept a lightly armed force yet veto a heavier one. The PK end of the PSO spectrum is therefore left a little more uncertain.

The US Army's most recent doctrine also stresses the more powerful end of the spectrum. *FM 100-20 Stability Actions and Support Actions* is in most respects extremely close to JWP 3-50, using similar terminology and placing a similar emphasis on force being used only impartially and with restraint against those who violate agreements or prevent the execution of the mission; any use of force is to be rapidly backed up with

STRATEGIC
DIRECTION

HIGH

C
O
N
S
E
N
T

PEACEKEEPING

Consent possibly sufficient
to preclude use of force

PEACE
ENFORCEMENT
Force necessary to
achieve objectives

Operations not

credible and tenable

LOW

LOW | **FORCE CAPABILITY** | **HIGH**

diplomatic activity to ensure that impartiality is not jeopardized. Yet this emphasis on restraint reads oddly alongside the injunction that PE forces be 'strong enough to engage successfully all the parties simultaneously, at least long enough for the force to extract itself or receive reinforcements'.[84] The possibility that the parties to the conflict might interpret the disparity between the power of such a force and its softly-softly approach as a sign of weakness – and so act against the interests of the operation, knowing that any reaction is likely to be muted – does not seem to be entertained. *Stability and Support Operations* thus ensures the continuation of the grey area even as it attempts to close it.

Yet perhaps the most significant aspect of these new doctrines is the proportion of the grey area they choose to leave unmapped, thus denying policy-makers other options. For instance, though JWP 3-50 acknowledges a substantial lingering grey area – the quarter of the quadrant where there is insufficient consent for PK yet insufficient combat capability for PE – its conceptual framework for this area consists of the injunction '[t]his quadrant should be avoided'.[85] The conceptual gap is all the more remarkable given that this prescription has remained intact throughout a gradually less prescriptive series of drafts. For instance, the First Draft's '[m]ilitary activities in PSO will be, *without exception*, part of a wider strategy in support of political goals' has become 'military activities *should be viewed* as only one of several lines of operation within a wider strategy directed towards an agreed end state'.[86] Yet there is still no conceptual provision made for interventions undertaken before, or independent of, any political process; the assumption is that there is a wider strategy and the possibility of an agreed end state. The grey area may have been narrowed, but gaps remain.[87]

This emphasis on political co-ordination is once again a back-to-basics reaction, this time to perceived failures in Somalia and Croatia/Bosnia, where UNITAF (Unified Task Force [Somalia]), UNOSOM II and UNPROFOR military operations were not integrated with any political process. Yet again, it misses the point. Much though they might like to, Western policy-makers can no longer afford to ignore internal conflicts in remote states. Dramatic reportage of huge human-rights abuses and population movements, the likelihood of regional destabilization, a state's need to maintain a global position, and painful awareness of the consequences of past inactivity, can all create an irresistible dynamic for intervention – even if the parties to the conflict are opposed to it, and there is nothing even approximating to a political process with which a military intervention can move in lockstep.[88] A perfect example of this is the explanation for French participation in UNITAF offered (three days after it began) by the man who initiated it:

> You see, it is soon going to be Christmas and it would be unthinkable to have the French public eat its Christmas dinner while seeing on TV all those starving kids. It would be politically disastrous. ...I also phoned several of our African friends ... They all agreed:... they would look ridiculous in Africa if the Americans went and we stayed home. But don't worry: as soon as all this stuff blows over and TV cameras are trained in another direction, we will quietly tip-toe out. With luck, it shouldn't last more than three–four months and in the meantime we will try our best not to do anything foolish.[89]

But at the beginning of the 21st century – in the wake of the international community's trauma of standing by while genocide was practised in Rwanda and 'ethnic cleansing' in Bosnia – political will may well be sufficient to authorize intervention against the wishes of the belligerents, yet be too weak either to authorize a genuine peace enforcement operation, or to provide any operation with enough backing to stop it joining the vicious circle of impotence.[90] The gradually increasing assertiveness of post–Cold War humanitarianism reflects this lack of will. Governments who have committed troops to the lowest common denominator policy of mitigating the effects of conflict, rather than addressing the conflict itself, try to mask their irresolution with 'humanitarian corridors', 'safe areas' and armed protection of aid convoys – while at the same time emphasizing the (implicitly contradictory) sanctity of state sovereignty.[91] This political fragility means troops will be committed to the low consent/ low force capability, or 'no go', quadrant, described in the UK doctrine's diagram. For instance, however much Britain might only want to be involved in PSOs with a clear political strategy, aim and exit date, its position as a significant player on the world stage means it will be asked to join muddier operations – and will join them to maintain that position.[92]

Even where Britain can remain aloof, other countries or organizations may not have the same freedom. According to UN Secretary-General Kofi Annan, states will launch middle ground interventions in response to their own imperatives – often under a UN framework. But '[t]he conventional wisdom … is that the Organization should do less peace-keeping, either by not getting involved at all in certain conflicts or by working only at their margins. Aside from the overriding fact that inaction in the face of massive violence is morally indefensible, non-involvement is an illusory option.'[93] The corollary of ongoing attempts to persuade developing country militaries to adopt British doctrine is that they will certainly find themselves committed to an operational area British doctrine writers would rather ignore. Thus the injunction to stay away is of little practical use. It may in fact worsen matters; knowledge that the zone exists, but that workable principles for operating in it do not, is unlikely to do anything other than weaken already precarious political backing.

JWP 3-50's no-go quadrant is in fact a cycle. Political incoherence leads to the deployment of a 'no go' (and thus by definition weak) force in a fluid environment, where ongoing conflict and a weak mission's need to assert itself combine to require the use of force. But conceptual incoherence makes policy-makers and practitioners uneasy with using force, and increases the likelihood that, when authorized, it will go wrong. Botched or tardy enforcement emphasizes force- and policy-level divisions; political approaches become yet more incoherent, and the force yet weaker.[94]

An excellent example of this process is UNOSOM II. Member-state unwillingness to extend the life, or broaden the mandate, of a multinational coalition meant that a traditional UN force with a bolted-on enforcement capability, weaker than its UNITAF predecessor, was deployed yet with a stronger mandate. The requirement to restore stability – i.e., confront the belligerents – meant that the traditional conceptual bedrocks, of being seen to be impartial and maintaining the consent of the parties, were inapplicable. Yet there was nothing to take their place. The need to use force – sometimes against women and children – and the absence of a sound conceptual basis for it, emphasized widely divergent competences and conceptual approaches. The casualties inflicted and sustained by the operation mounted, causing vigorous intra-coalition debate to degenerate into inter-contingent recrimination; this in turn precipitated the withdrawal of some contributor countries' political support, which contributed to the irrelevance, and ultimate failure, of the mission.[95]

If UK, US and French doctrines are all flawed, the PSO doctrine of the alliance under whose banner they often operate (NATO) is frankly counterproductive. NATO doctrine – like that of the UK – is being reappraised. But the final draft of the 1997 version places a debilitating emphasis – accentuated by being in bold print – on force protection. National publics expect PSOs to 'involve minimum cost in ... human life ... above all else the lives of their national contingents ... In political terms, this expectation translates itself into to [sic] the cliché of a [sic] conducting a "no casualties operation"... [A] Force Commander will afford the highest priority to protecting the members of his Force.'[96] On top of this, the broad thrust of the doctrine is not even bipolar; in a throwback to 'active impartiality', it emphasizes that many PK operations will need to be PE in nature, while one guiding principle (impartiality) is identified for both categories.[97] The result of this is that possible peacekeeping operations are unlikely to be undertaken – because a PE configuration will make them much more expensive than they need to be, so barring any intervention at all – while the emphasis on force protection rather than implementation means that any PE operations undertaken are unlikely (*pace* SFOR) to take risky, pivotal decisions and thus achieve very much. NATO doctrine ensures that PSO troops are, in the words of the World War I song, 'here/because we're here/ because we're here/ because we're here'.

It should not be thought that the recent developments in peacekeeping doctrine are universally bad. As Peter Viggo Jakobsen has pointed out, there is a common understanding in the Franco–British–American engineroom of NATO peacekeeping of the terms, concepts and broad-brush approaches required for successful peace operations, particularly when consent is in doubt.[98] This common understanding is also influencing regional/subregional military powers (particularly Nigeria and South Africa) through the efforts of donor-funded doctrine-writers and training initiatives such as the USA's ACRI and France's RECAMP.[99] The doctrines' emphasis on avoiding giving PE tasks to PK forces, and the need for PE-configured forces when consent is in doubt, is shared in the reports of the Lessons Learned Unit of the UN's Department of Peacekeeping Operations. This emphasis was also one of the key recommendations in the Report of the Panel on UN Peacekeeping Operations chaired by Lakhdar Brahimi and presented to the Security Council in August 2000.[100] This report is intended to create the political will to at last provide the UN with the resources and tailored mandates it needs to ensure its peacekeeping endeavours do not repeat the mistakes of the 1990s.[101] It is striking to note that in the consultation process that followed the presentation of the report both the Secretariat and the Security Council emphasized the need for a UN PSO doctrine.[102] When all of this is combined with the soul-searching reports on Srebrenica and Rwanda carried out at the Secretary-General's behest – both of which addressed the impossibility of asking traditional peacekeepers to carry out peace enforcement tasks – it is clear that the emerging consensus is shared at many levels across the UN. It is also clear that important actors in the UN's peace and security machinery are moving away from the obsession with consent and perceived impartiality that so hobbled the operations of the 1990s.[103] This broadening consensus is a considerable improvement over the contradictory incoherence of the UNPROFOR era. But the fact remains that the new coherence does not apply to the heart of the grey area.

The problem persists in part because the new coherence is illusory. For different armed forces' fundamentally different approaches to the application of this coherence suggests that contributor governments are not as convinced of its merits as they might appear. This has been highlighted in the recent 'grey area' operations in Kosovo and East Timor. KFOR's operations in Kosovo were planned on the basis of UK doctrine, with the force acting as the impartial executor of Security Council Resolution 1244.[104] But different contingents had fundamentally different approaches to the conduct of operations. US personnel concentrated on force protection, building a substantial camp and patrolling in vehicles and numbers; German forces imitated the US; Italian and French forces tended to be neutral (i.e., passive) rather than impartial when confronted with difficult decisions. In effect, the UK followed the more robust UK doctrine; other forces adhered to the much more passive NATO version. The corollary of this was seen in the early months of 2001 in the Presevo valley in extra-Kosovan Serbia and in northern Macedonia. Ex-KLA veterans attempted to widen their nationalist campaign by attacking Yugoslav and Macedonian forces; they believed they had the tacit support of Washington because their preparations had been laid in territory under the control or observation of US troops, who had refused to intervene. But the Albanian extremists were mistaken. The US military were not as omnipotent as the Albanians held them to be; their refusal to patrol on foot or leave their posts with any frequency meant they controlled neither their zone nor its borders; and when they were aware of extremist preparations, Washington's traditional reluctance to take difficult decisions intervened.[105] Tactical-level passivity and operational- and strategic-level evasiveness had combined to give the Albanian extremists an inadvertent green light. It is significant that when KFOR decided to control the US zone's external borders, it was British troops – with their extensive experience of foot patrolling and covert observation work, and readiness to grasp the nettle – who were brought in.[106]

The same disparity appeared (though with less dramatic results) in East Timor. The multinational intervention force for East Timor (Interfet) which restored order in the wake of the August 1999 referendum, was planned and led by Australia. Its rationale (based on Security Council Resolution 1264) was humanitarian.[107] But from the beginning of the planning process, the Australian command was keen to prevent the force acquiring any humanitarian tasks; it adopted the US tendency of trying to ensure that soldiers carried out only military tasks, thus limiting the chances for 'mission creep'. However, the principal problem on the force's arrival was humanitarian, not security-based – the militias refused to offer opposition. Even so, Australian troops followed the US emphasis on force protection, moving only in platoon-sized groups, and refusing to patrol outside Dili until they had established an extremely secure base – a process which took several days. By the second day, on the other hand, British Army Gurkhas were moving into the interior in small groups to determine humanitarian needs, and were well on the way to answering those needs before Australian forces joined in.[108]

These examples appear to show that doctrine can only achieve so much; the best doctrine is of no use at all if soldiers, or their political masters, will not apply it. But they also hint at a fundamental difficulty with existing doctrine. As we have seen it appears to offer coherence at the better-equipped end of the grey area spectrum; if consent is in doubt, deploy a heavy force and use both carrots and sticks to induce compliance. But even when this force sallies into the field replete with carrots and sticks, it appears reluctant (*pace* IFOR/SFOR & KFOR) to grapple with potentially dangerous or complicated tasks. And this is in part because existing doctrine does not offer timorous governments and militaries a concept for the use of force in the grey area convincing enough to dispel the ghost of the Mogadishu line. Timidity is undoubtedly partly a function of the fear of casualties. But it is also a function of the fear that robust action will embroil peacekeepers in something their governments would rather they stayed above.

CONCLUSION

The past decade has seen a fundamental shift in the nature and scope of peacekeeping operations. Peacekeepers have found themselves moving from the simple predictability of 'cook and look' – state parties, functioning chains of command, the consent of the belligerents, hardly any civilians – to the confusion of grey area operations, with multiple and apparently inchoate factions, a plethora of intervenors, evanescent political will and ever-present human rights abuses. Peacekeeping doctrine was slow to embrace this new environment, and initially took some dangerous missteps. Yet as we have seen, a degree of coherence has now arisen on how to approach grey area operations. But this coherence is replete with difficulties. It is too rigid and costly to apply to more than the grey area's most politically cohesive fringes, where the comparative clarity of the situation will be reflected in contributor country political will. If this approach is applied it provides no conceptual guidance for the grey area's murkiest reaches. And problems with the application of this coherence show that there is still no tactical-level principle for the use of force throughout the grey area which could liberate troops and governments alike from the ghost of the Mogadishu line.

The flaws in doctrines are understandable given the political imperatives behind them. As Rod Thornton has persuasively argued, *Wider Peacekeeping* was drafted partly to demonstrate to those who would embroil the British Army in the war in Bosnia that its limited role within UNPROFOR was the right course of action.[109] Current British doctrine was drafted in part to coalesce political thinking before any potential intervention, and so ensure that troops were not committed to the 'no go' quadrant – so answering the armed forces' institutional need to prevent a repetition of UNPROFOR's humiliating inertia.[110] French doctrine's insistence that even a traditional peacekeeping force have the capability to assert itself if the situation deteriorates reflects the ground-level humiliation of UNPROFOR. NATO doctrine had to provide a guide for non-NATO members soldiering under NATO command; it also had to demonstrate alliance unanimity. Its debilitating lowest common denominator emphasis on force protection thus reassures potential contributor countries and reflects the non-negotiable concern over casualties in Washington and Berlin.[111] And the Nigerian–South African spin on UK doctrine reflects the former's need to show it will not repeat some of the excesses of its troops in Sierra Leone and Liberia, and the latter's growing interest in providing a regional lead in conflict resolution. Yet these imperatives have guaranteed that PSO troops will be deployed with doctrines that do not fit the ground level reality. The grey area persists.

Yet these political imperatives have combined with another political imperative – the urge to heed what one senior British official has dubbed 'the "something must be done" school of public opinion'[112] – to create a double-edged sword. PSO troops will be deployed on grey area operations, and into British doctrine's 'no go' quadrant; but the politically influenced doctrines used as the basis for the planning and conduct of operations provide them with fundamentally unsuitable conceptual tools. The reality is that the work of the past decade has left the 'grey area' no clearer nor more certain than it was at the beginning of the doctrine revision process over ten years ago.[113] Only doctrine which embraces the confusion of the grey area, the vacillation of contributor country political will, the lack of resources, the need to take unpleasant decisions and the imperative to act against human rights abuses, can provide troops throughout the 'grey area' – but particularly in the 'no go' quadrant – with the conceptual bedrock they need to succeed.

NOTES

1. I would like to thank John Mackinlay, Peter Viggo Jakobsen and Nick Wheeler for their comments on different drafts of this article.
2. A brief note on terminology. Although I am unhappy with 'peacekeeping' being used to describe more than the classic, consensual, Chapter VI-based activity invented by the UN, the term has achieved such currency in its wider application that narrowing its use would seem pedantic. Accordingly I use 'peacekeeping', 'peace support operations' (the preferred UK term) and 'peace operations' (US) synonymously to describe the whole range of third party military operations, from small unarmed observer missions to air- and sea-supported Corps-sized multinational endeavours, intended to support or create peace. 'Traditional peacekeeping' describes the classic consensual Chapter VI-based activity mentioned above and is therefore a sub-category of peacekeeping. 'Enforcement' describes Gulf War or Korean War-style limited war authorized by the Security Council, and is outside the peacekeeping category. 'Grey Area operations' describes the whole range of operations – variously described in doctrines as peace restoration, peace enforcement or wider peacekeeping – which lie beyond traditional peacekeeping, but fall short of enforcement, and are covered by the rubric of peacekeeping.
3. It was formalized in the establishment of the General Assembly's Special Committee on Peacekeeping Operations in 1965. Maj.-Gen. Indar Jit Rikhye, *The Theory and Practice of Peacekeeping* (London: Hurst, 1984), pp.1–2.
4. Richard Connaughton, 'British Peacekeeping Doctrine: A Critique', in D. S. Gordon and F. H. Toase (eds.), *Aspects of Peacekeeping* (London: Frank Cass, 2001), p.200.
5. For instance, according to Maj.-Gen. John Kiszely the British Army has 'a strong antipathy for doctrine'. Kiszely, 'The British Army and Approaches to Warfare Since 1945', *Strategic and Combat Studies Occasional Paper*, No.26, p.10.
6. Rod Thornton, 'Cultural Barriers to Organisational Unlearning: The US Army, the "Zero-Defects" Culture and Operations in the Post-Cold War World', *Small Wars and Insurgencies*, Vol.11, No.3 (Winter 2000), pp.141, 146–7.
7. According to Richard Connaughton, troops in the 'Grey Area' are 'Dying … for want of a doctrine'. Richard Connaughton, 'Wider Peacekeeping – How Wide of the Mark?', *British Army Review*, No.111, p.60.
8. All peacekeeping thinking stresses the importance of having the parties to the conflict understand what the operation is intended to achieve, and how it intends to go about it. Widely disseminated doctrine – or at least a precis of it – can assist in the transparency process.
9. In fact many people deny the existence of a 'grey area' at all, claiming that there is traditional peacekeeping and enforcement and nothing between the two. But I would argue that IFOR/SFOR, KFOR, Interfet and other operations have shown this position to be a fallacy. For brevity's sake I have dealt only cursorily with the 'grey area' deniers; those interested should look at the mid-1990s writings of Alan James, or Boutros Boutros-Ghali's *A Supplement to an Agenda for Peace* (New York: United Nations, 1995).
10. United Nations PROtection FORce in Bosnia.
11. E.g. the Implementation FORce (IFOR) and Sustainment FORce (SFOR) in Bosnia during 1995–98, where civil tasks crucial to the success of the mission – for instance, refugee and IDP return, and the apprehension of indicted war crimes suspects – were ducked.
12. E.g. the United Nations Assistance Mission In Rwanda (UNAMIR) in April–May 1994.
13. E.g. Operation Alba, the Italian-led multinational intervention in Albania in 1997.

14. Paul Lewis, 'A Short History of UN Peacekeeping', in Barbara Benton (ed.), *Soldiers for Peace* (New York: Facts on File, 1996), pp.39–40.

15. John Mackinlay, 'Peace Support Operations Doctrine', *British Army Review*, No.113 (Aug. 1996), p.6.

16. During Brian Urquhart's visit to Cyprus in September 1975, he went to Varosha, a seaside tourist resort finished in 1973 only to be cut off a year later by the new ceasefire line drawn between Greek and Turk. Now it was deserted. 'The tables in the seaside restaurants were still laid for tourists who never came, and the boutiques displayed last year's fashions to empty streets. The grass had begun to grow through the paving stones. Varosha has remained a ghost city to this day, a monument to the foolishness of international politics.' Quoted in Urquhart, *A Life in Peace and War*, p.262.

17. Mackinlay, 'Peace Support Operations', pp.5–6.

18. *The Army Field Manual* Vol.V, Part I, pp.5–12.

19. Rikhye, *The Theory and Practice of Peacekeeping*, p.4.

20. United Nations Truce Supervisory Observers (Middle East, 1948–) and United Nations Force In Lebanon (S. Lebanon 1978–). Irbatt stands for IRish BATTalion.

21. Rod Paschall, 'UN Peacekeeping Tactics; The Impartial Buffer', in Barbara Benton (ed.), *Soldiers for Peace*, pp.52–5.

22. The fact that the Israelis sent such a substantial force on such a minor mission suggests that it was intended as much to test UNIFIL – only deployed the year before, and with an unusually strong mobile reserve – as to guarantee Israel's security.

23. John Mackinlay and Randolph Kent, 'Complex Emergencies Doctrine: The British are Still the Best', *The Journal of the Royal United Services Institute*, Vol. 42, No.2 (April 1997), p.40.

24. John Mackinlay, 'Peace Support Operations', p.7.

25. According to a British Army liaison officer deployed on the first day of Britain's UNPROFOR commitment, 'I arrived in Bosnia without a clue about our mission, specifically [what it was]. I asked Colonel Bob [Stewart, the battle group commander]. He said "We're not UNPROFOR. We're supposed to make it up".' Interview with ex-Capt., 9th/12th Lancers, 15 Nov. 1997. (The battle group used only UK symbols and flags for nearly a month after its deployment.)

26. For instance, ECOMOG (ECOwas Monitoring Group) in Liberia supposedly operated under the political authority of ECOWAS. But the Special Representative was withdrawn in 1991 and not replaced until 1995, leaving the Force Commander to fill both roles; funding shortages meant the Political and Legal Adviser posts were never filled; and the force had no civilian officials at all. 'Funmi Olonisakin, *Reinventing Peacekeeping in Africa* (The Hague: Kluwer Law International, 2000), p.166.

27. Sergio Vieira de Mello, 'UNHCR and the Military in Complex Emergencies', Paper given at the 'Aspects of Peacekeeping' Conference, RMA Sandhurst, 23 Jan. 1997.

28. A. James, 'The Problems of Internal Peacekeeping', *Diplomacy and Statecraft*, Vol.5, No.1 (March 1994), p.30.

29. Oliver A.K. Macdonald, 'Recent Developments in Peacekeeping – The Irish Military Experience', in Moxon-Browne (ed.), *A Future for Peacekeeping?* pp.46–51. For instance, military players in, over or off Bosnia in spring 1995 included UNPROFOR, European Union Military Monitors, a Western European Union naval task force in the Adriatic, an Organization for Security and Co-operation in Europe team, North Atlantic Treaty Organization forward observers (who changed from UN to own-nation headgear at will), and NATO air power. Military personnel in civilian clothes were also working for UN agencies.

30. UN High Commissioner for Refugees, World Food Programme, UN Children's Fund.

31. According to William Shawcross, Fred Cuny, who worked for the International Rescue Committee (a relief NGO) in Sarajevo, had had excellent connections 'at almost every level of the US government – in the White House, the Pentagon, the Central Intelligence Agency, the Agency for International Development' ever since Operation *Safe Haven* in 1991. William Shawcross, *Deliver Us from Evil* (London: Bloomsbury, 2000), p.6.

32. Mark Walsh, 'The Role of the Humanitarian Co-ordinator', in Jim Whitman and David Pocock (eds.), *After Rwanda: The Coordination of United Nations Humanitarian Assistance* (London: Macmillan, 1996), pp.218–21.

33. Cedric Thornberry, 'United Nations Peace Operations'. Fred Cuny (see note 31) warned Lt.-Gen. Rose on their first meeting that if the latter failed to be more robust with the Bosnian Serbs, 'he [Cuny] would do everything he could to undermine me'. Rose, *Fighting for Peace* (London: Harvill, 1998), pp.28–9.

34. Hugo Slim, 'Positioning Humanitarianism in War; Principles of Neutrality, Impartiality and Solidarity', Paper given at 'Aspects of Peacekeeping' Conference, RMA Sandhurst, 23 Jan. 1997.

35. Joint Publication 3-01, *UK Doctrine for Peace Support Operations* (Ratification Draft, 1997), p.2-2.

36. Chosen substances for abuse included vodka (former Soviet Union), *slivovic* (former Yugoslavia), and the mildly narcotic *qat* leaf (Somalia). The Irish Army transport company in UNITAF tried to mount their convoys in the four-hour period between the daily *qat* delivery and the disappearance of the initial gentle buzz the leaf bestows; a British Army UNPROFOR veteran informed me that the trick with checkpoints in Bosnia was to arrive when the guards were sober and then help them to get amiably drunk. Conversation with Irish Army officer, 20 Jan. 1997; inteview with Maj. M. Woolley 9/12 L. In Sierra Leone, RUF fighters relied on *destri blue*, among other substances. This blue narcotic paste was spread on the face, just before tiny cuts were made in the temples; the swift absorption into the brain was said to offer a better rush than cocaine. Dr Robin Poulton, Mission Report; Principal Findings of UNIDIR Mission to Freetown, 21–28 Nov. 1998, p.4.

37. Connaughton, 'Wider Peacekeeping', p.67.

38. Margaret Cecchine Harrell and Robert Howe, 'Military Issues in Multinational Operations', in Donald C. F. Daniel and Bradd C. Hayes (eds.), *Beyond Traditional Peacekeeping* (London: Macmillan, 1995), pp.196–8. This might apply to different units from the same contributor country. Different approaches to disarmament adopted by USMC and US Army units in UNITAF in 1992–93 created friction. See Bob Shacochis, *The Immaculate Invasion* (London: Viking Penguin, 1999) for relations between US Special Forces and the 10th Mountain Division in Haiti.

39. Mats Berdal, *Whither UN Peacekeeping?* Adelphi Paper 281 (London: IISS, 1993), p.39; Adam Roberts, 'The Crisis in UN Peacekeeping', *Survival*, Vol.36, No.3 (Autumn 1994), p.95.

40. On 22 Sept. 1994 Lt.-Gen. Sir Michael Rose, UNPROFOR commander in Bosnia, just arrived in the UK on leave, authorized a NATO air strike against a Bosnian Serb tank in the Sarajevo Total Exclusion Zone in response to a Serb attack on French peacekeepers. Gen. Sir John Wilsey, Joint Commander British Forces in the Former Yugoslavia (and his superior) then called to ask why RAF Jaguars were on their way to attack ammunition bunkers – an unauthorized escalation in the use of force. On being informed that the target had changed, Wilsey notified the pilots to abort the attack on the bunkers and wait for further instructions. Lt.-Gen. Rupert Smith then rang Rose from the Ministry of Defence; Robert Fox, the *Daily Telegraph*'s defence correspondent, had just called claiming he could see RAF Jaguars attacking targets near Pale and that smoke was rising from the area. British Ministers wanted to know what was going on. 'By now every level of command, from the tactical to the strategic, had become involved, each with a differing interpretation of events and each contributing to the confusion. For centuries, armies had tried to avoid this sort of muddle, but it was clear to me that the advent of modern communications had made the problem worse...' Rose, *Fighting for Peace*, pp.176–7. It is noteworthy that the complications arose in a contributor-country network which operated far more quickly than UN ones. The problem was generated, and resolved, entirely independently of New York.

41. The British Army uses the term 'strategic soldier' to describe the man or woman – perhaps only a private – whose actions, in the heightened political sensitivity and volatility of Peace Support Operations, can materially affect a mission's success. Briefing at United Nations Training and Assistance Team, 15 March 1997. An incident in Bosnia in the summer of 1994 offers an excellent example of the burden carried by a section commander in the new environment. Shortly after the 1st Bn Duke of Wellington's Regt deployed into C. Bosnia, RSA troops opened fire on a patrol led by a Cpl. Mills in an attempt to both test the mettle of, and achieve psychological dominance over, the new arrivals. Cpl. Mills initially tried to

break contact, as the UN rules required; but realizing that the Serbs were attempting to outflank, and so either capture or kill, his section, he instead launched a counter-attack. Eventually the Serbs broke contact, having sustained several casualties. The Serbs' commander was sufficiently impressed to ask 1 DWR's CO if his men might be taught the successful British tactics. Whether Cpl. Mills was aware of the strategic implications of his actions/inaction or not, he had the nerve to take a decision which might well have got him into considerable trouble (and which placed him at considerable risk). Rose, *Fighting for Peace*, p.122.

42. Donald C. F. Daniel, *Issues and Considerations in UN Gray Area and Enforcement Operations* (Newport, Rhode Island: US Naval War College Paper, 1994), p.5.
43. Though these relationships are crucial to the detachment being able to carry out its mission, they are so numerous that friction is inevitable. For instance, a British unit in UNPROFOR would have direct, or important indirect, links with: the British government and British political and public opinion (including the press); different levels of the UN, and NATO (political and military); the Bosnian government and army, local Bosnian authorities, and Muslim and pro-Bosnian State communities; Bosnian Serb representatives, military, and communities supporting the breakup of the Bosnian State; and Croat representatives, military, and communities ambiguous about that State. James Gow and Christopher Dandeker, 'Peace-Support Operations: The Problem of Legitimation', *The World Today*, Aug.–Sept. 1995, p.172.
44. For summaries of this new operational environment, see: Army Field Manual Peace Support Operations First Draft pp.2–2–3; Mats Berdal, *Whither UN Peacekeeping?*, pp.26–50; Berdal, *Disarmament and Demobilisation after Civil Wars*, Adelphi Paper No.303 (London: IISS, 1996) pp.9–23; Daniel, *Issues and Considerations*, pp.2–8; Mackinlay and Kent, 'Complex Emergencies Doctrine', pp.39–41; Goulding, 'The Use of Force by the UN', *International Peacekeeping*, Vol.3, No.1 (Spring 1996) pp.10–17; John Gerard Ruggie, 'The UN and Collective Use of Force', in Pugh (ed.), *The UN Peace and Force* (London: Macmillan, 1998), pp.4–10; A. B. Fetherston and C. Nordstrom, *Overcoming Conceptual Habitus in Conflict Management; UN Peacekeeping and Warzone Ethnography*, Working Paper No.147 (Australian National University, Peace Research Centre) (Canberra, April 1994) pp.11–14; Boutros Boutros-Ghali, 'The Evolution of Peacekeeping Policy', in Benton (ed.), *Soldiers for Peace*, pp.2–5.
45. United Nations Force In CYPrus.
46. Interview with ex-Capt. Justin Freeland, 9th/12th Lancers, 16 Aug. 1999.
47. Lt.-Col. Stewart had a strong relationship with the press. Following the Ahmici massacre – when his impassioned televised denunciation of an HVO officer made him even more of a household name – he was escorted everywhere by a media retinue. Many members of the bn group – particularly those not from Col. Stewart's own Cheshire Regiment – felt that he played up to the press. Justin Freeland believes that this incident would not have arisen had it not been for the presence of the media; Col. Stewart would have chosen a different route, and if obstructed, would have chosen a different way of resolving the issue. He also feels that the presence of the media ensured that the party could withdraw safely. Freeland interview, 16 Aug. 1999. For more on Col. Stewart's relationship with the press, see his book *Broken Lives* (London: HarperCollins, 1993).
48. Charles Dobbie, 'A Concept for Post-Cold War Peacekeeping', *Survival*, Vol.36, No.3 (Autumn 1994), p.121.
49. Dobbie, 'A Concept for Post-Cold War Peacekeeping', p.121.
50. Dobbie, 'A Concept for Post-Cold War Peacekeeping', p.145.
51. FM 100-23 *Peace Operations* (Washington, DC, Department of the Army, Headquarters, Dec. 1994), pp.12–15; Dobbie, 'A Concept for Post-Cold War Peacekeeping', pp.122–30, 144–5. The former talks of the 'consent divide'; the Rubicon analogy is Dobbie's.
52. FM 100-23, p.15.
53. Dobbie, 'A Concept for Post-Cold War Peacekeeping', p.135.
54. Dobbie, 'A Concept for Post-Cold War Peacekeeping', pp.136–7.
55. Mackinlay and Kent, 'Complex Emergencies Doctrine', pp.40–41.
56. John Mackinlay, 'Powerful Peacekeepers', *Survival*, Vol.33, No.3 (May/June 1990), p.245.

57.   Mackinlay and Kent, 'Complex Emergencies Doctrine', pp.40-41. For instance, Bo Huldt himself says that he has 'repeatedly' questioned the novelty of so-called second-generation operations. Bo Huldt, 'Working Multilaterally; the Old Peacekeepers' Viewpoint', in Daniel and Hayes (eds.), *Beyond Traditional Peacekeeping*, pp.116, 103–5. The British Army actually had considerable peacekeeping experience. It had been conducting peacekeeping operations continuously in Cyprus since 1963 (since 1964 as part of United Nations Force In CYPrus), had officers serving with Commonwealth contingents in ONUC (Organisation des Nations Unies Congo, 1960–64), led the CMF (Commonwealth Monitoring Force, Rhodesia/Zimbabwe, 1979–80), and contributed to MNF II (MultiNational Force II, Beirut, 1983–84) and MFO (Multinational Force and Observers, Sinai, 1982–). Yet it did not have a peacekeeping manual until 1988. In 1991 peacekeeping rated only one lecture in the Army Staff College's one-year syllabus, and soldiers were frequently reluctant (UNFICYP) or forbidden (MFO) to wear a peacekeeping service ribbon. John Mackinlay, 'Peace Support Operations Doctrine', p.10. (The medal for service in the CMF is not even accorded the status of a campaign award, being worn after commemorative medals like that for the Queen's Silver Jubilee.) See the Foreword to the Army Field Manual, *Peacekeeping Operations*, Vol.V, for the British Army's lack of institutional memory.

58.   Peter Viggo Jakobsen, 'The Emerging Consensus on Grey Area Peace Operations: Will It Last and Enhance Operational Effectiveness?', *International Peacekeeping*, Vol.7, No.3 (Autumn 2000), p.40.

59.   *Médecins Sans Frontières; Médecins du Monde.* According to Kouchner and Mario Bettati (a legal scholar who later became legal adviser to the French Ministry of Foreign Affairs), nations did not need the consent of the host country to intervene to alleviate the suffering of populations in emergencies. But France's strong stance on humanitarian intervention was weakened by the failure of the Bosnian 'safe havens', which she had outlined. See Philippe Guillot, 'France, Peacekeeping and Humanitarian Intervention', *International Peacekeeping*, Vol.1, No.1 (Spring 1994), particularly pp.31–2 and 34–8.

60.   French Ministry of Defence, *Principles for the Employment of the Armed Forces under UN Auspices*, Paper presented at UNIDIR conference 'Differing National Perspectives on UN Peace Operations' (March 1995), Sections 2;1 and 3;2; cited in Stephen John Stedman, 'Consent, Neutrality and Impartiality in the Tower of Babel and on the Frontlines; United Nations Peacekeeping in the 1990s', *Managing Arms in Peace Processes: The Issues* (Geneva: UNIDIR, 1996).

61.   General Philippe Morillon, in 'Only Passivity is Dishonourable', Ed Vulliamy, *The Guardian*, 12 Jan. 1996.

62.   *Principles for the Employment of the Armed Forces* Section 3;2. For a critique of other aspects of this doctrine, see Stedman, 'Consent, Neutrality and Impartiality', particularly pp.49–56. For other surveys, see Chilton, 'French Policy on Peacekeeping', in Clarke (ed.), *Brassey's Defence Yearbook 1995*, pp.139–43; Jean-Louis Dufour, 'Le Livre Blanc et les Conflits Regionaux', *Defense Nationale*, Vol.7, No.4 (July 1994).

63.   One Japanese was killed in the ambush (in the Ampil district) and three Japanese and five Dutch seriously wounded. Emotive accounts of survivors lying wounded and defenceless for nearly two hours while the Khmer Rouge looted their vehicles and threatened to finish them off, combined with the pleas of the Japanese CIVilian POLice (CIVPOL) commander that the detachment be withdrawn, created an atmosphere of near-hysteria in the Japanese media. Most Japanese CIVPOL abandoned their positions in the field without orders from UNTAC – many without orders from Tokyo – and retreated to the safety of Phnom Penh; the Japanese *jieitai* (Self-Defence Force) engineering battalion, already based in Cambodia's safest province, became base-bound and militarily ineffective for the rest of its tour. UNTAC refused Japanese requests that the CIVPOL detachment be reassigned, so a majority refused to stir from Phnom Penh until UNTAC gave many of the deserters sick notes and sent them home. See various reports in *The Daily Yomiuri* and *The Japan Times* from 6–8 May; 'A New World Role for Japan at Issue', *International Herald Tribune*, 25 Oct. 1993; 'Truce Unit from Japan Asks to Quit Cambodia', *International Herald Tribune*, 10 May 1993; 'Japanese UN Policeman killed in Cambodia', *Independent*, 5 May 1993; 'Cambodia Shatters Myth of Japanese Warrior' *Financial Times*, 25 May 1993. The fact that the Khmer Rouge looted the

vehicles without finishing off their occupants suggests that the ambush was a small demonstration of force aimed both at stopping Dutchbatt's mobile checkpoints and exploiting the contingents' existing mutual tensions as part of the KR's 'good UNTAC–bad UNTAC' attempt to fracture force unity. See Lt.-Gen. John Sanderson, 'UNTAC: Successes and Failures', in Hugh Smith (ed.), *International Peacekeeping: Building on the Cambodian Experience* (Canberra: Australian Defence Studies Centre, 1994), pp.25–6.

64. R. M. Connaughton, 'Military Support and Protection for Humanitarian Assistance Rwanda April–Dec. 1994', *Strategic and Combat Studies Occasional Paper*, No.18 (1996), p.21.

65. Special Representative of the Secretary-General; the overall commander in the field of all components of a UN peacekeeping operation.

66. Report of the Independent Inquiry into the Actions of the United Nations during the 1994 Genocide in Rwanda, Dated 15 Dec. 1999, p.8. President Habyarimana was supposed to inform UNAMIR within 48 hours of the steps he had taken in line with his responsibilities. He never did so. pp.8–9.

67. Connaughton, 'Wider Peacekeeping', pp.60–61. UNAMIR's inability to act made it clear to the Hutu extremists that opposition to genocide would be minimal, and shattered the force's legitimacy among Tutsis. The effectiveness of early, decisive action in averting catastrophe is indicated by UNAMIR commander Romeo Dallaire's repeated statements that he could have stopped the genocide much earlier had he had a highly trained brigade at his disposal. See Donald C. F. Daniel and Bradd C. Hayes, 'Securing Observance of UN Mandates Through the Employment of Military Force', in Michael Pugh (ed.), *The UN, Peace and Force* (Frank Cass, London, 1997) en.19, p.123. For a much more detailed analysis of the difficulties confronting KIBAT – the Belgian Paracommando battalion based in Kigali, which lost ten men in the early hours of the genocide on 4 April 1994 – see Astri Suhrke, 'Dilemmas of Protection: The Log of the Kigali Battalion', *International Peacekeeping*, Vol.5, No.2 (Summer 1998), and Linda Melvern, *A People Betrayed: The Role of the West in Rwanda's Genocide* (London, Zed Books, 2000). For an excellent survey of military intervention in Rwanda, 1993–96, see Larry Minear and Philippe Guillot, *Soldiers to the Rescue: Humanitarian Lessons from Rwanda* (Paris, OECD, 1996).

68. UN Document A/54/549 Report of the Secretary-General Pursuant to General Assembly Resolution 53/35 (1988) – The Fall of Srebrenica, para 473.

69. Kofi Annan ascribed the chain of command's reluctance to use air power to a fear that UNPROFOR would be seen to be taking sides, would lose control of the process, that its mission would be disrupted and that reprisals would ensue – classic concerns of a force trying to apply the traditional trinity. A/54/549, para 482. Nothing better demonstrates the changing operational environment than the fact that all the significant UN actors at every level conducted themselves like traditional peacekeepers, and disaster ensued. Karremans ordered his men to fire over the Serbs' heads, rather than at them; his Dutch superiors indicated that the mandate was secondary to the safety of his personnel; the UN in Zagreb showed a distinct lack of urgency in providing support; while those negotiating with the Serbs minimized the effect of their actions, and accepted their assurances at face value, so as not to jeopardize the possibility of a diplomatic resolution. It is perhaps Srebrenica's – and Karremans' – tragedy that the one individual in the chain of command who had been an adamant proponent of the measured use of air power (UNPROFOR BHC commander Lt.-Gen. Sir Rupert Smith) was away on family business during this period. It was Smith's Dutch deputy who dissuaded Karremans' first requests, even though they were in line with the mandate; Gen. Smith might have been readier to rock the overwhelmingly passive boat. It is striking that Smith's superior in Zagreb, General Janvier, who had been adamantly opposed to the use of air power, was himself absent when Smith gave the order to initiate Operation Deliberate Force later in the summer. See Shawcross, *Deliver Us from Evil*, pp.157–8.

70. A/54/549, para 264.

71. A/54/549, para 482.

72. This is despite the fact that in his original telegram indicating his intended course of action, Dallaire stated '[s]hould at any time during reconnaissance, planning or preparation, any sign of a possible contravening or possibility of an undue risky scenario present itself, the

operation will be called off'. Quoted in Report of the Independent Inquiry, p.8.

73.   A/54/549, para 488.

74.   Viggo Jakobsen, 'Grey Area Peace Operations', p.39.

75.   SCANdinavian BATTalion.

76.   K. Schork, 'Swedes Set New Standard for Peacekeeping in Bosnia', *Reuter News Service*, 6 Nov. 1993, and 'UN Hostages Freed in Bosnia', *Reuter News Service*, 7 Nov. 1993.

77.   According to Ruggie, 'In so far as the UN Secretariat ever expressed a common doctrine for the Bosnian military operation, this ["Wider Peacekeeping"] was it. … [T]he UN's civilian and military command more or less came to reflect Britain's concept of "Wider Peacekeeping".' Ruggie, 'The UN and the Collective Use of Force', p.10. A perfect example of this bipolar mindset is provided by a meeting in Split on 9 June 1995, in the midst of a hostage crisis, between SRSG Yasushi Akashi, UNPROFOR Commander Bertrand Janvier and UNPROFOR BHC commander Rupert Smith. Akashi expressed concern that UNPROFOR was 'on the edge of the Mogadishu line'. Crossing it would produce accusations of recklessness; failure to do so, charges of timidity. Smith stated that 'We have already crossed the Mogadishu line. The Serbs do not view us as peacekeepers.' Akashi asked if the force could return back over the line. 'Smith replied with some force, "Only by doing nothing, or by showing an absolute readiness to fight".' William Shawcross, *Deliver Us from Evil*, pp.138–9.

78.   Gow and Dandeker, 'Peace Support Operations', p.171.

79.   JWP 3-50 has, like its *Wider Peacekeeping* predecessor, been widely promoted; attempts are under way to have it adopted wholesale by African states. It has already influenced, and thus reflects, broader European and transatlantic perspectives. Lt.-Col. Philip Wilkinson MBE, 'Military Doctrine and Peace Support Operations', Presentation at 'Regional Security in a Global Context' Annual Graduate Research Conference, 1998.

80.   JWP 3-50, pp.3–4, para 308.

81.   JWP 3-50, pp.3–2–6. The quotation is from pp.3–6, para 313; the italic is mine.

82.   Wilkinson, 'Sharpening the Weapons of Peace', Appendix 1 in JWP 3-50, pp.1–5.

83.   UNOSOM II (United Nations Operation in SOMalia) had a wider, more intrusive mandate than its multinational predecessor (UNITAF – UNIfiedTAsk Force), yet far fewer resources. Intended to create stability and rebuild the Somali state, it instead saw some of its elements, particularly in Mogadishu, descend into warfighting – in large part because in the absence of any concept for the use of force short of war, troops found themselves overreacting when the security situation deteriorated. There is broad agreement that unrestrained use of force by certain contingents, combined with the identification of one faction leader as a criminal, created the widespread impression in Mogadishu that UNOSOM II, and the US forces operating alongside it, was the enemy. See, among others, Kenneth Allard, *Somalia Operations: Lessons Learned* (Washington, DC: NDU, 1996) and Walter Clarke and Jeffrey Herbst (eds.), *Learning from Somalia* (Boulder, CO: Westview Press, 1997). See also *super* fn 95.

84.   *FM100-20 Stability and Support Operations*, Final draft, no date, The Combined Arms Doctrine Directorate Library 1997, ch. 5, p.18.

85.   *FM100-20*, pp.3–6, para 312. In fact, according to *Peace Support Operations*' principal draughtsman, the UK does have a manual for the 'no go' quadrant: *Wider Peacekeeping*. The intention behind current doctrine is simply that the UK should never have to fall back on the old. (Conversation with Lt.-Col. Philip Wilkinson, OBE, 21 Jan. 2000.) The reliance on *Wider Peacekeeping* as a fall back is not mentioned in current doctrine, nor had Col. Wilkinson mentioned it in several discussions about the absence of 'no go' guidance before 21 Jan. 2000; it may therefore be the position of Col. Wilkinson alone. Even if it is not, the fact remains that *Wider Peacekeeping* does not provide guidance in the 'no go' quadrant; if it did, why draft a new doctrine, or identify the quadrant?

86.   Army Field Manual *Peace Support Operations* First Draft p.1-1, & JWP 3-50 p.1-1 para 101. The JWP sentence is identical to that in the Ratification Draft p.1-1. The italics are mine.

87.   Yet the definitions of Peace Enforcement in both drafts seem to allow for military activities as a precursor to a political process that may not yet be under way, or even contemplated. (First Draft, p.1-1; 'Coercive operations carried out … between parties who may not all consent to

intervention and who may be engaged in combat activities, in order to *help create the conditions for diplomatic and humanitarian activities...*' JWP 3-50, pp.1–2, para 101 c); 'PE operations are coercive in nature and undertaken under Chapter VII ... when the consent of any of the major parties is uncertain. They are designed to *maintain and re-establish peace or enforce the terms specified in the mandate.*' (The italics are mine.)

88. Glynne Evans, *Responding to Crisis in the African Great Lakes*, Adelphi Paper 311 (London: OUP/IISS, 1997), p.7. Patricia Chilton has equated France's grasp of the importance of peacekeeping in the international politics of the 1990s with the profile she ascribed to the possession of nuclear weapons from the 1960s on. 'Clearly, any country or group of countries which fails to make its mark in peacekeeping will lose rank in the new post-Cold War order.' Patricia Chilton, 'French Policy on Peacekeeping', in Michael Clarke (ed.), *Brassey's Defence Yearbook 1995* (London: Brassey's, 1995), pp.150–51.

89. Bruno Delhaye, head of the Africa Unit in the French President's office, to Gerard Prunier, 12 Dec. 1992. Quoted in Prunier, 'The Experience of European Armies in Operation Restore Hope', in Clarke and Herbst, *Learning from Somalia*, p.135.

90. Gow and Dandeker, 'Peace Support Operations', p.172.

91. Guillot, 'France, Peacekeeping and Humanitarian Intervention', pp.32–3.

92. 'The UK is invariably amongst the first to be asked to contribute [to PSOs] because the international community knows we deliver, and of course as a P5 member and a leading player in NATO we want to be involved in such operations, providing there is a clear political strategy, aim and preferably exit date. Even when such clarity is not possible, our position as a significant player on the world stage will mean that we continue to get asked. ... I should stress two points: first, multinationality is here to stay, either in formal alliances ... or in coalitions of the willing. Secondly, although some people speak of "wars of choice", where participation is discretionary ... the fact is that if we want to maintain our position as a leading player in NATO and on the Security Council we may well have an obligation to contribute even when we would rather not.' Gen. Sir Roger Wheeler (Chief of the General Staff), Address to the Royal United Services Institute, 17 Feb. 1999, pp.5, 7.

93. Kofi Annan, 'Peace Operations and the United Nations: Preparing for the Next Century' (unpublished paper, Feb. 1996), pp.4–5; quoted in Donald C. F. Daniel and Bradd C. Hayes with Chantal de Jonge Oudraat, *Coercive Inducement and the Containment of International Crises* (Washington, DC: USIP Press, 1999), pp.14–15.

94. Michael Wesley, *Casualties of the New World Order* (London: Macmillan, 1997), pp.79–80; Ruggie, 'The UN and the Collective Use of Force', pp.7–8.

95. Relations between the Italian and Nigerian contingents were particularly poor, the latter accusing the former of failing to come to their aid when attacked. See Mark Huband, 'Italians "Failed to Help Fellow UN Troops"', *The Guardian*, 6 Sept. 1993. The UN's killing of substantial numbers of non-combatants led Italy, France, Belgium, Sweden, Norway and Germany to withdraw, or threaten to withdraw, their contingents over the summer of 1993. Following the 3/4 Oct. battle in Mogadishu's Bakhara Market, the US pledged to withdraw its contingent by March 1994. See April Oliver, 'The Somalia Syndrome', in Roderick von Lipsey (ed.), *Breaking the Cycle* (London: Macmillan, 1997), pp.131–46; Wesley, *Casualties of the New World Order*, pp.68–81; John L. Hirsch and Robert B. Oakley, *Somalia and Operation Restore Hope* (New York: USIP, 1995), pp.115–30.

96. *Bi-MNC Directive for Nato Doctrine for Peace Support Operations* Final Draft 27 July 1998 para 1-5 (b) 1 & 2, pp.4–5.

97. *Bi-MNC Directive*, paras 2-2 (b), 2-4 (c). PSO 'are multi-functional operations conducted impartially in support of a UN/OSCE mandate ... They include peacekeeping (PK) and peace enforcement (PE)...' *Bi-MNC Directive*, p.9.

98. Viggo Jakobsen, 'Grey Area Peace Operations', pp.40–42. When consent is in doubt the third parties should 'deploy a force capable of using both carrots and sticks to promote consent, deter non-compliance and, if necessary, enforce compliance.' Ibid, p.51.

99. The Economic Community of West African States (ECOWAS) and the Southern African Development Community are jointly reinterpreting British doctrine in developing a Working Draft Manual for African Military Forces in Peace Support Operations, with considerable input from the principal draughtsman for JWP 3-50. John Mackinlay, 'Mission Failure', *The*

World Today (Nov. 2000), p.9. For a summary of ACRI and RECAMP and the Western attempts to assist African peacekeeping initiatives see Eric Berman and Katie Sams, *Peacekeeping in Africa* (Geneva: UNIDIR/ISS, 2000). RECAMP has been fairly successful, particularly in breaking down the traditional francophone/anglophone divide in the continent's militaries: funding provided under the scheme was also essential in launching the (unfortunately curtailed) ECOMOG operation in Guinea Bissau in 1999. ACRI (Africa Crisis Response Initiative), on the other hand, has seen the absurdity of an army which loathes peacekeeping despatch troops who have never served in a PSO to train some of the African stalwarts of UN peacekeeping, such as Senegal.

100. Viggo Jakobsen, 'Grey Area Peace Operations', p.46.
101. Interview with senior political officer, DPKO, 12 May 2001. The Brahimi Report makes a series of highly sensible recommendations, focusing on information and analysis, mandate formulation, conflict prevention and mission manning. Yet it is also a 'last war' proposal. See Mackinlay, 'Mission Failure'.
102. The author represented the Office of the Special Representative of the Secretary-General for Children and Armed Conflict in many of these meetings.
103. Interview with senior political officer, Department of Peacekeeping Operations, United Nations, 10 May 2001.
104. Conversation with senior British Army officer at Franco–British Council 'Peacekeeping and International Crisis Management' Seminar, 30 May 2001.
105. Put simply, US forces could only establish a presence in a very limited area. Two-thirds of their troops had force protection duties (so rarely if ever left Camp Bondsteel). This left only one-third available for other duties (including, crucially, executing the mandate). These troops could only patrol in platoon sized (approx. 35 men) or larger formations; they kept to roads and tracks, and rarely patrolled on foot, because of the mine threat; those occupying fixed posts did not venture outside them. Contrast this with the British approach; patrolling in sections (8 men) or fire teams (4), on foot, off-track, and establishing excellent contacts with local people through their appearance (soft hats not helmets, no visible body armour) and cheerful mien. Interviews with former Lt.-Gen., USMC, 4 Nov 1999; British KFOR battalion commander, 16 Aug 2000; senior political officer, Department of Political Affairs, United Nations, 4 May 2001.
106. Interview with senior political office, Department of Political Affairs, United Nations, 4 May 2001. British troops were also brought in to reinforce French troops in Mitrovica during disturbances there, in part because 'everyone thinks they're the most proactive. They're the best, they're the model for robust action in KFOR.' *Ibid.*
107. James Cotton, 'Against the Grain: The East Timor Intervention', *Survival*, pp.129–30.
108. Interview with former Operations Officer, British element of Interfet, 16 Aug. 2000.
109. *Wider Peacekeeping* was not aimed at the military at all but those agencies outside military circles who 'had the power to alter policy to the detriment of military wishes that what the Army was doing in Bosnia was right'. See Rod Thornton, 'The Role of Peace Support Operations Doctrine in the British Army', *International Peacekeeping*, Vol.7, No.2 (Summer 2000) pp.58–9.
110. Lt.-Col. Philip Wilkinson OBE, Military Doctrine and Peace Support Operations; Presentation at Department of War Studies 'Regional Security in a Global Context' Annual Graduate Research Conference, 7 April 1998. The current joint doctrine writers considered dropping the 'no go' quadrant diagram from the next draft, until a senior British officer suggested that the 'no go' quadrant was too useful a warning to the Ministers he advised to dispose of. Member of Joint Doctrine Concepts Centre staff at Aberystwyth, May 2000.
111. Conversation with senior official, French Ministry of Defence, and with senior British Army officer, at Franco–British Council 'Peacekeeping and International Crisis Management Seminar', 30 May 2001.
112. Senior official, British Ministry of Defence, Franco–British Council 'Peacekeeping and International Crisis Management Seminar', 30 May 2001
113. There is also a substantial academic debate about the 'grey area', the most interesting element of which focuses on suggesting different approaches to be adopted in the field. For those interested, I would recommend the following works as a primer of 'grey area' thinking.

Berdal, *Whither UN Peacekeeping?*; Berdal, *Disarmament and Demobilisation*; Boutros Boutros-Ghali, *An Agenda for Peace* & *Supplement to an Agenda for Peace* (New York: United Nations, 1995); Jarat Chopra, *Peace Maintenance* (London: Macmillan, 2000); Connaughton, 'Wider Peacekeeping'; Donald C. F. Daniel, *Issues and Considerations in UN Gray Area and Enforcement Operations*, (Newport, RI: US Naval War College Paper, 1994); Daniel and Hayes (eds.), *Beyond Traditional Peacekeeping*; Daniel and Hayes with de Jonge Oudraat, *Coercive Inducement*; Dobbie, 'A Concept for Post-Cold War Peacekeeping'; Marrack Goulding, 'The Use of Force by the United Nations'; James Gow and Christopher Dandeker, 'The Legitimation of Strategic Peacekeeping', in Gordon and Toase, *Aspects of Peacekeeping* (London: Frank Cass, 2001); Mary Kaldor, *New & Old Wars* (Cambridge: Polity Press, 1999); anything by John Mackinlay, but including *A Concept for Second Generation Peacekeeping Operations* (Thomas J. Watson Institute, 1993); 'Peace Support Operations Doctrine', in *British Army Review*, No.113 (Aug. 1996); Mackinlay and Kent, 'Complex Emergencies Doctrine'; 'Funmi Olonisakin, *Reinventing Peacekeeping in Africa*; Adam Roberts, 'The Crisis in UN Peacekeeping', *Survival*, Vol.36, No.3 (Autumn 1994) and 'From San Francisco to Sarajevo', *Survival*, Vol.37, No.4 (Winter 1995–96), p.23; John Ruggie, 'The UN and the Collective Use of Force'; Hugo Slim, 'Positioning Humanitarianism in War', in Gordon and Toase; Stephen John Stedman, 'Consent, Neutrality and Impartiality in the Tower of Babel and on the Frontlines; United Nations Peacekeeping in the 1990s', in *Managing Arms in Peace Processes: The Issues* (Geneva: UNIDIR, 1996).

Fighting For Freetown: British Military Intervention in Sierra Leone[1]

PAUL WILLIAMS

Writing in mid-1998, Abiodun Alao argued that events in Sierra Leone stood as 'a salutary lesson in the lack of concern about the fate of small nations in the post-Cold War era'.[2] In light of Britain's military intervention in Sierra Leone in May (and again in October) 2000, should we reassess Alao's conclusion? Shortly after its 1997 general election victory, Foreign Secretary Robin Cook announced that New Labour would take 'the ethical dimension' of foreign policy more seriously than had the previous Conservative administration.[3] An important part of the debate about New Labour's foreign policy revolved around the questions of when and whether to intervene militarily in what Tony Blair called 'other people's conflicts'.[4] Although a wide consensus now exists that intervention is by definition a failure of prevention and that the use of military force should always be a last resort, New Labour has used force in Iraq, the Federal Republic of Yugoslavia (FRY), East Timor and most recently Sierra Leone.

With specific reference to sub-Saharan Africa, British foreign policy is designed – forcibly or otherwise – to promote peace, prosperity and democracy.[5] Purportedly in defence of these values, in early May 2000 approximately 1,300 British troops were deployed to Sierra Leone as part of Operation Palliser. Within six weeks the majority of these troops were withdrawn and a smaller contingent of approximately 200 left behind to train an accountable and effective Sierra Leone army that, in tandem with the United Nations (UN) peacekeeping force UNAMSIL, would hopefully restore order to the country. In October and November, the British government deployed the Amphibious Ready Group and the Headquarters of the 1st Mechanized Brigade (comprising approximately 650 personnel) to Sierra Leone to bolster the beleaguered UN force.[6]

This use of force follows similar instances of military intervention by New Labour purportedly in defence of values rather than territorial ambitions. The aim of this article is to provide a tentative evaluation of Britain's military intervention in Sierra Leone, particularly the deployment in May 2000. Admittedly, since the intervention is ongoing it is still too early to assess fully its impact on Sierra Leone's future. Nevertheless, enough information has entered the public realm to merit a discussion of whether Britain's use of force has helped promote its foreign policy objectives.

The article proceeds in three stages. In order to evaluate the success of Britain's military intervention it is necessary to understand the political context in which the intervention took place. The first two sections therefore analyse the factors fuelling Sierra Leone's conflict and Britain's role in the Lomé Accord of 7 July 1999 respectively. The third section then outlines the rationale behind Britain's intervention and discusses five imperatives that influenced the decision to deploy troops to West Africa. It concludes by assessing how far Britain's intervention has contributed to the promotion of peace and security in Sierra Leone. While external military intervention alone cannot resolve the country's problems I argue that it represents a positive contribution to the process of reconstructing a viable and accountable polity. In particular, Britain's military intervention can play an important role in constructing a space in which Sierra Leoneans themselves can think how best to reconfigure the country's patrimonial system of governance.

THE POLITICAL ECONOMY OF VIOLENCE IN SIERRA LEONE

Sierra Leone's violent conflict can be understood as a combination of two primary factors: first, the existence of endemic poverty and the country's patrimonial system of governance; and second, the desire of various individuals and groups, both insiders and outsiders, to profit from Sierra Leone's natural resources at the expense of national development. As discussed below, the violence is not random, nor does it result from the senseless activities of psychopaths. Rather it follows a clear logic: the pursuit of commercial gain within the context of the country's complex patrimonial system.

The Context for Violence: Poverty and Patrimonialism in the Global Periphery

The violence that has characterized Sierra Leone's recent history must be seen in relation to the country's peripheral status in the global political economy. Since the late 1970s in particular, Sierra Leone's economy has collapsed. Between 1980 and 1990 the country's GDP fell from US$1.1 billion to $857 million; by 1992 its international reserves stood at just $5 million; by 1995 it had accrued $1,226 million of external debt; and between 1990 and 1995 not a single economic sector or activity registered any growth.[7] Public expenditure also plummeted as the social base from which the government could extract direct taxation virtually disappeared.[8] To take two examples: by 1993 the country received almost twice as much development aid ($204 million) as the internal revenue it produced. In addition, whereas in the late 1960s diamonds had generated about $200 million in profits in Sierra Leone's formal economy, or about 30 per cent of national output, and had provided 70 per cent of foreign exchange reserves, by 1987, formal revenue from diamonds was valued at only $100,000.[9] These dire statistics were exacerbated by IMF and World Bank policies that forced successive governments to end subsidies for basic commodities, deregulate the economy, devalue the national currency, and reduce public expenditure.[10] Poverty thus became endemic and Sierra Leone became a regular feature of the UNDP's list of the world's most impoverished countries.[11] The worsening economic situation drove many of the country's youth to the cities in search of nonexistent jobs; instead they ended up as petty criminals, pimps or hired thugs for a variety of political patrons and strongmen. However, not everyone drifted to the cities. Some sections of this youth drifted to the country's mining areas to seek their fortune as so-called *san san* boys. It was primarily this uneducated and unemployed subclass that provided a fertile pool from which all parties to the conflict were later to recruit fighters.[12]

Sierra Leone's violence is inextricably linked to the widespread poverty and social exclusion that characterizes those countries on the periphery of the global political economy. This point was not lost on the British Foreign Office (FCO). As its 1999 Human Rights Annual Report noted, 'poverty increases the risk of violent conflict when people are economically marginalised or lack access to basic services, or where there are high levels of inequality'.[13] But in spite of such statements the British government has failed to ask, let alone seriously engage with, a series of uncomfortable questions about how the global economic system that it helps run through the G-8 increases the likelihood of violence in countries like Sierra Leone.[14]

The global economy has local as well as foreign agents, which in Sierra Leone's case have helped to impoverish the majority of its people.

Since at least its independence, politics in Sierra Leone has been based upon corrupt patrimonial networks that have operated across both the country's formal and informal economies.[15] Indeed, William Reno coined the term 'shadow state' to explain the peculiar relationship between corruption and politics in Sierra Leone whereby the power of a succession of rulers was based upon their ability to control both formal and informal markets rather than upon some concept of popular legitimacy.[16] In patrimonial systems an individual rules by dint of personal prestige and power. Authority is thus entirely personalized, shaped by the ruler's preferences rather than any codified system of laws. In spite of what may be written in official constitutions, this patrimonial logic infuses what bureaucratic institutions actually exist.[17] The problem is that such 'systems lack the capacity to create any sense of moral community amongst those who participate in them, let alone among those who are excluded'.[18] In times of economic crisis this lack of community is especially evident and threatens the basis of patrimonial systems in at least two ways: first, as resources dwindle the social glue that holds the ruling coalition together will start to dissolve; and second, as fewer and fewer resources trickle down to the ordinary population, the ruling coalition's legitimacy erodes and the likelihood of violent revolt from below increases. Since patrimonialism encourages the dismantling of public institutions and the erosion of the rule of law, ordinary citizens are left with few means of redress other than violence.

Corruption within this patrimonial system intensified after Siaka Stevens' All Peoples Congress (APC) took power in 1968. In practice, Stevens turned politics in Sierra Leone into 'an affair for and by APC members and supporters ... that made access to resources impossible for non-members; it made membership of the party a *sine qua non* to get by; exclusion literally meant death by attrition'.[19] In this process of privatizing power and wealth within certain patrimonial networks, Afro–Lebanese businessmen such as Jamil Sahid Mohammed played a crucial intermediary role between the global economy and patrimonial accumulation.[20] Since these Lebanese dealers had few local social networks from which they could challenge Stevens' rule, they were allocated the bulk of diamond mining licences in preference to African dealers. They also had access to international diamond markets and credit networks, particularly in the Middle East, that helped make collaborative ventures with Stevens a success. But as the state's institutions withered in the 1970s and 1980s, Stevens became increasingly dependent upon Lebanese management of the economy to provide his supporters with resources.

In short, the corrupt patrimonial manipulation of educational and employment opportunities that has characterized successive leaders of Sierra Leone has increased the likelihood that those excluded from its benefits will use violence as a means of redress.[21]

The Value of Violence: Diamonds, Despots, and Dogs of War

For some Sierra Leoneans, the resort to violence has brought considerable profits. It was the trade in diamonds in particular that enabled successive leaders of Sierra Leone to finance their personal networks of patronage and preserve them by force if necessary.[22] However, the existence of lucrative informal markets and the increasing inability of the patrimonial system to regulate such activity encouraged local strongmen to compete for a share of the national cake. The importance of the diamond trade in fuelling the violence in Sierra Leone is something the British government is well aware of. For instance, the then Minister of State for Africa, Peter Hain, acknowledged that there would 'be no long-term … solution … unless stability and order [were] established in the diamond mining areas'.[23] Hain also singled out Liberia's president Charles Taylor as one of the chief exporters of the Revolutionary United Front's (RUF) diamonds to the extent that Liberia's diamond exports are now considerably larger than its diamond production.[24] In response, the British government has taken a leading role in international efforts to regulate the diamond trade to ensure that illicit diamonds sold on the European markets will not fuel conflict in Africa and elsewhere.[25]

The winners and losers in this privatization of Sierra Leone's resources have been determined by the use of force as various politicians, miners, rebels, and 'sobels' (soldiers by day, rebels by night) have competed to alter the distribution of resources in their favour. The continuation of violence in Sierra Leone is thus linked inextricably to the pursuit of profit by those individuals and groups able to command the necessary force.[26] This economic agenda also provides a powerful disincentive to work towards building legitimate and accountable forms of governance. As part of the strategy to privatize resources, successive leaders of Sierra Leone have learnt to use the mantle of state sovereignty to exploit and manipulate external creditors and diplomatic partners.[27] In so doing, they have contributed to perpetuating the kleptocratic political economy that fuels the violence. In this regard they have not been alone.

A variety of foreign actors have seriously aggravated Sierra Leone's turmoil in their rush to profit from this regrettable set of circumstances. Most prominent among the private external actors have been firms such as the Israeli LIAT Finance and Construction,[28] the US–Australian Sierra Rutile and mercenary organizations such as Gurkha Security Guards and Executive Outcomes.[29] Although a number of commentators have posed the question of whether mercenaries represent the most likely source of Sierra Leone's salvation,[30] any positive humanitarian and political outcomes they may have helped secure have been brief and incidental to their primary goal of profiting from the country's civil war. For the purposes of this discussion, the fact that foreign firms and mercenaries have played such a significant role in Sierra Leone's recent history highlights: first, the way in which, until recently, international society abdicated its responsibility to help resolve the crisis in favour of supporting, or at least tolerating, mercenaries; and second, the kleptocratic political economy that underlies the violence – it is, after all, economic incentives that attract private firms and mercenaries to Sierra Leone, not the plight of its people.

The violence has also been stoked by a number of African states, most notably Liberia, but also Libya and Burkina Faso. It is important to recall that the immediate catalyst for Sierra Leone's civil war in 1991 was the earlier eruption of violent conflict in Liberia that presented Charles Taylor with the opportunity to support the RUF's invasion on 23 March 1991. Liberian warlord-turned-President, Taylor had been thwarted in his protracted campaign to gain control of the capital, Monrovia, by the ECOWAS Monitoring Group, ECOMOG. In Taylor's opinion, Sierra Leone's government was guilty of trying to play the role of peacemaker in Liberia while simultaneously allowing ECOMOG to use its airport facilities to bomb territories controlled by his faction, the National Patriotic Front of Liberia. Taylor therefore supported the RUF's initial invasion of Sierra Leone not only to exact revenge for the country's interference in his campaign, but also because it served his commercial interests since he became the pivotal link in ensuring that the RUF's diamonds could be exchanged for arms and logistics.[31]

Sierra Leone's conflict must therefore be understood in the context of an ongoing struggle over resources, most notably diamonds, located within a state at the very bottom of the global economy. In this struggle the ability of a succession of Sierra Leone's leaders to lay claim to the mantle of state sovereignty has allowed them to build powerful alliances not only with a variety of favoured insiders but, even more importantly, with outsiders willing to risk the country's political instability in the pursuit of profit.[32] The problem for ordinary Sierra Leoneans is that their rulers have been able to privatize the country's resources and to call on an array of outsiders to help them do so.[33] Crucially, since the benefits of this resource extraction have fallen disproportionately to the leaders' favoured clients, some of those excluded from this process have sought a piece of Sierra Leone's national cake through the only means at their disposal: force.

In the RUF's case, the recourse to violence was the outcome of a mobilization of segments of the country's lumpen youth by a small group of people angry at their exclusion from an opaque and corrupt patrimonial system that did not provide for their needs.[34] For example, an RUF lecture to new 'abductees' attempted to rationalize their abduction on the grounds that,

> There was no fairness and transparency in the system in Sierra Leone. Despite mineral riches, there was no development of roads, schools and health centres in rural areas. No one in government was listening. Thus the time for talking had passed. Violence was now the only option. Young people had been abducted for guerrilla training to regain their birthright.[35]

While the RUF's demands for a slice of the national cake are understandable, the methods it has employed in pursuit of these demands are unjustifiable. Prior to the British intervention it was clear that the RUF had alienated the vast majority of Sierra Leoneans through its attacks on civilians and had failed to generate a coherent programme of societal transformation.[36] Nevertheless, as President Kabbah correctly noted, 'while we [may] unreservedly condemn the junta and its RUF allies, we must not forget to ask ourselves why it happened'.[37] The fact remains that in order to safeguard against the emergence of another RUF-type organization in the future, any resolution of Sierra Leone's political conundrum must address the severe levels of poverty and social exclusion, particularly among its lumpen youth, that the combination of its peripheral position in the global economy and its corrupt patrimonial system of governance has produced. Unfortunately, repeated attempts to engineer a peaceful cessation of hostilities have failed to achieve this admittedly arduous task. It is the most recent of these attempts, and specifically Britain's role within it, that occupies the next section.

BRITAIN AND THE LOMÉ ACCORD

Recent attempts to resolve Sierra Leone's crisis have taken the form of three peace agreements.[38] The first was the Abidjan Accord signed on 30 November 1996 by the government of Sierra Leone and the RUF. Unfortunately, neither party took the accord seriously. It subsequently collapsed after a coup d'état, led by Major Johnny Paul Koroma, deposed President Kabbah and set up the Armed Forces Revolutionary Council (AFRC) junta in partnership with the RUF on 25 May 1997. However, one part of the agreement that was honoured was the formal departure of Executive Outcomes in January 1997. It is widely believed that the coup was the result of a combination of the resulting security vacuum; Kabbah's alienation of the army through his attempts to turn the *kamajors*[39] into a private army; and the increasing 'sobelization' of the army.[40] In response to these events, ECOWAS brokered the Conakry Peace Plan on behalf of Kabbah's exiled government in October 1997. Yet again, however, the AFRC/RUF junta reneged on its commitments. This triggered military intervention by ECOMOG to restore Kabbah to office by force.

The Lomé Accord was thus the third attempt to broker a peace agreement. The dynamics behind it remain the subject of heated debate. On 7 July 1999 the accord officially ended the armed conflict between the government and the AFRC/RUF. It provided for a political settlement through power-sharing within the framework of a constitution whereby a broad-based government of national unity was created. Under Lomé, RUF leader Foday Sankoh was appointed director of the National Resources Commission, a post that gave him the status of vice-president and more importantly legitimated his access to the country's diamond fields. Perhaps most controversially of all, he and his followers were also granted a blanket amnesty for the war crimes and gross human rights abuses they had committed since the start of the conflict in March 1991. International involvement in Lomé was co-ordinated under the auspices of the British-led International Contact Group.[41] At the time, statements from the British government welcomed the agreement. Tony Blair, for instance, suggested it offered the people of Sierra Leone 'the prospect of an end to the terrible suffering they have endured over the past eight years of conflict'.[42] For his part, Foreign Secretary Robin Cook emphasized that Britain expected 'both sides to honour the agreement and to implement it fully'.[43] Little mention was made of the agreement's fragility or the way in which it bartered crimes against humanity in exchange for the hope of gaining a degree of peace and stability.[44]

The British government has subsequently come under fire for the role it played in promoting the agreement, particularly its appeasement of the RUF. David Francis, for instance, recently argued that Lomé,

> reveals the double standards of the international community. The government of Sierra Leone, having been encouraged along a path of military options as late as 1998 by its international backers, especially Great Britain, was later forced to negotiate the cheapest exit out of the bloody civil war. After years of de-legitimizing the RUF and branding Sankoh a war criminal, London and Washington pressured the Kabbah regime to do business with him as a 'legitimate' political actor.[45]

Francis's claims are supported by several other commentators. William Shawcross, for example, argued that Lomé 'was an absurd deal' in which the British government 'forced' Kabbah 'into alliance with the rebels'.[46] Kayode Fayemi, a Nigerian present during the negotiations, was another critic who denounced Lomé as a 'pact with the devil' whereby 'Western liberals in Britain' had 'created' a 'Frankenstein in the name of so-called ethical foreign policy'.[47] Similarly, Tim Spicer of Sandline International was equally damning when he claimed that, 'thousands of lives could have been saved ... if the Blair Government had not acted in such an unseemly rush to get a peace accord at all costs'.[48] While these critics certainly have a point it is important to consider a number of factors when evaluating Britain's role at Lomé: the approach to resolving 'internal wars' that currently predominates in international society; the role of the United States; and the question of the alternatives available.

The Ideological Context

First, British involvement in the Lomé Accord should be seen in the wider context of those attitudes that currently dominate international approaches to the resolution of 'internal' conflicts. Although this issue remains the source of considerable international debate, the norm of non-intervention based upon Articles 2(4) and 2(7) of the UN Charter still sets the structural context in which debates about international responses to 'internal wars' are played out. To date, a norm of intervention, even for 'humanitarian' purposes, has yet to emerge.[49]

More specifically, Charles King observed that in the post–Cold War era a policy of 'promoting negotiations has supplanted victory as the chief objective of Western involvement in civil wars'.[50] An earlier example of the dominance of this type of thinking, that several commentators have argued contributed to preparing the ground for the 1994 Rwandan genocide, was the Arusha Accord signed by the Rwandan government and the Rwandan Patriotic Front in August 1993. Other examples include the Lusaka Accord (1994) in Angola which granted UNITA's leader Jonas Savimbi impunity, and the Cotonou Accord (1993) in Liberia that granted impunity to several of the country's warlords. Crucially, from this perspective, the consent of all belligerent parties is considered necessary to attain peace.

This approach has been questioned by a number of commentators. David Shearer, for instance, has argued convincingly that in 'internal wars' it is often only the use of military force that can produce the change in fortunes on the battlefield that are needed to convince intransigent parties to accept settlements.[51] Writing in 1997, Shearer argued that in Sierra Leone's case 'support for one warring side against another is a valid response that can hasten the end of the conflict and restrict the loss of life', which falls disproportionately upon civilians.[52] Such criticism aside, Lomé was the logical result of the norm of non-intervention and the Contact Group's theoretical assumption that consensual negotiations are the most appropriate methods for resolving 'internal wars', the blame for which cannot simply be laid at Britain's door.

The American Dream?

Second, in spite of its position as head of the Contact Group, it is far from clear that Britain was the key player in securing the Lomé Accord. Speaking before the House of Commons Foreign Affairs Select Committee, Peter Hain rejected the interpretation of events supplied by the government's critics and defended Britain's role at Lomé as supporting an African solution. In Hain's view, Lomé was 'a West African agreement' to which Britain gave its backing. There 'is a myth', Hain argued, 'that Britain and the US foisted' [the Lomé Accord] 'on the people of Sierra Leone; on the contrary, it was negotiated by President Kabbah ... and supported by the various African organisations involved'.[53]

Hain's view that Britain was not the primary player in the process leading up to Lomé is supported by evidence from the US – although the same sources cast doubt upon his claim that Lomé was a 'West African agreement'. According to Ryan Lizza, Lomé was 'conceived and implemented by the United States', American officials 'drafted entire sections of the accord', and Clinton's special envoy to Africa, the Rev. Jesse Jackson, and US Ambassador to Sierra Leone, Joseph Melrose, in particular encouraged Kabbah to sign the agreement.[54] The critics were given added ammunition when in September 1999, Assistant Secretary of State for African Affairs, Susan Rice bragged,

> the US role in Sierra Leone ... has been instrumental. With hands-on efforts by the president's special envoy Jesse Jackson, Ambassador Joe Melrose, and many others, the United States brokered the ceasefire and helped steer Sierra Leone's rebels, the Kabbah government, and regional leaders to the negotiating table.[55]

In comparison with the enthusiastic support exhibited by US officials for the RUF's legal representative in Washington, Omrie Golley, British diplomats had shown a significant level of disdain for his organization. Thus although the US should take some of the 'credit' for Lomé, but it is unlikely that it would have been able to push the accord through without some level of support from President Kabbah himself and other members of the Contact Group, including Britain. Indeed, immediately after Lomé very few states were prepared to publicly criticize the accord, The Netherlands being a notable exception in this regard. As the Dutch representative, Mr van Walsum, later explained to the UN Security Council,

> The Netherlands delegation expressed its dismay at these provisions [that gave a blanket amnesty to the RUF and its leaders] at the time because we felt they conveyed a dangerous message, namely, that committing unspeakable atrocities pays. We proposed to include a reference to our concerns in resolutions 1260 (1999) and 1270 (1999) but we were prevailed upon not to insist because any talk of accountability was likely to prolong the war.[56]

In light of these comments, the US has to assume a significant part of the responsibility for the Lomé Accord. However, it was not alone in arguing that there was simply no alternative: it was either Lomé or continued war.

No Alternative?

In one sense, Lomé's imperfections, especially its treatment of the RUF as a legitimate and sincere participant in the peace process, reflected the balance of military forces on the ground in the spring of 1999. At that time, according to Hain, 'there was an elected government without the necessary foundations' such as an effective army and bureaucracy. Consequently, the RUF 'were the major aggressive force'.[57] When asked by Sir John Stanley why 'the Foreign Office supported taking Sankoh into government as the Vice-President, as Minister for Natural Resources, in July' 1999, Hain responded in the following manner:

> Together with the international community, we felt it necessary to support a very imperfect Lomé Agreement in which that was provided for ... because *there was literally no alternative* ... We were in a situation where the RUF had again attacked ... Freetown. The elected government had no army ... The Nigerian troops which had been supported and had previously repelled the rebel forces were about to pull out, so he [Kabbah] felt the only option he had ... was to strike the best deal that he could.[58]

In other words, Lomé's imperfections reflected the fact that the RUF remained militarily effective in mid-1999. Other commentators have agreed that Kabbah was left with few alternatives but suggested this was primarily due to 'lacklustre international support' that stood 'in marked contrast to the greater generosity displayed towards Kosovo and East Timor'.[59]

The other factor that New Labour claimed left it with little room for manoeuvre was that it was not until 22 October 1999 that UNAMSIL, the UN peacekeeping mission in Sierra Leone, was created (under Chapter VII of the UN Charter). This situation severely limited British options. Short of a massive British military intervention, which was not requested by either the regional African states that brokered Lomé, the Organization of African Unity or the Commonwealth, and given the military situation on the ground, there was little alternative but to engage in negotiations. As Hain made clear, this would have been 'unilateral British action ... which might look very clever with hindsight but was simply not a realistic, serious policy objective for the British Government then to pursue, especially when there was no United Nations mandate to do so'.[60] Although Britain had intervened militarily

in the FRY earlier that year without the explicit authorization of the UN
Security Council, it could – and did – point to previous Security Council
resolutions when defending its actions (specifically numbers 1160, 1199
and 1203, all of which were authorised under Chapter VII of the UN
Charter). In Sierra Leone's case there was no comparable raft of
resolutions on which to draw. Moreover, given the timing of the Lomé
negotiations, overlapping as they did with NATO's bombing of the FRY,
it would in all likelihood have been difficult to persuade the British
public that their troops should become involved in yet another 'just war'.
Hain's point that British intervention was not a viable substitute for the
Lomé agreement thus seems reasonable.

However, while Peter Hain was correct that the RUF (with support
from Liberia, Libya and Burkina Faso) remained a potent fighting force,
he neglected to mention two important factors. First, it was not only the
RUF that was responsible for dismantling 'the necessary foundations' of
an elected government. Since Stevens' rule successive leaders of Sierra
Leone, including Kabbah, had dismantled the means to combat the
RUF, such as an effective and accountable army, in order to preserve
their patrimonial networks.[61] Second, Hain was also loath to mention
that a major reason why the RUF still constituted a 'major aggressive
force' and the primary catalyst for UNAMSIL's expansion was the
inability of international society to adequately support the Nigerian-led
ECOMOG force in its earlier efforts to bring stability to Sierra Leone.
This was noted by Kofi Annan when he observed in January 2000 that
ECOMOG's withdrawal left 'no alternative to expanding UNAMSIL in
order to keep the peace process … on track'.[62] Similarly, speaking at the
UN Security Council, Nigeria's Mr Mbanefo had reminded his
illustrious audience that ECOMOG and Nigeria in particular had borne
'a disproportionate burden' in the international effort to bring stability
to Sierra Leone. Although the ECOMOG force had managed to contain
the crisis, this was 'in spite of limited resources and inadequate logistical
support and amid considerable international apathy'.[63] Algeria's
representative at the UN Security Council reiterated these concerns
when he recalled that 'many appeals by ECOWAS for significant
international logistic and financial assistance for ECOMOG went
unanswered'.[64] Such support could have made a vital difference because
although ECOMOG undoubtedly suffered from poor co-ordination,
according to former ECOMOG Force Commander Timothy Shelpidi,
his troops could have defeated the rebels if they had possessed

appropriate counter-insurgency military equipment such as the MI-24 helicopter gunship.[65] In Britain's defence, it had done more than any other country to support ECOMOG, particularly the contingents from Ghana and Mali, allocating some US$7m for logistical support, maps and intelligence sharing by mid-1999.[66] However, because Britain refused to offer direct assistance to ECOMOG while Sani Abacha remained in power in Nigeria, such support proved too little, too late. Although reliance upon ECOMOG highlighted the way in which international society would have preferred to abdicate its responsibility for intervening in Sierra Leone, adequate support for ECOMOG could potentially have averted the need to seek an end to hostilities at the heavy price of appeasing the RUF.

Thus for all its imperfections, Lomé should be understood as the logical outcome of international society's failure to adequately support ECOMOG; US diplomatic pressure (supported by the Contact Group and probably by Kabbah himself); the ideological context guiding Western responses to 'internal wars'; and the lack of explicit UN authorization for intervention. Some of the factors that altered this situation are discussed below.

BRITISH MILITARY INTERVENTION: MISSION AND MOTIVES

According to *The Guardian*, the decision to deploy British troops in the largest unilateral overseas military operation since the Falklands war was taken amid some confusion.[67] The impending crisis in Sierra Leone came at a time when Blair was preoccupied with the situation in Northern Ireland and the IRA's latest statement on decommissioning. In addition, the paper suggested, ministers were acting on flawed military intelligence, both from the UN and from the 15-man British 'technical assistance' team in Sierra Leone led by Brigadier David Richards. The main catalyst appears to have been what the paper described as a 'panic-stricken report' from the UN claiming that Freetown was poised to fall to the rebels. While in hindsight certain individual reports may have exaggerated the immediacy and degree of the threat to Freetown, given the RUF's atrocities in January 1999 and its increasingly flagrant breaches of Lomé, there is no doubt that a significant threat existed. This added up to a turbulent baptism for the new British High Commissioner Alan Jones, who had just arrived in Freetown. He too filed an anxious report. The first public hint that a decision had been taken to send a 'spearhead battalion' of approximately 700 troops came early on 7 May 2000. That evening, Foreign Secretary Robin Cook gave Jones the power to 'trigger' the evacuation of British citizens. The following day, the High Commissioner did just that and set Operation Palliser in motion.

Initially the operation went smoothly with the troops securing Lungi airport and evacuating British citizens and others to whom Britain had consular responsibility. However, on 17 May British paratroopers and Nigerian troops killed four rebels about 20 miles from Lungi airport. This incident sparked a series of debates not only about the risk to British soldiers but also about the nature of their mandate in Sierra Leone.[68] The next serious incident concerned the capture of 11 British soldiers by a group of rebels known as the 'West Side Boys'. According to the Ministry of Defence (MoD), on 25 August, an 11-man patrol from the First Battalion The Royal Irish Regiment, with a Sierra Leone liaison officer, travelled from the Benguema training camp to visit – by invitation – a Jordanian battalion at Masiaka.[69] The patrol was approved by the Commander of British Forces as part of routine liaison with adjacent friendly units to gain increased warning of any threats. On the return journey the patrol's commander visited the village of Magbeni, where the patrol encountered armed members of the West Side Boys. Very quickly the patrol was enveloped, the soldiers disarmed, and moved in two boats to Gberi Bana on the other side of Rokel Creek. After negotiations to release all 12 hostages collapsed, a rescue mission was launched on 10 September in which one British soldier was killed and several others were seriously injured. Although there were calls, most notably from the Conservative Party, for British troops to withdraw following this incident, the British contingent was instead scaled down as the situation in and around Freetown stabilized. It was subsequently reinforced during October and November.

Britain's geostrategic interests and investments in Sierra Leone are negligible. It is apparent that Britain would have preferred the Nigerian-led ECOMOG force to play the role of guardian of Sierra Leone's peace process. However, as the former colonial power,[70] and leader of the International Contact Group, expectations naturally turned to Britain – not least those of Freetown's inhabitants and President Kabbah – when it became clear that ECOMOG was no longer prepared to shoulder the burden of keeping the peace. It is therefore inaccurate to portray the government's intervention as simply a public relations exercise to grab some much-needed attention by making a 'drama' out of Sierra Leone's crisis.[71] Nor is it the case, as Richard Dowden suggested, that 'Sierra Leoneans have nothing to induce Britain to send troops there except their imperilled humanity'.[72] Unfortunately, even more is at stake in Sierra Leone than the 'imperilled humanity' of its inhabitants, not least the continued credibility of the UN as it decides whether or not to commit a similar mission to the Democratic Republic of Congo, and the New Labour government as it wrestles with the dilemmas thrown up by the FCO's new mission statement. And, by definition, questioning UN credibility is in reality another way of questioning the ethical claims made by the great powers. Events in Sierra Leone thus had – and continue to have – significance far beyond the country's borders.

Nevertheless, British military intervention in Sierra Leone was by no means a foregone conclusion. As Malcolm Chalmers argued in 1997, a British presence in major operations outside Europe remained unlikely, partly because of its strategy to enhance the peacekeeping capacity of African governments and organizations, and partly because most practical peacekeeping activity would probably take the form of infrastructural support for other nations, especially in Africa.[73] Britain's intervention was therefore something of a surprise. It was also not revealed in its entirety until Cook's statement to the House of Commons on 6 June.[74] Having successfully averted the immediate threat to Freetown, British strategy had three objectives. The first priority was to equip the government of Sierra Leone with an effective and accountable army.[75] The second was to restore momentum to the peace process – in September Cook suggested that Britain would help achieve this by supporting an expanded UNAMSIL and funding the disarmament process.[76] The third priority was to reduce the incentive that the illicit trade in diamonds had provided for the violence.

The British government's decision to intervene militarily in Sierra Leone in May 2000 can be understood as a combination of five imperatives: a concern to protect British citizens; the humanitarian impulse to 'do something' as Sierra Leone teetered on the brink of a crisis that could be averted by the use or threat of military force; the defence of democracy; the need to live up to the commitment it made about the 'ethical dimension' of foreign policy; and the perception that the future credibility of UN peacekeeping operations was at stake, particularly in Africa. The remainder of this section discusses each in turn.

Protecting British Citizens

Initially, the most common justification for the intervention was the protection of approximately 500 British citizens who were threatened by Sierra Leone's political instability. As Defence Secretary Geoffrey Hoon suggested, 'British troops are in Sierra Leone to get British nationals out, and help get UN reinforcements in'.[77] Cook was more specific. 'Our first duty', he argued, 'is to protect the lives of British citizens ... and others to whom we have a consular responsibility ... In view of the limited commercial opportunities to leave Sierra Leone and the current insecurity, we have taken the precautionary measure of deployment of a number of British military assets to West Africa.'[78]

The pragmatics of the evacuation dictated that the British army secure a suitable exit point – Lungi airport was the obvious choice. Hain later told the House of Commons' Foreign Affairs Select Committee that this entailed securing 'the airport and its perimeter because you do not secure an airport in this kind of operation unless you are able to have a wide deployment area, perhaps at least four miles around'.[79] The fact that such an operation precipitated an engagement with the RUF, and also meant that Britain could 'assist in the build-up of the UN forces',[80] gave rise to a somewhat confused debate within certain segments of the British media. This debate focused primarily on the nature of the mandate governing British forces but often digressed to the relationship between Operation Palliser and the mayhem in Zimbabwe. *The Daily Telegraph*, for instance, accused New Labour of operating without a clear set of objectives and of double standards in its response to the crises in Zimbabwe and Sierra Leone, the clear inference being that Britain should do more to help Zimbabwe's white commercial farmers.[81]

The Humanitarian Impulse

To legitimate the intervention, British ministers regularly pointed to the fact that Sierra Leone's inhabitants were living under the threat of 'brutal rebel force'. While all sides to the conflict were guilty of severe human rights abuses, it was the RUF in particular that attracted the condemnation of the West after its attack (in conjunction with the AFRC) on Freetown on 6 January 1999. This had unleashed an unprecedented level of carnage upon the city. In addition to destroying roughly 90 per cent of the buildings in the eastern suburbs of Freetown, RUF/AFRC forces killed an estimated 5,000–6,000 people and injured,

maimed, raped and abducted thousands more.[82] Then, after the last
ECOMOG troops had been replaced by a poorly armed and
uncoordinated UNAMSIL in early May 2000, the RUF gained further
notoriety – and effectively shattered the Lomé Accord – when it attacked
disarmament, demobilization and reintegration camps in central and
eastern Sierra Leone, killing four Kenyan members of UNAMSIL and
detaining approximately 500 others. Widespread reports of the RUF's
often drug-induced atrocities, the tendency of its members to mutilate
(and allegedly sometimes eat) their victims, and the portrayal of its
leader Foday Sankoh as a psychopath fuelled the moral outrage evident
in Britain.[83] As Cook commented shortly after the arrival of British
troops in Freetown, 'I don't see how we could maintain our self-respect
if we turned away from this kind of savagery'.[84]

In spite of such noble motivations, the government initially
emphasized the intervention's more traditional concerns with the rescue
of British citizens rather than its humanitarian credentials. *The Guardian*
offered a convincing explanation as to why the humanitarian impulse –
although present – was played down. 'For most members of the public',
the paper argued, 'Sierra Leone is more likely to be mistaken for a car
model off a Ford assembly line, and as to the competing virtues of rebel
leader Foday Sankoh, or President Kabbah, fewer than one in 100,000
could even pretend to have an opinion'.[85] Unlike the humanitarian crisis
generated by severe flooding in Mozambique and parts of South Africa,
in which the victims obviously deserved assistance in the face of an
overwhelming natural disaster, the catastrophe facing Sierra Leone was
obviously man-made. More importantly, in an incredibly influential
essay that was widely distributed amongst US officials on the African
continent, Robert Kaplan had depicted the violence as lacking any clear
political purpose. Rather it was the work of criminals and bandits.[86] In
this interpretation, Sierra Leone's crisis was of its own making – an
example of Kaplan's 'coming anarchy' thesis – and therefore less
deserving of outside help. The fact of the matter remained that despite
the impending threat to Freetown, for most British citizens Sierra Leone
was a far away place of which they knew (or cared?) little.

Defending Democracy

A third justification for British military intervention were Kabbah's
democratic credentials. As Cook stated in October, 'Britain is standing
up for democracy … in Sierra Leone'.[87] The promotion of democracy

abroad is a crucial element of New Labour's foreign policy doctrine, and one of the three key themes of its policy towards sub-Saharan Africa.[88] Having suffered the ignominy of the so-called 'Arms-to-Africa' scandal, the British government was understandably keen to prevent a repeat of the May 1997 coup.[89] Kabbah, leader of the Sierra Leone People's Party, itself the leading party of a coalition, had been elected president in the second round of voting on 15 March 1996 with 59.9 per cent of the vote.[90] In accordance with the demands for political change made by a strong civic movement made up of women's groups and civic leaders including many tribal chiefs, the British and American governments pressurized Brigadier Maada Bio, then the country's latest military leader, not to abort the proposed elections.[91] They were duly held in the midst of a raging conflict without adequate attempts to establish any meaningful ceasefire or demobilization of the combatants.[92] Consequently, less than 25 per cent of the population voted as no one in contested or rebel-held areas was able to do so.[93]

The plan had been to establish a constitutional government upon a base of popular legitimacy and the rule of law. In practice, however, the elections helped consolidate a reconfigured political alliance that, lacking effective domestic military support, was heavily dependent on the presence of foreigners, most notably Executive Outcomes, but also related firms such as Branch Mining. With help from such outsiders to protect him from the demands of his own population, and with the privileged international ties that came with being the sovereign representative of Sierra Leone, Kabbah was able to construct a political network to facilitate private business operations to attract political supporters and disable opponents.[94] While such activities are understandable given Sierra Leone's patrimonial system of governance, they are hardly the actions of a genuine democrat. Nevertheless, it is reasonable to conclude that even with less than perfect democratic credentials Kabbah currently represents Sierra Leone's least worst option. The British government's decision to support Kabbah is therefore understandable.

Sticking to Foreign Policy Principles

A fourth imperative that encouraged New Labour to intervene in Sierra Leone was the principles it had outlined in the FCO's May 1997 Mission Statement. As part of its desire to give greater consideration to the 'ethical dimensions' of foreign policy, New Labour sought to promote the interrelated goals of peace, prosperity and democracy on the African continent. In particular, the debate over British intervention in Sierra Leone came after Tony Blair's so-called 'Chicago speech' in which he claimed, 'the most pressing foreign policy problem we face is to identify the circumstances in which we should get actively involved in other people's conflicts'.[95] In the speech, Blair also identified five considerations that should govern British thinking about whether or not to intervene:

> First, are we sure of our case? ... Second, have we exhausted all diplomatic options? ... Third, on the basis of a practical assessment of the situation, are there military operations we can sensibly and prudently undertake? ... Fourth, are we prepared for the long term? ... And finally, do we have national interests involved?[96]

Sierra Leone represented a test case in which all five of these questions could be responded to positively: New Labour had outlined the moral imperative, had clearly exhausted diplomatic initiatives after Lomé collapsed, set limited and attainable military objectives, pledged a number of long-term contributions to aid in Sierra Leone's reconstruction,[97] and referred to Britain's national interests on numerous occasions both in terms of protecting its citizens and in promoting international peace and security. In addition, an intervention in West Africa provided the perfect opportunity to display Britain's rapid reaction capability as outlined in the 1998 Strategic Defence Review.[98] As Defence Secretary Geoff Hoon put it at the time, 'the deployment of British forces for a limited period on these tasks is a model of the rapid deployment concept that was at the heart of the Strategic Defence Review'.[99] While this was a successful test of Britain's rapid reaction capability there is little evidence to suggest that it was a major motivation behind the intervention.

To some degree therefore, it is fair to say that the principles outlined in the FCO's Mission Statement, and more recently those enunciated by Blair in his Chicago speech, made it very difficult for Britain to abandon Sierra Leone once the going got tough. This was reflected in the fact that the public debate in Britain moved rapidly from discussing the question of whether or not to intervene, to arguing what form British intervention should take and what its objectives should be. Based on their assessment of the situation on the ground, New Labour concluded that in this instance, the threat and use of military force could be deployed effectively in defence of its foreign policy principles.

Fighting for the UN

The final imperative pushing New Labour to intervene was the credibility of future UN peacekeeping operations, especially in Africa. Not only was the utility of the traditional doctrine of UN peacekeeping at stake, but also the organization's ability to successfully implement its resolutions, traditional or otherwise, in the field. For example, the UK had argued at the UN Security Council in October 1999, that Sierra Leone represented 'a test case' that would 'be seen by many as a litmus test of the commitment of the international community to resolving conflict'.[100] In February 2000, Sir Jeremy Greenstock had reiterated this point at the UN Security Council stating,

> Sierra Leone may be a small country, but this is an enormous challenge for the United Nations. It is in effect no less of a test of the United Nations commitment to conflict resolution in Africa than what we are contemplating for the Democratic Republic of the Congo. It is a test not just of our willingness to intervene ... but of the United Nations' actual ability to deliver effective peacekeeping of lasting impact and value.[101]

The Economist was one of several publications that echoed these concerns. 'Sierra Leone', it pointed out, 'is a test – if we fail here, what hope is there for peacekeeping anywhere else in the world?'[102] The Guardian's Hugo Young was of a similar opinion. At the time of the British intervention he outlined the problem facing UNAMSIL in more detail:

> Intended to be 11,000-strong, the force there is the largest UN peacekeeping army in the world. Yet it is pathetically failing. It has become hostage ... to the armed gangs of rebel forces who are destabilising the regime it should be defending ... If this massive UN presence is incapable of sustaining peace, against a disorderly and largely untrained rabble, one must ask what future there can ever be for the entire principle of humanitarian peacekeeping intervention by the UN.[103]

Faced with the potential disintegration of its mission, the UN Secretary General appealed to Britain, amongst others, for assistance.[104] As noted above, Britain initially dispatched an advisory team to Freetown shortly followed by Operation Palliser. In spite of Sierra Leone's importance as a test of the UN's effectiveness, British ministers were loath to use this line of argument at the time of the intervention when defending their actions to the British media and public. Instead, when dealing with domestic audiences they tended to use a combination of the other four imperatives. For example, it was only when defending the continued role of British troops in Sierra Leone in September 2000 that Cook alluded to the UN's crisis as a reason for British intervention. British troops, he argued, were there partly 'because we are a leading member of the UN, [and] we are committed to UN peacekeeping'.[105] Again, with the benefit of hindsight, Hain had acknowledged that the Sierra Leone experience highlighted the limitations of UN peacekeeping forces, 'the need to modernise and upgrade them and the need to look at a rapid reaction capability for the UN'.[106]

It is significant that at the time, statements by ministers to domestic audiences did not frame the intervention in terms of safeguarding the future of UN peacekeeping. There are at least two possible explanations for this. First, given the general lack of knowledge within Britain about the way in which the UN functions and the situation in Sierra Leone noted above, New Labour probably believed that domestic opinion would not support the deployment of British troops if it was couched in terms of defending the UN's credibility. The second explanation is more cynical in that it casts doubt upon the depth of British commitment to uphold the UN's reputation. Although under the previous Conservative administration Britain had prevaricated in the UN Security Council as the 1994 Rwandan genocide unfolded,[107] New Labour had proclaimed a greater degree of support for the organization upon its election to office.[108] The primary factor that casts doubt on the depth of New Labour's commitment is its refusal to deploy British troops under the UNAMSIL flag in anything other than a token presence – on 22 May 2000 just 15 military observers were part of the UN force.[109] Britain has repeatedly ruled out direct participation in UNAMSIL on a larger scale while simultaneously offering assurances that it will not be allowed to collapse. 'All options', Hain recently argued,

> are being explored with member countries, including NATO countries, but Britain is very overstretched in Kosovo, with Iraq and in Northern Ireland. There will be a fully fledged UN

peacekeeping operation in Sierra Leone. It will be a better force with an improved command structure.[110]

Britain's reluctance to operate within UNAMSIL may well be because, like the US, it is wary of the operational efficiency and calibre of significant numbers of troops participating in UN peacekeeping operations. It may also reflect pragmatic concerns that Britain can achieve more constructive results in Sierra Leone by operating outside – but in co-operation with – UNAMSIL. Whatever rationale lies behind British activities, the bottom line remains that despite recent pledges of extra troops from Bangladesh and Ghana, extra equipment and support personnel from Ukraine, extra equipment from Slovakia, and the decision to increase UNAMSIL's authorized maximum strength to approximately 20,000 troops, in practice its future looks uncertain with the Indian and Jordanian contingents, which provide the bulk of the current UN force, set to withdraw. Britain's relationship with UNAMSIL will thus continue to be the subject of some debate.[111]

CONCLUSION

How, then, are we to judge Britain's intervention? In many respects, it is still too early to tell what impact the British intervention will have on Sierra Leone's future. In May 2000, Hugo Young argued that

> The pocket generals at the Foreign Office and the fervent moralist in Downing Street need alike to restrain themselves. There is a clear limit to what Britain can or should do ... This could yet become a modest case-study in focused interventionism, provided it acknowledges that a deeply imperfect situation has to be left behind.[112]

Young's argument is a powerful one. Britain cannot save Sierra Leone on its own, and nor should it – the country's fate should be decided by its own inhabitants. And after more than 20 years of turmoil, Sierra Leoneans have just cause to be suspicious of external involvement in their country's politics. Nevertheless, outsiders have the capacity to help in important ways. Indeed, in a country as devastated as Sierra Leone outside help is a prerequisite for the country's reconstruction.

In committing its troops to Sierra Leone as part of a broader political package, the British government deserves credit on several counts. First, for averting a potential crisis in Freetown similar to that which occurred in January 1999. Second, it has ceased to condone the use of mercenaries to help implement its policy objectives. Third, it has been prepared to stand by at least some of its foreign policy principles, perhaps most notably by not withdrawing its troops after the hostage rescue mission at Rokel Creek. Such a withdrawal would have been foolish, for it would have signalled to the world that the British army is as casualty-shy as its US counterpart and would simply encourage groups in other parts of the world to ensure they surpass the necessary casualty threshold.[113] Finally, although Britain's aversion to operating under the UN umbrella has caused some commentators to question its motives, the presence of British troops has undoubtedly aided UNAMSIL in its arduous task and generated overwhelming support within the UN Security Council.[114]

The poverty, social exclusion and patrimonial networks that lie at the root of Sierra Leone's violence can only be resolved through the co-ordinated activities of a combination of insiders and powerful outsiders like the G-8 states. Nevertheless, Britain's intervention and ongoing assistance is a step in the right direction. As Paul Richards has suggested, a plausible objective for Britain and international society in general would be to try and open up a space for rethinking patrimonialism in Sierra Leone. 'A wise international community', Richards argued,

> might seek to focus some of its help on funding popular participation in seeking answers to the crisis of patrimonialism [and deciding] whether its good points (a parental sense of commitment to the needs of the young) can be separated from the bad (a chronic tendency towards factionalization between those who 'enjoy' and those who feel excluded).[115]

The key to preventing the emergence of another RUF-type movement lies in combating the social exclusion and poverty that is generated by patrimonialism and intensified in times of economic crisis. New Labour is well aware that in the final analysis military means cannot achieve political ends, and that intervention reveals the stark failure of both prevention and earlier diplomatic initiatives that relied upon the consent of the RUF. Britain's military intervention must therefore be considered in light of its involvement in other areas designed to reconstruct a viable state in Sierra Leone, such as support for a Truth and Reconciliation Commission and various civic associations, efforts to train an effective and accountable army, its ongoing attempts to reform the country's security sector,[116] and assistance to rebuild the country's shattered economy and social infrastructure. And here Britain has done more than any other country. Thus, from this admittedly precarious vantage point, describing New Labour's actions as 'a modest case-study in focused interventionism' seems entirely reasonable.

However, to get beyond intervention and begin the serious business of conflict prevention, Britain and the rest of the G-8 need to seriously consider how the global economy they manage increases the likelihood of violence in countries peripheral to their interests. In this sense, recent events in Sierra Leone stand as a salutary lesson in the lack of concern about the fate of peripheral nations in an increasingly iniquitous global economy.

NOTES

1. Thanks go to Rita Abrahamsen, Alex Bellamy, David Francis, Thomas Jaye and Ian Taylor for their constructive criticisms.
2. Abiodun Alao, *Sierra Leone: Tracing the Genesis of a Controversy* (London: RIIA, Briefing No.50, 1998).
3. Robin Cook, 'British Foreign Policy', speech at the launch of the Foreign Office (FCO) Mission Statement, Locarno Suite, FCO, London, 12 May 1997. Unless otherwise stated, all speeches and other FCO material are available at www.fco.gov.uk.
4. Tony Blair, 'Doctrine of the International Community', speech to the Economic Club of Chicago, 22 April 1999.
5. For a discussion see Rita Abrahamsen and Paul Williams, 'Ethics and Foreign Policy: The Antinomies of New Labour's "Third Way" in Sub-Saharan Africa', *Political Studies*, Vol.49, No.2 (June 2001), pp.249–64.
6. Ministry of Defence press release 270/00, 'Military Assistance to Sierra Leone', 10 Oct. 2000. This also reaffirmed the government's readiness to deploy, if required, a rapid reaction capability, up to Brigade strength (approximately 5,000 personnel), based in the UK and centred on the Joint Rapid Reaction Force.
7. Jimmy D. Kandeh, 'Ransoming the State: Elite Origins of Subaltern Terror in Sierra Leone', *Review of African Political Economy*, Vol.26 (1999), pp.353–4.
8. For more detail on Sierra Leone's recent past see Paul Richards, *Fighting for the Rain Forest: War, Youth & Resources in Sierra Leone* (Oxford: James Currey, 1998); William Reno, *Corruption and State Politics in Sierra Leone* (Cambridge: Cambridge University Press, 1995) and *Warlord Politics and African States* (Boulder, CO: Lynne Rienner, 1999), pp.113–45.
9. Reno, *Warlord Politics*, pp.115–16.
10. William Reno, 'Ironies of Post-Cold War Structural Adjustment in Sierra Leone', *Review of African Political Economy*, Vol.67 (1996), pp.7–18; Kandeh, 'Ransoming the State', p.358.
11. In 2000 Sierra Leone was bottom of the 174 states ranked by the United Nations Development Programme's Human Development Index. The *Human Development Report 2000* is available at www.undp.org.
12. Abdel-Fatau Musah, 'A Country Under Siege: State Decay and Corporate Military Intervention in Sierra Leone', in A-F. Musah and J. 'Kayode Fayemi (eds.), *Mercenaries: An African Security Dilemma* (London: Pluto Press, 2000), p.82.
13. *Human Rights: Annual Report 1999* (London: FCO & DFID, CM 4404, 1999), p.34.

14. See Ken Booth, 'Military Intervention: Duty and Prudence', in Lawrence Freedman (ed.), *Military Intervention in European Conflicts* (Oxford: Blackwell, 1994), pp.56–75.
15. Kandeh, 'Ransoming the State', pp.351–8.
16. Reno, *Corruption and State Politics in Sierra Leone*.
17. M. Bratton and N. van de Walle, *Democratic Experiments in Africa* (Cambridge: Cambridge University Press, 1997), ch.2.
18. Christopher Clapham, *Africa and the International System: The Politics of State Survival* (Cambridge: Cambridge University Press, 1996), p.59.
19. Ibrahim Abdullah, 'Bush Path to Destruction: The Origin and Character of the Revolutionary United Front/Sierra Leone', *Journal of Modern African Studies*, Vol.36, No.2 (1998), p.206.
20. See Reno, *Corruption and State Politics in Sierra Leone*, pp.72–5, 89–90, 109–12, 143, 149–52 and Kandeh, 'Ransoming the State', pp.351–2.
21. Richards, *Fighting for the Rain Forest* and Kandeh, 'Ransoming the State'.
22. See Ian Smillie, Lansana Gberie and Ralph Hazleton, *The Heart of the Matter: Sierra Leone, Diamonds and Human Security* (Ottawa: Partnership Africa Canada, 2000) available at www.Sierra-Leone.org.
23. Foreign Affairs Select Committee (FAC), *Minutes of Evidence for Monday 22 May 2000 Sierra Leone: Mr Peter Hain MP and Mr J. Bevan* (London: The Stationery Office, 20 July 2000), response to question 40.
24. FAC, *Minutes of Evidence*, response to question 40.
25. Robin Cook, 'Statement on Sierra Leone', transcript of his interview with the BBC and Reuters, the Azores, 7 May 2000.
26. See David Keen, *The Economic Functions of Violence in Civil Wars* (Adelphi Paper 320, Oxford: Oxford University Press for the IISS, 1998); Mats Berdal and David M. Malone (eds.), *Greed and Grievance: Economic Agendas in Civil Wars* (Boulder, CO: Lynne Rienner, 2000).
27. Reno, *Warlord Politics*, p.114.
28. See Reno, *Corruption and State Politics in Sierra Leone*, pp.158–62.
29. For a comprehensive overview of mercenary and corporate activities in Sierra Leone see Reno, *Warlord Politics*, pp.113–45 and Musah, 'A Country Under Siege'.
30. For example Reno, *Warlord Politics*, p.139, and William Shawcross, see his 'Send in the mercenaries if our troops won't fight', *The Guardian*, 10 May 2000 and 'A bloody continent wracked by war and disastrous leadership', *The Sunday Times*, 14 May 2000.
31. See Richards, *Fighting for the Rain Forest*, pp.2–4, 19–20; and Adekaye Adebajo and David Keen, 'Banquet for Warlords', *The World Today* (July 2000), p.9. For more detail of the links between Taylor's policies and the violence in Sierra Leone see Reno, *Warlord Politics*, pp.91–107, 123–4.
32. Reno, *Warlord Politics*.
33. This is extrapolated from Reno's argument about ordinary Zaireans in *Warlord Politics*, p.219.
34. See Richards, *Fighting for the Rain Forest*, and Abdullah, 'Bush Path to Destruction'.
35. Richards, *Fighting for the Rain Forest*, p.177.
36. Adebajo and Keen, 'Banquet for Warlords', p.8, and Abdullah, 'Bush Path to Destruction', pp.222–7.
37. Cited in Kandeh, 'Ransoming the State', p.349.
38. This paragraph draws heavily from David J. Francis, 'Torturous Path to Peace: The Lomé Accord and Postwar Peacebuilding in Sierra Leone', *Security Dialogue*, Vol.31, No.3 (2000), pp.359–64.
39. These were predominantly ethnic Mende militia based on traditional hunting societies that by May 1997 numbered some 20,000. See Musah, 'A Country Under Siege', p.95.
40. See for example, Richards, *Fighting for the Rain Forest*, p.171; Abdullah, 'Bush Path to Destruction', p.230; and Kandeh, 'Ransoming the State', pp.362–4.
41. The International Contact Group includes representatives from the governments of Belgium, Canada, China, Egypt, France, Germany, Italy, Japan, the Netherlands, New Zealand, Nigeria, Norway, Sierra Leone, Sweden, United Kingdom, United States, the Commonwealth Secretariat, Economic Community of West African States (ECOWAS),

European Commission, United Nations (UN) and World Bank. The Contact Group was first convened by the United Kingdom in London on 5 Nov. 1998.

42. Tony Blair, statement, 'Sierra Leone Peace Agreement', 8 July 1999.
43. Robin Cook, statement, 'Sierra Leone Peace Agreement', 8 July 1999.
44. Francis, 'Torturous Path to Peace', p.366.
45. Francis, 'Torturous Path to Peace', p.364.
46. See Shawcross, 'A bloody continent', and 'Send in the mercenaries'.
47. 'Sandline boss blames Blair for carnage in Sierra Leone', *The Sunday Telegraph*, 14 May 2000.
48. 'Sandline boss blames Blair'.
49. For a comprehensive discussion of this debate see Nicholas J. Wheeler, *Saving Strangers: Humanitarian Intervention in International Society* (Oxford: Oxford University Press, 2000).
50. Charles King, *Ending Civil Wars* (Adelphi Paper 308, Oxford: Oxford University Press for the IISS, 1997), p.81.
51. David Shearer, 'Exploring the Limits of Consent: Conflict Resolution in Sierra Leone', *Millennium*, Vol.26, No.3 (1997), pp.845–60.
52. Shearer, 'Exploring the Limits of Consent', p.858.
53. FAC, *Minutes of Evidence*, response to question 13.
54. New Jersey Congressman, Donald Payne also played an important part in drumming up US domestic support for Foday Sankoh and Charles Taylor. In Feb. 1999, for example, Payne wrote a letter to Kabbah telling him that 'successful negotiations must be without preconditions and include the permanent release of Mr Foday Sankoh', in Ryan Lizza, 'Sierra Leone: The Last Clinton Betrayal', *The New Republic Online*, 24 July 2000. See also 'Diamonds and Death', *The American Spectator*, Oct. 2000.
55. Lizza, 'Sierra Leone: The Last Clinton Betrayal'.
56. S/PV.4139, 11 May 2000, p.12.
57. FAC, *Minutes of Evidence*, response to question 14.
58. FAC, *Minutes of Evidence*, response to question 16. Emphasis added.
59. Adebajo and Keen, 'Banquet for Warlords', p.10. See also Mr Olhaye's (Djibouti) comments as Co-ordinator of the East African sub-region at the UN Security Council emergency session, S/PV.4139, 11 May 2000, p.26.
60. FAC, *Minutes of Evidence*, response to question 22.
61. See Reno, *Warlord Politics*, p.8.
62. Second Report of the Secretary General on the United Nations Mission in Sierra Leone, S/2000/13, 11 Jan. 2000, para 24.
63. S/PV.4054, 22 Oct. 1999, p.7.
64. S/PV.4139, 11 May 2000, p.5.
65. Cited in Eric G. Berman and Katie E. Sams, *Peacekeeping in Africa: Capabilities and Culpabilities* (Switzerland: UNIDIR/2000/3, 2000), p.119.
66. Berman and Sams, *Peacekeeping in Africa*, pp.125–6, 327–8.
67. 'Flawed evidence led to "mission creep"', *The Guardian*, 16 May 2000.
68. See 'Four die in first clash with British', *The Guardian*, 18 May 2000.
69. MoD press release 14 Sept. 2000.
70. In a press statement on 'Britain's role in Sierra Leone', broadcast on 19 May 2000, Blair argued that as the former colonial power Britain had 'historic responsibilities' to Sierra Leone.
71. Victoria Brittain, 'Making a drama out of an African crisis', *The Guardian*, 10 May 2000.
72. *The Observer*, 14 May 2000.
73. Malcolm Chalmers, 'The Strategic Defence Review – British Policy Options', *RUSI Journal*, (Aug. 1997), pp.36–8.
74. Robin Cook, statement to the House of Commons, 6 June 2000.
75. Ironically, in May 1991 Britain had rejected Joseph Momoh's appeal for British military advisers to boost the Sierra Leone Army's capacity to deal with the terror threat, and to improve its communications and intelligence capabilities. Although individual officers were highly sympathetic to Momoh's request for help, the Ministry of Defence turned it down. See *Africa Confidential*, Special Report: *Chronology of Sierra Leone* (1998) available at

www.africa-confidential.com.
76. Robin Cook, 'British Commitment in Sierra Leone', edited transcript of a press conference, Heathrow Airport, London, 11 Sept. 2000.
77. Statement to the House of Commons, 23 May 2000. See also Statement by the Prime Minister's Office on Sierra Leone, 11 May 2000.
78. Robin Cook, 'Britain will not abandon its commitment to Sierra Leone', statement to the House of Commons, 8 May 2000.
79. FAC, *Minutes of Evidence*, response to question 3.
80. Cook, 'Britain will not abandon'.
81. See 'We're there because we're there', *The Daily Telegraph*, 13 May 2000; 'Cook's Double Trouble', *The Daily Telegraph*, 15 May 2000; and 'A very risky venture', *The Daily Telegraph*, 16 May 2000.
82. See *Sierra Leone* (Briefing Paper: FCO, 8 May 2000) and Francis, 'Torturous Path to Peace', p.361.
83. See for example, Jon Swain, 'The making of a monster', *The Sunday Times*, 21 May 2000.
84. Cited in *The Daily Telegraph*, 15 May 2000.
85. 'In the line of fire', *The Guardian*, 15 May 2000.
86. Robert Kaplan, 'The Coming Anarchy: How scarcity, crime, overpopulation, and disease are rapidly destroying the social fabric of our planet', *Atlantic Monthly* (Feb. 1994), pp.44–76. In contrast see the sustained critique of Kaplan in Richards, *Fighting for the Rain Forest*.
87. Statement by Robin Cook, 10 Oct. 2000.
88. See for example Robin Cook, 'Promoting Peace and Prosperity in Africa', speech to the UNSC, 24 Sept. 1998; Tony Lloyd, speech to the Africa Day Conference, Lancaster House, London, 26 May 1999; and Peter Hain, 'Africa: Backing Success', speech to the 'Challenges for Governance in Africa' conference, Wilton Park, 13 Sept. 1999.
89. This revolved around FCO complicity in Sandline International's contravention of the UN arms embargo on Sierra Leone in order to return Kabbah to office. See *House of Commons Foreign Affairs Committee, Second Report: Sierra Leone, Vol. I* (London: The Stationery Office, 1999).
90. *Africa Confidential*, Special Report.
91. Musah, 'A Country Under Siege', p.90; *Africa Confidential*, Special Report.
92. Musah, 'A Country Under Siege', p.90.
93. 'The darkest corner of Africa', *The Economist*, 9 Jan. 1999, p.37.
94. Reno, *Warlord Politics*, pp.134-7. For Kabbah's less than perfect track record see A. B. Zack-Williams, 'Kamajors, "Sobel" and the Militariat: Civil Society and the Return of the Military in Sierra Leonean Politics', *Review of African Political Economy*, Vol.73 (1997), pp.377–9; Kandeh, 'Ransoming the State', pp.355–6.
95. Blair, 'Doctrine of the International Community'.
96. Blair, 'Doctrine of the International Community'.
97. For example, on 13 Jan. 2000 Britain donated £250,000 to fund the work of Sierra Leone's Truth and Reconciliation Commission, see Peter Hain, statement at a press conference, Freetown, Sierra Leone, 13 Jan. 2000. Since March 1998, Britain has committed approximately £70 million to support the peace process in Sierra Leone, see Robin Cook, statement to the House of Commons, 6 June 2000.
98. For a discussion see Colin McInnes, 'Labour's Strategic Defence Review', *International Affairs*, Vol.74, No.4 (1998), pp.823–45.
99. Geoffrey Hoon, statement on Sierra Leone to the House of Commons, 15 May 2000. Defence sources have also justified the redeployment of extra British troops to Sierra Leone in Oct. 2000 in similar terms. See 'UK forces grow in Sierra Leone', *The Guardian*, 30 Oct. 2000.
100. S/PV.4054, 22 Oct. 1999, p.8.
101. S/PV.4099, 7 Feb. 2000, pp.3–4.
102. 'A line in the sand', *The Economist*, 16 Sept. 2000, p.25.
103. Hugo Young, 'We are good at getting in, not so good at getting out', *The Guardian*, 18 May 2000.
104. 'Sierra Leone cruelly exposes UN's crisis', *The Guardian*, 6 May 2000. See also S/2000/13,

11 Jan. 2000, para 25.

105. Cited in *The Guardian*, 12 Sept. 2000.

106. FAC, *Minutes of Evidence*, response to question 28.

107. See Linda Melvern, *A People Betrayed: The Role of the West in Rwanda's Genocide* (London: Zed Books, 2000).

108. See Cook, 'British Foreign Policy' and the Mission Statement itself, which promised Britain would use its status to make the UN a more effective tool for securing peace in the world.

109. FAC, *Minutes of Evidence*, Mr Bevan (Head of the FCO's African Dept.), response to question 44.

110. Cited in *The Guardian*, 22 Sept. 2000.

111. See for example, 'A line in the sand'; and Menzies Campbell's comments in *The Guardian*, 12 Sept. 2000 and *The Observer*, 29 Oct. 2000.

112. Young, 'We are good at getting in'.

113. See 'A line in the sand'.

114. See the minutes of the Security Council's deliberations in S/PV.4139, 11 May 2000.

115. Richards, *Fighting for the Rain Forest*, p.162.

116. Most notably perhaps through Keith Biddle's lengthy attempts to reform Sierra Leone's police force; see Chris McGreal, 'Whitehall launches second colonisation', *The Guardian*, 19 May 2000.

The Role of Monitoring and Verification

TREVOR FINDLAY

Monitoring and verification are playing an increasingly important role in international intervention in the affairs of states, whether in crisis or conflict situations or in the normal course of events. It is, for instance, almost axiomatic now that the Organization for Security and Co-operation in Europe (OSCE) will, in the face of a political crisis in one of its member states, dispatch some sort of monitoring mission. National elections in the developing world, often being used for the first time to effect genuine and peaceful political change, will be monitored and verified by international observers. The UN Human Rights Commission continuously monitors human rights situations in a variety of countries, while international monitoring of civilian police is now an accepted part of the peacekeeping package for comprehensive peace settlements, from Cambodia to Kosovo.

But in the military sphere, too, monitoring and verification are assuming a new importance. This article will consider these aspects of military intervention. Naturally monitoring and verification can only play a role once an agreement has been reached to end armed conflict, or at least curtail it. This is not to say that monitoring and verification cannot be done while fighting is continuing, as was the experience of the OSCE's Kosovo Verification Mission (KVM) in 1998–99. However, such circumstances are not ideal and usually lead to withdrawal or pressure to re-establish or even re-negotiate from scratch the ceasefire or peace accord on which a monitoring role for outsiders is predicated.

For the purposes of monitoring and verification, this article will consider 'intervention' to be the deployment of an observer mission, peacekeeping operation or some other type of peace operation mounted by the international community or some part of it. Such a mission will be designed to help implement an agreement between warring parties, whether it be a simple ceasefire or a comprehensive peace agreement, using a mix of incentives and disincentives. The latter may include some elements of peace enforcement, either through sanctions or military action. Given such a focus, the article will *ipso facto* mostly be concerned with United Nations (UN) operations, but other multilateral peace operations will also be considered where necessary.

WHAT ARE VERIFICATION AND MONITORING?

Despite the enormous range and volume of research into peace operations that has been carried out since the early 1990s, and the increasing importance of verification and monitoring in the implementation of peace agreements, verification and monitoring remain a neglected backwater of study in the peace operations field. The conceptualization of verification and monitoring with regard to peace agreements owes more to traditional arms control theory than to thinking about conflict resolution, while the practice often owes more to standard military concepts of operations than to any innovations designed specifically with monitoring and verification in mind.

Verification is the process by which compliance with an agreement is determined. This involves using information to make a judgment about the behaviour of parties to an agreement. While such judgments are meant in theory to be impartial, verification judgments take place in a political context: they are invariably made by a political body which perforce is obliged to take into account the political implications of any verification judgment reached. Monitoring, on the other hand, is essentially the technical process of collecting information on which a verification judgment is to be made. It may be done remotely or on–site, by human beings or by technical means. It is, at least in theory, meant to be apolitical and impartial.

Verification theory posits several roles for verification. Although these were developed in the context of arms control and disarmament, mainly that dealing with nuclear, chemical and biological weapons, they are also applicable to the role of verification in peace operations. The three main roles of verification are:

(1) the detection of violations;
(2) the deterrence of potential violators; and
(3) confidence-building, including by allowing compliant states the opportunity to credibly demonstrate their compliance.

While 100 per cent verifiability of a particular agreement is rarely achievable, verification nonetheless should raise the cost of non-compliance for the violating party. It does this by increasing the risk of exposure and subsequent sanctioning, by other parties and the international community generally, and by forcing a determined violator to expend more resources in attempting and concealing a violation. Verification also serves the interests of compliant parties by providing early warning of potential or actual violations, permitting them to take precautionary steps or counter-measures, and by providing a sound legal or quasi-legal basis for undertaking unilateral or collective action against violators.

Verification and Monitoring in the Context of Peace Operations

Verification and monitoring can be applied to a whole range of elements that make up a peace implementation process, most notably electoral, human rights and civilian police aspects. However, the monitoring and verification of the military aspects of peace operations has the longest lineage of all. In particular ceasefire agreements have historically often provided for monitoring by a neutral third party. Essentially any military aspect of peace agreements can be verified, provided there is some type of accord that sets benchmarks or standards against which the behaviour of parties can be judged and verification decisions made. Oddly, even though verification judgments have frequently been made in assessing compliance with peace agreements, it is only relatively recently that the term 'verification' has been used in relation to them. There seems to have been a preference for describing peace agreements as being 'monitored', apparently because the term was perceived to have less rigorous and coercive connotations.

There are significant differences between the verification of arms control and disarmament agreements on the one hand and of peace agreements on the other. The verification of peace agreements is usually less well defined and less well organized than in the case of arms control agreements. This is particularly so in the case of arms control agreements dealing with weapons of mass destruction, where even minor breaches can have enormous strategic and political implications: verification systems are minutely negotiated and highly organized. In peace agreements, on the other hand, there is almost an expectation of imperfection, since it is recognized that during the winding down of armed conflict there is often a period of prolonged uncertainty before the situation settles down. Minor infractions are often overlooked on the grounds that they may not necessarily presage the emergence of more significant challenges to an agreement and that to over-react to them might jeopardize the continuing peace process. In the implementation of peace agreements there is often an expectation that monitoring and verification activities will not be prolonged and that therefore they can be makeshift and hence easily terminated. In arms control it is at least implicitly recognized that monitoring may be required in perpetuity. More robust systems therefore tend to be instituted. Perhaps the most crucial difference is that the monitoring and verification of peace agreements is but a small part of a larger process designed to move the status quo – the end of fighting – towards a sustainable peace. As long as the process is moving in the right direction, monitoring and verification need not be fetishized, as sometimes appears to be the case in arms control and disarmament.

Notwithstanding these differences, there are also strong similarities between the two fields of arms control/disarmament and peace agreements. Impartiality, transparency and confidence-building are *leitmotifs* of monitoring and verification in both cases. The verification of declared items is also easier in both cases than the verification of non-declared items. And finally, in both fields, monitoring and verification are devoted to discovering veracity in an essentially political context, in which allegation and counter-allegation can rapidly sour the atmosphere of trust that monitoring and verification are designed to establish and sustain.

TRADITIONAL ACTIVITIES AND NEW ROLES

The most conspicuous verification and monitoring activity, and the one most often associated with the early UN peacekeeping missions such as those in the Middle East, was the monitoring of a ceasefire line. This simply involved the stationing of peacekeepers along a line, equipped with the normal military means of surveillance and detection. As time went on fixed monitoring positions would be established. Often the whole monitoring environment would become entrenched, static and increasingly routine and neglected in terms of funding and personnel. An example is the UN Military Observer Group in India and Pakistan (UNMOGIP), which has languished in the disputed state of Jammu and Kashmir since 1949.[1] Nonetheless, the mission continues to file reports with the UN Security Council about violations of the so-called ceasefire between the two states. Another example is the UN Disengagement Observer Force (UNFOF), established in 1974, which observes the ceasefire and buffer zone between Syria and Israel.

Such monitoring missions are not only often neglected, but they are usually detached from any political processes which may be swirling around them. These missions may from time to time engage in limited local 'peace making' between local communities or among low-level military commanders or factions in addition to their monitoring activities. They may even indulge in limited peacebuilding through assisting local communities with medical support or modest aid projects. But they are essentially divorced from the larger political issues at stake. Indeed, they can often become pawns in a larger political game, as has been the fate of the inaptly named UN Interim Force in Lebanon (UNIFIL), which has been alternatively ignored, attacked or manipulated by the Israelis, the Syrians and the Lebanese and their various factions since being deployed in 1978.

The end of the Cold War, however, resulted in more peace operations, with greater complexity and size, often integrating a number of implementation tasks in one operation. Peace missions suddenly became an integral part of comprehensive peace processes rather than mere stopgap measures to allow political processes to begin. In these missions, such as those in Cambodia, Somalia, the former Yugoslavia, East Timor and Kosovo, monitoring and verification came to be part of a much larger undertaking, rather than the main undertaking. In such missions, however, monitoring and verification have paradoxically become politically more important: such means are used to determine not simply the compliance of the parties to the agreement, but the success of the mission and its progress through various stages of an evolving and complex peace process. Such a process often aims at nothing less than the re-establishment of democratic governance, the rule of law and respect for human rights. In Cambodia in 1994, for example, military observers on the Thai–Cambodia border were able to prove through their monitoring activities that the arms embargo imposed on the Cambodian parties was being violated by Thai military personnel supplying arms to the Khmer Rouge. Since Thailand was also a key party to the Paris Peace Accords on Cambodia, public exposure of Thailand risked undermining the whole peace process. The issue eventually went all the way to the UN Security Council, resulting in political pressure being applied to the Thais, mostly on a bilateral basis by the United States. Similarly, the political importance of monitoring and verification was highlighted when the UN mission, known as the UN Transitional Authority in Cambodia (UNTAC), was obliged to undertake strenuous efforts, including the dispatch of verification teams throughout the country, to verify that no Vietnamese soldiers remained there after their announced withdrawal. A failure to disprove Khmer Rouge allegations in this matter would have given credence to the guerrilla group's allegations that the peace process as a whole was stacked against them, including through the illicit presence of Vietnamese forces.

The greater importance of monitoring and verification in peace operations is due not just to a higher political salience, however, but to the heightened media attention paid to peace operations and the instantaneous transmission of information. An incident that violates or is presumed to violate a peace accord can be flashed around the world by the news media before a peace mission has had time to thoroughly investigate it and make a sober assessment of its significance. Peace missions have thus been required to improve their monitoring and verification capabilities, and their capacity to deal with alleged violations, accordingly.

Although an increasing number of aspects of peace processes overall are being subjected to monitoring and verification, military matters remain at the forefront. The military aspects of a peace process that may require monitoring and verification include:

- ceasefire/separation of forces
- withdrawal of forces
- establishment of buffer zones or demilitarized zones
- disarmament
- cantonment
- demilitarization
- demobilization
- re-integration of armed personnel into society, and
- arms embargoes.

The increasing demands on peace operations for monitoring and verification have appeared at the same time that other demands are being imposed on the military and other components of peace operations. For instance, in contrast with the Cold War period, military observers can today be involved in assisting the negotiation of accords as well as overseeing their implementation. In both Cambodia and Mozambique, UN military observers offered technical advice on the ceasefire-monitoring aspects of the peace agreement as it was being negotiated. Such involvement helps insure that monitoring and verification tasks are realistic, affordable and manageable within a given time frame. This situation is quite different to that found in the arms control and disarmament world, where implementation and verification functions, for instance within international implementation bodies, are normally kept quite distinct.

As in arms control agreements, the easiest task of monitors in peace agreements is to confirm the presence or absence of declared items or activities (for example surrendered weaponry or numbers of troops deployed along a border). It is much more difficult to verify the existence of undeclared items or activity, since it is impossible for verification to prove a negative. In Kosovo, for instance, although the Kosovo Liberation Army committed itself to surrendering all of its weaponry once the province came under UN and NATO control, in fact it has proved impossible to verify complete compliance with this undertaking. In Northern Ireland, it has proved possible to verify that a limited number of arms identified by the Irish Republican Army (IRA) and sealed in arms dumps have not been used between visits by international inspectors; but it has not proved possible to determine what proportion of the total IRA holdings this amounts to, since that has not been declared. Verification of the total amount is not therefore in prospect.

MULTI-LAYERED VERIFICATION PACKAGES

Jane Boulden has identified what she terms 'multi-layered verification packages' for military monitoring operations, in which each element has its own purpose but supports all of the others.[2] The package includes:

- observers
- information provided by the parties (baseline data)
- inspections to confirm the accuracy of information (baseline inspections)
- data provided by outside parties

- ongoing inspections
- patrols and observation in the case of ceasefires and agreed troop levels or positions
- aerial surveillance
- other remote monitoring, including by automatic sensors
- a joint commission process.

Such 'packages' include a chain of command for dealing with reported and alleged violations. Violations that are sufficiently serious and which cannot be handled in the field are usually reported to field headquarters, both to the military commander and the representative of the UN Secretary-General or other 'political' representative in the case of non-UN missions. Often some type of liaison body, or joint commission comprising representatives of the parties to the conflict as well as of the mission, will have been established to handle allegations of non-compliance. In Cambodia this was called a Military Mixed Commission. However, it may also be a civilian body, such as the so-called Security Committee established in Somalia by the US Special Envoy to Somalia, Robert Oakley, during the US-led United Task Force (UNITAF) intervention in 1994–95.

If violations are serious and persistent, UN headquarters in New York and the UN Secretary-General will be notified. Political pressure may then be applied to the party or parties concerned. If this fails to rectify the situation, the Secretary-General may report to the Security Council, which could take appropriate action, such as imposing sanctions. In any event, the Council is kept informed of all notable violations through regular reports by the Secretary-General on the progress of each peace operation in the field.

Military Observers (MilObs) tend to be the backbone of monitoring and verification tasks in respect of peace accords. They are usually unarmed and may or may not be in military uniform. They may be deployed and organized separately from regular peacekeeping contingents deployed in the same theatre contemporaneously. In this way they maintain their separate identity, which can be seen as enhancing their impartiality. A military observer force often comprises individual military officers from a wide variety of nations. Many of the problems encountered by military observers in the field reflect those of civilian police monitors. They lack the level of military support that fielded battalions of peacekeepers have, their chain of command is usually less robust and they are often deployed in remote locations. They are also vulnerable to attack, hostage-taking, harassment, and, perhaps surprisingly, boredom. Since they are forward-deployed, often unarmed, they represent a vulnerable target to warring factions wishing to put pressure on a peace operation as a whole, as happened in Bosnia during the deployment of the UN Protection Force (UNPROFOR) in the mid-1990s.

The increasing use of force in peace operations, both by parties to the conflict and by the military component of peace operations, can have a profound effect on the monitoring and verification environment. The substantial use of force can render monitoring and verification activities completely useless (because conditions are changing too quickly) or impossible (because access is completely denied). The parties to conflicts may be unable or unwilling to distinguish between military observers and normal peacekeeping troops, regarding them all as part of the UN 'machine'. Military observers are liable to be taken hostage or killed, as in Sierra Leone and Bosnia. They are more vulnerable even than lightly armed peacekeepers because they are unarmed and often deployed in small numbers in remote locations. States have increasingly proved unwilling to provide military observers to UN missions as a result of the apparently increased dangers being faced. Providing military protection for MilObs would draw resources away from other peacekeeping tasks or require larger deployments of armed peacekeepers. While technology may be able to supplant or supplement some of the monitoring functions of human observers, thereby lessening the element of danger, they are unlikely to ever be entirely replaced.

Aside from military observers on the ground, naval and air forces are increasingly being used in monitoring and verification tasks. For example, naval forces helped monitor the arms embargo imposed on the states of the former Yugoslavia.[3] In the case of the UN Special Commission (UNSCOM) for Iraq, which for several years monitored Iraqi compliance with a key aspect of the Gulf War ceasefire agreement – Iraq's pledge to dismantle its weapons of mass destruction capabilities – the US Air Force actually loaned a U2 aircraft to the monitoring body to assist in its verification effort. The acquisition by an international body of such a powerful monitoring tool was unprecedented.

Less powerful but nonetheless significant air monitoring capabilities are envisaged under the 1992 Open Skies Agreement. The agreement, which is likely to come into force in the near future, opens the entire territory of each state party to aerial observation by any other state party, using unarmed fixed-wing aircraft with an agreed suite of sensors and fixed imagery resolutions.[4] Day and night capability is available. In addition to using such capabilities for monitoring compliance with arms control and disarmament agreements, Open Skies can also be used to monitor peace agreements involving the parties. Although the sensor resolutions have been set to permit detection and identification of heavy conventional weaponry, such as tanks, helicopters and artillery pieces, they could also detect large-scale troop movements. In addition to the 25 European states that negotiated the treaty, Open Skies is currently open to any former Soviet state that did not participate in the negotiations and, after it enters into force, any member of the OSCE. In future any state may apply to the Open Skies Consultative Commission to join.

Since monitoring is essentially the gathering of information, it has some similarities with intelligence-gathering. Traditionally, the UN and other international bodies have officially been averse to intelligence-gathering to support their verification functions. However, the UN has often collected information surreptitiously and unofficially, as in the case of its peacekeeping mission in the Congo in the 1960s, or relied on national contingents to provide the necessary information. Increasingly it is being recognized by the UN that intelligence information, whether it calls it that or not, is essential in the most difficult monitoring cases, such as that of Iraq. Quite apart from helping ensure the safety of its personnel, intelligence information can immeasurably bolster the UN's credibility in determining compliance with a peace agreement.

Yet there remain continuing dilemmas over the UN's use of intelligence information and its involvement in collecting it, especially with regard to the tension between the UN's advocacy of transparency versus the requirement for secrecy in intelligence-gathering. Since peace operations are designed to increase the confidence of the parties involved that the implementation of a peace process is proceeding fairly and effectively, particularly by encouraging transparency in military matters, it would appear to be counterproductive for the UN to be gathering and using secret information. The UN in any event often lacks competent personnel to interpret intelligence information, especially that which may be foisted on it by a party with its own agenda. It may, moreover, be impossible to use secret information for verification purposes, since a decision on non-compliance has to be based on information that can be released. A determination that a party is in serious breach of its obligations needs to be shown to be just and safe in the court of international opinion.

TECHNOLOGY

It is surprising, perhaps, given the capacity of new technologies, that the monitoring and verification of the military aspects of peace operations is still so dependent on the humble human observer. Apart from improved military surveillance capabilities which come with national troop contingents (for example night vision goggles and better communications), there has been little recognition that technology may play a larger, more systematic role in co-operative multilateral verification missions. One notable exception is the long-standing non-UN mission in the Sinai, the Multilateral Force and Observers (MFO), which from its inception in 1982 has used relatively high technology, including ground sensors and aerial imagery, for monitoring and verification purposes.

One might imagine a number of ways in which technology could help improve monitoring and verification of the military aspects of peace missions in the future:

- the use of satellite reconnaissance with increasingly sophisticated sensors and improved resolution (commercial satellites are supplying information comparable to that of the early military satellites, at low cost and to any customer)[5]
- manned or unmanned overflights either at high altitudes, using such aircraft as the U-2 used by UNSCOM, at lower levels using such craft as the US Global Hawk unmanned vehicle, or better still, the cheap microcraft which are currently under development[6]
- ground sensors and automatic sentries, linked to monitoring centres, which can help reduce the number of ground troops needed[7]
- information technology (IT), including data fusion techniques
- use of the Global Position System (GPS), which is no longer subject to signal degradation by the US military, to pinpoint monitoring stations, objects of observation and violations more accurately[8]
- electronic communications, including the Internet, email and mobile telephony, to speed the monitoring process, the verification decision-making process and the implementation of compliance measures
- hand-held detectors for detecting and monitoring landmines,

    unexploded ordnance and chemical and biological warfare agents
•   underground radar to detect hidden caches of weapons.[9]

There are several drawbacks for UN and other multilateral forces in attempting to deploy and successfully use new monitoring and verification technologies. First, it can be expensive, although the cost of new technology often declines rapidly once it becomes widely available. Second, expert training is needed to permit personnel to use advanced technology, especially when troops are drawn from a wide variety of countries and military backgrounds. In UN operations training is often seriously lacking even for conventional military tasks. Third, new technology may produce information overload, overwhelming the capacity of missions in the field to successfully use the information that becomes available. Peace missions will need to invest in analytical capabilities as well as data–gathering ones. Fourth, technology may come to be deployed and used for its own sake, rather than as a useful adjunct to human capabilities. Technology may not be as flexible or creative as human monitors, who can be readily switched to different tasks, who may notice activities for which they are not programmed and who will understand the subtleties of situations better.

MONITORING THE MONITORS – REGIONAL PEACE OPS WITH A UN OVERSIGHT MISSION

There have now been several instances in which regional peacekeeping operations have been monitored by small UN monitoring missions to ensure that they fulfil their mandate properly and act according to agreed peacekeeping procedures and standards. The regional missions are invariably dominated by their military component and military tasks, rather than the full range of personnel and activities found in comprehensive UN missions. Hence these are mostly cases of (UN) military personnel observing the activities of other (regional) military personnel. One of the most prominent and controversial examples to date has been the UN Observer Mission in Liberia (UNOMIL), which from 1993 to 1997 observed the troubled peacekeeping operation mounted by a regional organization, the Economic Community of West African States (ECOWAS). Another example is the UN Mission of Observers in Tajikistan (UNMOT), which to this day monitors the activities of a peacekeeping mission fielded by the Commonwealth of

Independent States (CIS). These are difficult undertakings, since regional organizations are often dominated by a local hegemon – Nigeria and Russia in the aforementioned cases – making the regional operations less multilateral than the UN would normally countenance. The regional operation is thus invariably less impartial and more subject to national political and military agendas than a pure UN operation. While the presence of another monitoring mission, fielded by the UN, may add an extra layer of complexity to what might already be a complex monitoring environment, by 'monitoring the monitors' such UN missions can be a cost-effective use of limited UN resources. The alternative may be the deployment of a full-scale UN mission.

CONCLUSION

Monitoring and verification are playing increasingly important roles in the military aspects of peace operations. As comprehensive efforts are made to resolve armed conflict through substantial peace operations, so it becomes more necessary to ensure that compliance difficulties do not jeopardize the large investment that the international community is obliged to make. Despite their increased importance, however, the basic concepts behind monitoring and verification have remained the same over the past decade. Like peacekeeping in general, monitoring missions always start from scratch, they are assembled piece by piece using voluntary contributions and they rarely have sufficient human or financial resources to undertake their mission effectively and efficiently. They tend to be low-technology operations, reliant on the unarmed, often untrained, military observer for their effectiveness. This can no longer be acceptable in situations where the stakes in achieving a successful conflict resolution outcome are so high. Hence there is a need for professionalization, training, lessons-learned activities, centres of excellence, the drafting of operational manuals and concepts of operation, and the use of appropriate technology. There is also a need for the yawning gap in academic studies to be filled and the issues of verification and monitoring to be placed higher on the research agenda.

NOTES

1.   A. Blixt, *Kashmir's Forgotten Guardians: United Nations Military Observer Group in India and Pakistan* (Stockholm: SWEDINT, 1994).

2. J. Boulden, 'Monitoring and Verifying the Military Aspects of Peace Accords', in *Verification Yearbook 2000* (London: Verification Research, Training and Information Centre (VERTIC) 2000), pp.175–6.
3. See J. Ginifer, 'The UN at Sea? The New Relevance of Maritime Operations', *International Peacekeeping*, Vol.1, No.3 (Autumn 1994), pp.320–35.
4. See M. D. Miggins, 'Whatever Happened to Open Skies?', *Trust & Verify*, No.91 (May 2000), pp.5–6.
5. See B. Jasani, 'Remote Monitoring from Space', in *Verification Yearbook 2000*, (London: Verification Research, Training and Information Centre (VERTIC) 2000), pp.200–213. The US government in December 2000 licensed a Colorado company, Space Imaging, to sell extremely high-resolution photographs to customers worldwide, effectively relinquishing the monopoly that the intelligence agencies previously had over precision imagery from space, *International Herald Tribune*, 18 Dec. 2000, p.3.
6. See 'Backpack drone that sees behind enemy lines', *New Scientist*, 21 Oct. 2000, p.10.
7. See report on British research into remote sentries in H. McManners, *The Times* (London), 4 Oct. 1998, p.8.
8. US President Bill Clinton announced on 1 May 2000 that the US had switched off the built-in error signal – called Selective Availability – in the GPS. This makes the system 10 times more accurate for all users. The US maintains the ability to deny access to GPS in future if it believes that US national security is threatened. See 'Getting a Better Fix', *New Scientist*, 6 May 2000, p.5 and Statement by the President Regarding the United States Decision to Stop Degrading Global Positioning System Accuracy, White House Press Release, 1 May 2000.
9. B. Bender, 'Radar Breakthrough Could Help DoD "See" Underground', *Jane's Defence Weekly*, 22 Dec. 1999, p.8.

Bosnia and Kosovo: Interpreting the Gender Dimensions of International Intervention

JAYNE RODGERS

This contribution builds upon an article on gender and intervention in Bosnia published in 1998.[1] In that article I argued that intervention in Bosnia was, as in other post–Cold War conflicts to that point, based on principles of territoriality rather than upon humanitarian concerns. In effect, the international community based its decisions on intervention on traditional principles of state sovereignty and inter-state conflict which were of little, if any, relevance to the intra-state war in Bosnia. One of the main criticisms of the position outlined in that article was that abuses of the human rights of women were largely ignored and were not, therefore, treated as relevant criteria for intervention. The suggestion made was that human rights abuses, and in particular crimes of sexual violence against women, were subsumed to a 'state-strategist' agenda. The general picture presented in the article was one of dismay at the lack of regard paid to human rights abuses, tinged with optimism regarding the ways criteria for intervention could and should be developed to incorporate feminist agendas. This optimism was based on the apparently increasing interest of some governments and international organizations in the humanitarian dimensions of intervention.

Moving on from those arguments, and in response to the 1999 NATO campaign in Kosovo, this article suggests that there is a fundamental feminist dilemma at the heart of debates on the ethics of intervention. The concern lies in the difficulties of promoting a feminist agenda for acceptance by a male-dominated, masculinist and militaristic international community whilst also taking into account the unique local gender constructions that must be acknowledged in any decision on intervention. The main premise of this article is that it is not sufficient to persuade organizations such as NATO and the UN, and powerful states such as the US and Russia, to recognize the gendered aspects of conflict, important though this is. The key question is reflected back to feminists: how can we promote feminist criteria on intervention to the *international* community while respecting the needs and cultural diversity of *local* communities? In the case of Kosovo, we need to ask how feminist calls for equality and non-discrimination can be reconciled with the extremely patriarchal construction of gender relations among Kosovar Albanians.

Specific constructions of gender and nationalism create localized differences which the international community has limited mechanisms for addressing. This issue is exemplified in the very specific constructions of gender and nationalism which the Serb–Kosovar relationship over centuries has engendered. It is the very specificity of such constructions which poses problems of universalism and particularism for feminists: the recognition and punishment of crimes of sexual violence is a fundamental element of feminist conceptions of justice, while the gender relationships of nationalist communities may militate against debate about such acts.

To situate this issue in context, this article will examine some of the arguments posed in the initial article on Bosnia, to draw out the strengths and weaknesses of the position taken therein. The questions of universalism and particularism which feminists thought they had resolved long ago[2] have, the article suggests, a renewed relevance in an age where internal conflicts are increasingly seen by the international community as falling within their area of responsibility. The article will therefore address how different constructions of gender and national identities may require the acknowledgement and acceptance of cultural differences that may be anathema to some feminists.

The article concludes by arguing that there are two dominant perspectives on advancing a feminist ethics of intervention, but that neither of these is particularly satisfactory at present. The first would be to accept that some forms of sexual violence will, given local constructions of gender and nationalism, go unpunished. That is, the threat of retribution and exclusion of raped women by their own community may be too high a price to pay for the punishment of rapists. The second, the proposal of flexible, feminist-friendly approaches to the ethics of intervention, cannot at present be accommodated by a slow-moving, highly bureaucratized and still largely state-centric international security system.

THE CONCEPT OF INTERVENTION

We need first to address what intervention is and why it is undertaken. Although the concept is clear to most scholars of international relations, it is useful to address the differences between intervention in Bosnia and Kosovo in order to establish a context for the feminist debates that follow. For Weiss 'intervention is not a single phenomenon. It is generally understood as constituting the spectrum of possible actions *intended to alter internal affairs elsewhere*' (emphasis added).[3] As far as *military* intervention is concerned, the basis for action has traditionally operated according to very restrictive codes of conduct. Although the ethics of intervention have been widely discussed, the acceptable reasons for undertaking military activity inside a sovereign state have been subject to the international norm of state autonomy. That is, states have the right to conduct themselves as they please within the confines of their own borders, with self-determination for nationalist groups running a poor second to governmental authority. For this reason, altering the internal affairs of a state through military intervention has not, as a rule, been a popular choice for the leaders of major states, and other tactics such as diplomacy, sanctions and embargoes have been preferred as a means of demonstrating approbation.

When fighting broke out in Bosnia the international community was confronted with a conflict where it was difficult to identify clearly either territorial violations or the 'real' victims. In addition, the rhetoric of the 'new world order' which was heralded at the start of the 1990s still dominated the agendas of both political practitioners and theorists as the conflicts began. As a consequence, the codes of ethics and responsibility which the international community should have applied to the conflicts were unclear, as the usual norms of territorial invasion did not apply and the notion of human rights abuse as a punishable offence under international humanitarian law was not yet adequately established. It has been widely argued, of course, that intervention in Bosnia came too late and failed to offer any real security to civilians in the region. As it was the first large-scale internal conflict following the end of the Cold War, there was no convenient precedent for international organizations to follow and there was an absence of both mandate and experience in a structure designed to handle inter-state conflicts. While the EU floundered as it tried to establish authority over negotiations in the region, key players in the UN and NATO, still regrouping (almost literally) following the Gulf War, were keen to avoid entanglement in what was viewed from outside as an essentially European problem.

No one can make the same claims of indecision in respect of the Kosovo intervention. However one views the merits of the action taken and the motives of the parties to intervention, there was a clear and obvious contrast between the degree of confusion over international reaction to the Bosnian conflicts and the determined approach to the Kosovo crisis. In this sense, international organizations moved from the position of seeing intra-state conflict as a purely internal affair towards a stance where violation of human rights could be viewed as a moral concern extending beyond state borders.[4] The international community, through the auspices of NATO, adopted the human rights of Kosovar Albanians as the guiding principle for action.[5] As Julie Mertus has argued, the principles of 'territorial integrity' and 'human rights' need not conflict: the former cannot be had without the latter and the realization of human rights can support the integrity of territory.[6]

The NATO response to the crisis in Kosovo signalled a massive shift in interpretations of international humanitarian law and led to the first violation of state sovereignty by NATO in its 50-year history. This suggested that the code of ethics which international organizations apply has undergone something of a sea-change, with territorial integrity no longer viewed as the defining conceptual boundary against intervention.

Primarily a critical examination of political practice and theorizing on intervention, the article on Bosnia outlined three key arguments: that the international community largely ignored human rights abuses on the ground (and gendered abuses in particular); that humanitarian issues were given less consideration than territorial divisions; and that it would be necessary to assess the needs of local communities before intervention is undertaken in future conflicts. Many would argue that NATO intervention in Kosovo addressed all of these concerns, in that the humanitarian crisis was met with a military response apparently designed to relieve the suffering of oppressed peoples.

What such claims would fail to address, however, is the degree to which the intervention is conducted by *external* actors, working to criteria which *they* have established. That is, although the reasons given for intervention may have changed to accommodate human rights violations, the interpretations of such violations were based on much the same conceptualizations of conflict as the traditional, state-centric ones.

The genocide and population transfers of the Kosovar Albanian population essentially related as much to claims to territory as to issues of ethnicity. In deference to age-old assertions of political might, in 'reclaiming' Kosovo the Serb authorities aimed to demonstrate their power over the people in the region.

In this sense, although international intervention in Kosovo may have been about righting human wrongs, it was also about countering the resurgence of the Milosevic regime. In addition, for both the Yugoslav authorities and the international community, Kosovo represented the unfinished business of the Bosnian wars. Milosevic rose to power in the late 1980s on an anti-Albanian nationalist ticket and neither he nor Western leaders had fully addressed the Kosovo problem in the Dayton Accords or during the ensuing period of reconstruction in the former Yugoslavia. So, although human rights concerns provided the justification for action, territory and its governance remained the underlying concern. It would be useful here to examine briefly some of the differences between gender relations in Bosnia and Kosovo, as this gives some insight into the environment which interventionist organizations entered.

SEXUAL VIOLENCE IN BOSNIA AND KOSOVO

One of the obvious differences in comparing the gender relations in Bosnia and Kosovo lies in the nature of inter-ethnic relations in the two regions. Although nationalist sentiments ran high on all sides as the Bosnian wars developed, prior to the conflict the province was the most racially integrated of the six Yugoslav republics, with around two million people (both spouses and children) from ethnically mixed marriages.[7] For women in Bosnia prior to the break-up of Yugoslavia, nationalism played only a limited role in the construction of gender identity.[8]

The survival of the Kosovar Albanian nation has, by contrast, depended upon the construction of a single national identity, built over centuries in direct contrast to Serb national identity. Mertus notes that the way gender has been constructed in Kosovo has helped solidify a particular Albanian identity which is unique to the powerful oppressor.[9] This creation of a unified conception of 'the nation' has had a clear impact on the ways in which gender identity has evolved, as the survival of the nation has demanded very specific gender roles. In this situation, the interests of the nation take precedence over the interests of women

as individuals. One of the outcomes in this particular case has been the
development of an extremely patriarchal society, where women, most
notably those in the rural communities, have been viewed as wives and
homemakers, with few rights as individuals.

Hansen has argued that in such circumstances a dual construction of
identity is evident, with both a gendered construction of national
identities and a nationalized construction of gendered identities
occurring.[10] Here, gender is both based upon and informed by the
concept of nation. In each case, the rights of women take second place to
the fight for the nation and this has important implications for the ways
Kosovar Albanians have portrayed their struggles to the outside world.
In turn, of course, this affects the ways the outside world may respond
to internal strife.

Through the identification of the struggle for nationhood as the
dominant feature of Kosovar community, relationships between the local
population and the international community have been framed by a
limited and fairly specific vision of how that nation should be
constituted. Atrocities committed by Serb forces[11] against Albanian
women in Kosovo have, as a consequence, been given fairly limited
coverage, particularly in comparison with the publicity surrounding
such acts in Bosnia. Rape as a war crime is not incidental; it is a
calculated feature of ethnic cleansing and the destruction of enemy
morale. 'It routinely serves a strategic function in war and acts as an
integral tool for achieving particular military objectives.'[12] The brutal
and systematic rapes in Kosovo followed a pattern established in Bosnia
and there was a concerted effort on the part of Serb forces to 'taint' the
ethnic stock of the Albanians.[13]

It is not unusual in any society for women to feel a reluctance to
report rape. A woman's experience of rape is almost always one of
extreme psychological trauma and the legal requirement for proof
militates against conviction in most cases. In Kosovo, however, to
highlight women's rights is to undermine the patriarchal system.
Consequently, to produce testimonies of widespread sexual violence and
torture is to betray the very nation women as well as men are seeking to
liberate. Dominique Serrano's report for the United Nations Population
Fund suggests that many of the women raped in Kosovo are willing to
talk about their experiences but only under conditions of strict
anonymity.[14] Many fear the risk of divorce or exclusion from their
community or family, and many others suggest that they will never

discuss what has happened to them in order to protect themselves and their families, either from the revenge of the perpetrators or from the consequences of reprisals by their own partners.

A mass of disturbing evidence on the crimes of sexual violence committed in Kosovo is beginning to emerge. The figures are inevitably confused, largely because women are reluctant to talk of their experience but also partly because of the likelihood that many raped women were then murdered.[15] Estimates vary from the low hundreds to 20,000.[16] Evidence suggest that sexual violence escalated following the onset of NATO's bombing campaign, with three standard venues for rape: in public, as women fled in refugee convoys, in women's homes and in abandoned buildings. The acts were often committed in front of large numbers of people and women were frequently subject to other acts of abuse.[17]

There is a strong sense that many women in Kosovo are avoiding discussion of rape and crimes of sexual violence committed against them during the recent conflicts. Given the strength of ethnic solidarity among the Albanian population in Kosovo, to admit sexual abuse by the 'enemy' is to undermine the solidarity of the national group, to risk rejection and to foreground gender identity over national identity. In addition, the cultural taboo associated with rape means that many women feel ashamed to admit that such acts have been committed against them. Serrano even found reluctance among medical personnel to discuss incidents of rape among the Kosovar refugees.

RAPE AS A WAR CRIME

As Cynthia Cockburn has noted, women have always known that rape is an endemic and not an incidental feature of war.[18] In order to overcome difficulties experienced in ending the appalling history of impunity for rape and other gendered war crimes, rape in conflict must be understood as an abuse that targets women for political and strategic reasons. One of the main problems which has been faced in promoting feminist agendas on intervention has been the legal framework which the international community applies to war crimes. In particular, the system has an inherent requirement to testimony and visibility: women who have been subject to sexual violence are required to provide evidence to international courts or to their representatives.

The body of law which can be applied in this area has grown in recent years, and the *opportunity* for women to bring action against the perpetrators of crimes against them has risen accordingly. That said, the processes relating to prosecution are complex and there has been very little success to date in convicting criminals from the Bosnian conflicts. Human Rights Watch has identified the following aspects of international humanitarian law[19] as relevant to the issue of rape as a war crime. Firstly, acts of sexual violence in internal armed conflicts are forbidden. Common Article 3 of the 1949 Geneva Conventions prohibits 'violence to life and person', 'cruel treatment', 'torture' or 'other outrages upon personal dignity'. Protocol II Additional to the 1949 Geneva Conventions, governing the protection of civilians in internal armed conflicts, explicitly outlaws 'outrages upon personal dignity, in particular humiliating and degrading treatment, rape, enforced prostitution and any form of indecent assault' at Article 4(2)(e). These violations have been made criminal offences under the statute of the International Criminal Tribunal for Rwanda (ICTR). Similarly, the statute of the International Criminal Tribunal for the Former Yugoslavia (ICTY) lists 'torture or inhuman treatment' and 'wilfully causing great suffering or serious injury to body or health'.

Secondly, a single rape can be a war crime: it is not necessary to find that rape and sexual violence take place systematically or on a wide scale in order to prosecute the perpetrators. Just as a single case of murder of a civilian can be prosecuted, so too can a single rape. Where acts of sexual violence are widespread, they may also constitute a crime against humanity.

Thirdly, sexual violence can be viewed under international humanitarian law as a crime against humanity. Widespread or systematic commission of acts of sexual violence may also be prosecuted as crimes against humanity, regardless of whether such acts take place in the context of war or peace. Crimes against humanity include acts such as murder, torture, enslavement, imprisonment, rape or other inhumane acts when committed systematically or on a mass scale against civilians.

Finally, sexual violence may be considered to be a form of torture in some circumstances: even where the statutory definitions of war crimes or crimes against humanity do not explicitly specify rape or other sexual assaults, they are typically understood to be acts of torture and inhuman treatment. As such, they can be charged as grave breaches of the laws of war, as war crimes or as crimes against humanity.

All this, of course, is grist to the mill of feminists and enables us to see the extent to which feminist agendas have influenced the workings of the international community. The legal framework within which such acts are prosecuted, however, places the responsibility for dealing with the issue of rape squarely on the shoulders of women: provide testimony and (possibly) achieve justice. Within the international legal system, to say nothing is not an option. It is possible to argue therefore that it is necessary to define rape and other abuses of women more directly in political terms – that is, as part of the strategy of war and potentially subject to intervention criteria. This would allow for the prosecution of rape without the automatic need for women's testimonies. In addition, this mechanism would permit the inclusion of rape and other crimes of sexual violence on evolving intervention agendas. As a political, rather than a legal, issue, rape would thus fall into the human rights category which the international community appears keen to use as a justification for intervention.

There are two problems with adopting this strategy though. Firstly, political and military criteria are not always compatible; what politicians want may not always be what the military can, or want to, provide. There are some very complex issues which arise when we consider asking soldiers to prevent other soldiers from committing acts of violence against women. Male soldiers, whether allies or enemies, do not live in gender-free environments. On the one hand they invariably work within male-dominated, heterosexual (whether real or imagined) organizations, whilst on the other they are sons, brothers, husbands and fathers.

Secondly, and perhaps most pertinently for this article, looking for political solutions does not resolve the problem of identifying ways of promoting flexible feminist agendas which are responsive to cultural difference. Even if gendered war crimes are included on political agendas as a potential criteria for intervention, feminists will still be caught in a conflict between international and local value systems. In effect, feminists need to decide whether they wish to defend a broad conceptualization of women's human rights or to accept that some cultural contexts will fall outside of Western feminist ideas on fairness and justice.

These issues can be understood most clearly by a return to discussion of the conflict in Kosovo. Internally, states have responsibility for collective security of citizens. Yugoslavia clearly was not protecting the security of Kosovar Albanians throughout 1998 and into 1999.[20] State violence against the Albanian population in Kosovo had the effect of consolidating their sense of otherness, leading them in turn to deepen their own notions of collective security and 'alter-nationalism'. This alter-nationalism was based both on the fear of physical harm and on the cultural norms of the Albanian community. This concept reflects not simply a nationalist ideal on the part of Kosovar Albanians but is based also on opposition to real and imagined oppression by Serbs. To a significant degree, the characteristics of Kosovar Albanian nationalism are based on their 'non-Serbian' nature, rather than upon specifically Albanian traditions. As is evident from the action taken by the international community, the first of these concerns – physical threat – can be dealt with where the call exists through sanctions, diplomacy and ultimately through military action.

Cultural norms, however, are beyond the remit or imagination of any of the major international institutions as they are currently structured. That is, where it is just about possible to imagine a situation where intervening states or organizations would use crimes of sexual violence as a determining factor in future interventions, it is impossible at present to believe that local considerations as to the ways these crimes should be treated could be taken into account. Laura Reanda's overview into the glacial pace of change at the UN offers an insight into the problems involved in updating the agendas of these organizations,[21] while the long-running debate on the expansion of NATO illustrates the difficulties of reaching agreement on shared interests where military security is at stake.

The difficulties involved in achieving organizational change both at the macro level and within internal bureaucracies indicate that, where difference needs to be accounted for, the international community simply cannot operate effectively. Thus, where it is feasible to imagine future interventions based on rape as a war crime, it is, for this author, hard to believe that the sensitivities of local communities regarding how to treat the victims and perpetrators of these crimes can be adequately addressed.

CONCLUSION

On the one hand, although the implementation of the body of law relating to crimes of sexual violence has been more rigorous in recent years, there are two key problems for feminists in interpreting the international and local dynamics relating to such crimes. Firstly, the requirement for personal testimony rather than other forms of evidence discriminates against women whose culture will not permit open discussion of such violations. In peacetime, rape is usually a hidden crime and it is incumbent upon victims to prove the veracity of their accounts. The international legal system reflects this requirement and expects testimony from rape victims. In cases of conflict, however, eyewitness accounts of rape are often available. Indeed, part of the strategic logic of rape as a war crime is to make visible the violation of women as the 'property' of the enemy. The visibility of such acts during civil conflict should render the need for women to relate their ordeals unnecessary in many instances. The need for witness protection programmes is also evident: at present neither rape victims nor those who testify on their behalf receive any form of protection from possible reprisals.

Secondly, although the *legal* system has moved towards recognition of gendered crimes, there remains a profoundly gender-blind body of legislation relating to *military* intervention. In effect, decisions on intervention at state and institutional level, though apparently now paying some attention to human rights abuses, show little concern for gendered war crimes and there is no case to date of such crimes being applied as criteria for action by the international community. This is not to detract from the work of the ICTY in bringing rapists to justice (few though these cases have been). It should be noted that legal action comes after the fact and that mechanisms to prevent crimes of sexual violence during conflict and/or before intervention are entirely absent from the agendas of the international community. In this vein, too, there is little evidence to indicate that commanders of forces which perpetrate such crimes will be held accountable for the actions of individual soldiers.

The simple response, of course, is to argue the need for feminists to lobby the UN, ICRC, and other IOs and NGOs active in conflict regions and involved in decision-making to promote gender issues onto international agendas. This would be an important step towards recognition of gendered war crimes on both political and military agendas. It is not enough, however, simply to call for feminist concerns to be acknowledged by the international community. This is important but the real problem needs to be addressed by feminists themselves, particularly those who have assumed that the universalist–particularist debate is no longer an issue.

In the case of gendered war crimes, feminists face the dilemma of not only acknowledging but also accepting difference, even where such difference may appear at odds with the rights of women. In the case of Kosovo, this may mean accepting that a patriarchal and, to Western eyes, discriminatory system is the reality within which many Kosovar Albanian women live. It is possible to promote a universalist feminist position where issues such as rape as a war crime must be included in overview of conflict, in international legal, political *and* military systems. This, however, could actually cause greater damage in the long term to women like the Kosovar Albanians whose cultural norms frequently call for the rejection of women who have been sexually violated. The social stigma and near impossibility of earning a living for women ostracized by their families in a system with little or no welfare service may be too high a price to pay for Western conceptions of 'justice'.

Feminists have the option of promoting a particularist position, where acknowledgement of all of the myriad cultural contexts of gendered abuses can be expected. To seek such a flexibility from international organizations within the current system stands little chance of success. Where the gender dimensions of war are ignored at structural level, expecting women's rights to be first acknowledged and then contextualized seems something of a long shot.

NOTES

1. Jayne Rodgers, 'Bosnia, Gender and the Ethics of Intervention in Civil Wars', *Civil Wars*, Vol.1, No.1 (Spring 1998), pp.103–16.
2. Debates on universalism and particularism were a staple of feminist discussion during the 1980s. Western feminists were criticized for an imperialistic approach to the defining of women's rights and needs. There is now a broad acceptance that the needs of particular groups of women cannot be subsumed to a universal feminist agenda, but that a range of 'feminisms' is more appropriate.
3. Thomas G. Weiss, 'The United Nations and Civil Wars at the Dawn of the Twenty-First Century', in Thomas G. Weiss (ed.), *The United Nations and Civil Wars* (Boulder, CO and London: Lynne Reinner 1993), p.199.
4. The Kosovo conflict was, of course, subject to more 'spin' than any other in living memory, so it is sometimes very hard to interpret the basis on which decisions were made. See 'The Media and the Kosovo Conflict', *European Journal of Communications Special Edition*, Vol.15, No.3 (2000).
5. Even if we accept the view that the adoption of humanitarian principles was a smokescreen for ulterior motives, there is little doubt that the principle is now accepted as adequate justification for action on the part of many governments and citizens.
6. Julie Mertus, 'Beyond Kosovo: Evaluating the NATO Intervention', paper presented at ISA 2000 Convention, Los Angeles, March 2000, p.6.
7. See Maja Korac, 'Understanding Ethnic–National Identity and its Meaning – Questions from Women's Experience', *Women's Studies International Forum*, Vol.19, No.1-2, p.133.
8. For discussion of gender constructions in the Balkans see Sabrina P. Ramet (ed.), *Gender Politics in the Balkans – Women & Society in Yugoslavia and the Yugoslav Successor States* (University Park, PA: Pennsylvania State UP, 1999).

9. Julie Mertus, 'Women in Kosovo: Contested Terrains – The Role of National Identity in Shaping and Challenging Gender Identity', in Ramet, *Gender Politics in the Balkans*, pp.171–86.
10. Lene Hansen, 'Gender, Nation, Power: Bosnia and the Construction of Security', paper presented at the BISA Annual Conference, University of Sussex, Dec. 1998.
11. This refers to both serving troops and paramilitaries. See http://www.hrw.org/reports/2000/fyr/kosovo
12. Dorothy G. Thomas and Regan E. Ralph, 'Rape in War: The Case of Bosnia', in Ramet (ed.), *Gender Politics in the Balkans*, p.206.
13. Human Rights Watch have comprehensive reports on rape and other gendered war crimes in Kosovo, compiled from both their own research and that of other organizations in the region. See http//www.hrw.org/reports/2000/fry/kosovo03.htm
14. http://www.unfpa.org/news/pressroom/1999/kosovo-report.doc
15. At present, there is no requirement for war crimes investigators to examine women's bodies for evidence of rape or sexual abuse. See http://www.unfpa.org/news/pressroom/1999/kosovo-report.doc
16. See Helena Smith, 'Revealed: the cruel fate of war's rape babies', *The Observer*, 16 April 2000, pp.1, 8, 9.
17. http//www.hrw.org/reports/2000/fry/kosovo03.htm
18. Cynthia Cockburn, *The Space Between Us – Negotiating Gender and National Identities in Conflict* (London/New York: Zed Books, 1998).
19. http://www.hrw.org/reports/2000/fry/kosovo
20. Indeed, Kosovar Albanians had suffered discrimination at the hands of the Serb authorities for decades, some would argue centuries. See Miranda Vickers, *Between Serb and Albanian – A History of Kosovo* (London: Hurst & Company, 1998) and Julie A. Mertus, *Kosovo, How Myths and Truths Started a War* (Berkeley/Los Angeles/London: University of California Press, 1999).
21. Laura Reanda, 'Engendering the United Nations – The Changing International Agenda', *European Journal of Women's Studies*, Vol.6 (1999), pp.49–68.

Abstracts

Introduction: The Political and Moral Limits of Western Military Intervention to Protect Civilians in Danger
by Nicholas J. Wheeler

Although in many respects the wars of the 1990s are not as new as is sometimes suggested, what is new is the complete breakdown of traditional state structures resulting in complex emergencies. What is also new is that the language of a threat to 'international peace and security' has been stretched from its traditional inter-state referent to encompass the protection of civilians, leading to calls for international action in response. The article describes how the various contributions to this volume help us understand Western reaction to these emergencies.

Fatal Attraction? Air Power and the West *by Colin McInnes*

This article identifies why air power has proved attractive to the West. But this does not mean that air power is unproblematic. In particular precision guidance does not mean a 'bloodless war', while there is still insufficient evidence to demonstrate that air power can successfully act alone. The manner in which air power is used is also subject to debate, particularly between strategic and theatre strikes. The issue of how best to use air power for coercive purposes, and even the viability of coercion, also remain subject to debate.

The RMA and Intervention: A Sceptical View *by Colin S. Gray*

Much of the West's contemporary willingness to intervene in foreign quarrels is highly contingent on a very demanding set of military expectations keyed to zero–low friendly casualties. An information RMA appears to enable advanced militaries to wage war (including intervention in others' quarrels) far more cost-effectively than before. It also appears to coincide with the West's preference for a permissive military environment which allows immaculate bombardment from altitude. This article takes a sceptical view of the impact of the RMA. It concludes that the first decade of the 21st century and beyond could see Western military power bloodily repulsed by a regional polity which had taken its asymmetrical warfare options seriously.

Implications of the Weinberger Doctrine for American Military Intervention in a Post-Desert Storm Age *by Cori E. Dauber*

This article argues that the Weinberger Doctrine is very much in play in the public debate over military intervention in the United States. It embeds a strong bias against humanitarian intervention – which led to a strange distortion of mission structure in the 1990s, as humanitarian missions were in a sense 'disguised' to look like Weinberger missions. In response, the Bush Administration may hold to the Weinberger line in a way that will lead to a form of isolationism in outcome if not intent.

Missing the Story: The Media and the Rwandan Genocide *by Linda Melvern*

The Rwandan genocide was conducted with extraordinarily little international response. This was enabled by an inaccurate portrayal of the killing as 'tribal violence' by the international press. The basic inference was that the killing represented uncontrollable tribal savagery about which nothing could be done – a portrayal which was not only wrong but which proved influential in permitting Western inaction to go unchallenged.

The Doctrine Gap: The Enduring Problem of Contemporary Peace Support Operations Thinking *by Dominick Donald*

Traditional peacekeeping thinking evolved out of operational experience. The past decade has, however, seen a fundamental shift in the nature and scope of peacekeeping operations. Peacekeeping doctrine was slow to embrace this new environment, and initially took some dangerous missteps. A degree of coherence has now arisen, but doctrine remains replete with difficulties. Importantly, whereas doctrine provides guidelines on the type of crises where troops should not be deployed, these are precisely the crises that political imperatives and public opinion will continue to require troops to go into. Until doctrine embraces this 'grey area' it will remain unsatisfactory.

Fighting for Freetown: British Military Intervention in Sierra Leone *by Paul Williams*

In order to evaluate the success of Britain's military intervention it is necessary to understand the political context in which the intervention took place. The first two sections of this article therefore analyse the factors fuelling Sierra Leone's conflict and Britain's role in the Lomé Accord of 7 July 1999 respectively. The third section then outlines the rationale behind Britain's intervention and discusses five imperatives that influenced the decision to deploy troops to West Africa. It concludes by arguing that, while external military intervention alone cannot resolve the country's problems, the British intervention represents a positive contribution to the process of reconstructing a viable and accountable polity.

The Role of Monitoring and Verification *by Trevor Findlay*

Monitoring and verification are playing increasingly important roles in the military aspects of peace operations. Despite this, the basic concepts behind them have remained the same. Monitoring missions start from scratch, they are assembled piece by piece using voluntary contributions and they rarely have sufficient human or financial resources to undertake their mission effectively and efficiently. They tend to be low-technology operations, reliant on the unarmed, often untrained, military observer for their effectiveness. This can no longer be acceptable in situations where the stakes in achieving a successful conflict resolution outcome are so high.

Bosnia and Kosovo: Interpreting the Gender Dimensions of International Intervention *by Jayne Rodgers*

This article suggests that there is a fundamental feminist dilemma at the heart of debates on the ethics of intervention. The concern lies in the difficulties of promoting a feminist agenda for acceptance by a male-dominated, masculinist and militaristic international community whilst also taking into account the unique local gender constructions that must be acknowledged in any decision on intervention. It is not sufficient to persuade organizations such as NATO and the UN, and powerful states such as the US and Russia, to recognize the gendered aspects of conflict, important though this is. The key question is reflected back to feminists: how can we promote feminist criteria on intervention to the *international* community while respecting the needs and cultural diversity of *local* communities? In the case of Kosovo, we need to ask how feminist calls for equality and non-discrimination can be reconciled with the extremely patriarchal construction of gender relations among Kosovar Albanians.

Notes on Contributors

Cori E. Dauber is a faculty member of the Department of Communication Studies at the University of North Carolina, Chapel Hill.

Dominick Donald served in the British Army and has worked as a leader writer for *The Times* and a Programme Officer at the Office of the Special Representative of the Secretary-General for Children and Armed Conflict at the United Nations. He is completing a PhD on Peace Support Operations Thinking at the Department of War Studies, King's College London.

Trevor Findlay is the Executive Director of the Verification Research, Training and Information Centre (VERTIC) in London.

Colin S. Gray is a Professor in the Department of Politics, University of Reading.

Colin McInnes is a Professor in the Department of International Politics, University of Wales, Aberystwyth.

Linda Melvern is a freelance journalist and the author of *A People Betrayed: The Role of the West in Rwanda's Genocide*.

Jayne Rodgers is a lecturer in the Institute of Communication Studies, University of Leeds.

Nicholas J. Wheeler is a Senior Lecturer in the Department of International Politics, University of Wales, Aberystwyth.

Paul Williams is a lecturer in the Department of Politics, University of Birmingham.

Index

Aideed, General, 18, 37, 61, 63
air power, 4, 7–8, 28ff, 58, 62, 177–80
Annan, Kofi, 4, 15, 16, 20, 22, 124, 152
asymmetric warfare, 40–1, 61, 62
Australia, 16–17, 127

Blair, Tony, 5–7, 10, 21, 58–9, 147, 153, 159
body bag problem see casualty aversion
Bosnia, 6, 17, 18, 23–4, 28, 33, 35, 42, 45, 48,
    73, 77, 78, 114–16, 120, 123–6, 129, 177,
    183, 185 see also Gorazde and Srebrenica
Boutros-Ghali, Boutros, 101
Brahimi Report, 19, 126
British Army, 109, 115–17, 127–9, 140, 153–4,
    156, 159, 163

Cambodia, 22–3, 92, 118, 173–4, 176
casualty aversion, 7–12, 19, 21, 25, 30, 33–4,
    39, 52, 61, 77ff, 163
civilian casualties see collateral damage
Clinton, William, 11–14, 73, 76, 78–80, 97,
    105, 150
CNN effect see media
coercion, 38, 41–3
Cook, Robin, 5–6, 10, 58–9, 60, 63, 140, 148,
    154–5, 157, 158, 161
collateral damage, 7, 30, 32–3, 36, 43–4, 47, 57
complex emergencies see humanitarian
    emergencies

Daillaire, General Roméo, 13–14, 16, 92, 96–7,
    100, 102, 104, 118
diamond trade, 144–6, 155

East Timor, 1, 5, 15–17, 127, 140, 173
ECOMOG, 23, 145, 147, 152–4, 157
ECOWAS, 145, 147, 152, 180
ethical foreign policy, 140–1, 158–60 see also
    Robin Cook, morality
Executive Outcomes, 145, 158

Falklands War, 31, 38, 39, 153
FM (Field Manual) 100-23, 115–17

genocide, 13–14, 91, 95–103, 161, 187
Gikondo massacre, 92–5
Gorazde, 103
Gulf War, 28, 30–3, 37, 43, 48, 56, 73, 85, 108,
    185

Hain, Peter, 144, 149, 151–2, 156, 161–2
Haiti, 3, 73
human rights, 5, 24–5, 142, 171, 183, 187
humanitarian emergencies, 3, 7, 21, 111
humanitarian intervention, 4, 6–8, 10, 12, 20,
    32, 34–5, 52, 62, 76–81, 84, 124, 140,
    148–9, 156–7, 162, 183, 185–7, 193

IFOR – see Bosnia
Indonesia, 1, 15–17
intelligence, 30, 36–7, 45, 47, 55, 178
international law, 24, 99–100, 189–91, 192–3
Iraq, 28, 177–80 see also Gulf War
Israel, 1, 110, 173

just war, 57
JWP (Joint Warfare Publication) 3-50, 120–3

Kabbah, President, 146–8, 150–4, 157–8
Keating, Colin, 98–9
KFOR see Kosovo
Kosovo, 3–4, 6–8, 11, 23–4, 29–40, 45–6, 48,
    56, 59, 73, 76–8, 85, 127, 173, 175, 183ff
Kosovo Liberation army (KLA), 4, 45, 127
Kosovo Verification Mission (KVM), 169

Liberia, 144, 145, 152, 180
Libya, 31, 33, 48, 145, 152
Lomé Accord, 20, 22, 141, 147–53, 159

Major, John, 97
media, 12–13, 15, 17, 75–9, 91ff, 174
mercenaries, 145, 158, 163 see also Executive
    Outcomes
Milosevic, Slobodan, 5, 28, 35, 45, 61, 85, 107
Mogadishu Line, 116, 121
morality, 52, 57–9, 63 see also ethical foreign
    policy

no-fly zones, 28, 35, 116
non-governmental organizations (NGOs), 112,
    193 see also Oxfam
North Atlantic Treaty Organization (NATO),
    3–4, 6, 8, 10, 19, 23–4, 29–31, 33–8, 46,
    58–9, 85, 126, 129, 175, 183, 186, 189

Organization for Security and Co-operation in
    Europe (OSCE), 169, 178
Owens, Admiral William, 53–4

Oxfam, 5, 98, 102–3

Pakistan, 1–3, 18
peace enforcement, 3, 18–19, 115ff, 120–2,
    125–6
peace support operations, 107–8, 111, 115ff,
    172–3
peacekeeping, 2, 13, 15, 17–20, 79, 92ff, 98,
    104, 107, 109ff, 116ff, 125–6, 151, 155,
    160–2, 172–3
Powell Doctrine, 10–11, 72–3 see also
    Weinberger Doctrine
precision guidance, 30, 32, 40, 45–7, 58 see also
    collateral damage

rape as a war crime see sexual violence
RUF see Sierra Leone
Russia, 2–4, 37, 184
Rwanda, 6, 12–16, 18–19, 78–80, 91ff, 118,
    124, 126, 161

Sankoh, Foday, 147–8, 157
Schelling, Thomas, 41, 58
Serbia, 8–9 see also Bosnia and Kosovo
sexual violence, 187–91
SFOR see Bosnia
Short, USAF Lt.-General Michael, 35–6, 46
Sierra Leone, 20–2, 60, 129, 140ff, 177
Somalia, 6, 8, 11, 17–18, 60, 77–9, 82, 89, 98,
    116, 121, 123, 125, 173, 176, 179
sovereignty, 3, 23–4
Soviet Union see Russia
Srebrenica, 18, 118–19, 126

Stewart, Lt.-Colonel Bob, 114–15
strategic air power, 29–30, 37, 43–4, 46–7
strategic bombing see strategic air power
Summers, Colonel Harry, 68ff, 85

Thailand, 22

UNAMSIL see Sierra Leone
UNITAF see Somalia
United Kingdom, 20–1, 52, 59, 60, 97, 100ff,
    124–5, 140ff see also Blair, Cook and Hain
United Nations, 1–4, 6, 13–16, 19–22, 25,
    92–3, 96ff, 109, 114, 117–19, 125–6, 149,
    152, 155, 160–3, 169, 172–81
United States, 1–2, 9–12, 14–16, 18, 21, 29,
    38–40, 43, 52–3, 59–60, 66ff, 125, 127–8,
    140, 149–50, 184–5 see also Clinton,
    Weinberger Doctrine
United States Army, 115–17, 127–8
UNOSOM see Somalia
UNPROFOR see Bosnia

Vietnam, 8, 9, 11, 21, 34, 58–60, 62, 66ff, 82,
    84–5

weapons of mass destruction (WMD), 62, 171
Weinberger Doctrine, 10–11, 66, 70ff
West Side Boys, 154
Wider Peacekeeping, 115–17

Yugoslavia, 4–5, 8, 10, 31, 59, 140, 152, 173,
    177

Books of Related Interest

International Security in a Global Age

Securing the Twenty-first Century

Clive Jones, *University of Leeds* and **Caroline Kennedy-Pipe**,
University of Sheffield (Eds)

> '... offers a very broad and thoughtful reading of the way in which some of the major
> contemporary players in the "security business" conceive of their roles, dangers and
> opportunities as well as some very useful discussions of certain themes that are widely
> perceived as central to the new frameworks.'
>
> **From the foreword by Nick Rengger**

This book contains a series of essays which centre upon the question of what is new, if anything, about the conflicts which have come to be seen as defining the character of the post-Cold War world.

These accounts of conflict cover both the role of key state actors, as well as international organisations, and the more diffuse threats associated with the environment, religious radicalism and the proliferation of weapons of mass destruction. In examining these issues, International Security in a Global Age highlights that the security dilemmas of the past, so often ignored in the era of globalisation, remain the security challenges of the future.

256 pages 2001
0 7146 5061 7 cloth
0 7146 8111 3 paper

FRANK CASS PUBLISHERS
Crown House, 47 Chase Side, Southgate, London N14 5BP
Tel: +44 (0)20 8920 2100 Fax: +44 (0)20 8447 8548 E-mail: info@frankcass.com
NORTH AMERICA
5824 NE Hassalo Street, Portland, OR 97213 3644, USA
Tel: 800 944 6190 Fax: 503 280 8832 E-mail: cass@isbs.com
Website: www.frankcass.com

US National Defense for the Twenty-First Century

And the Grand Exit Strategy

Edward Olsen

Most books about US foreign or defense policy fall within two broad categories: apologia for the status quo and constructive criticism designed to improve the status quo around the margins. A small minority takes the less travelled path – analysis, which is deliberately iconoclastic, dismantling geopolitical shibboleths. This is an intellectually proud – if often politically unpopular – tradition. This volume is of that ilk. Although it offers policy recommendations based on consistent non-interventionist strategic logic and its tone is consciously moderate, the points it makes are blunt and intended to rattle cages. Critics of American neo-isolationists (who can be on the left or right, sometimes leading to accusations of a McGovern–Buchanan coalition) often accuse the left of thinking the world would suffer by having US hegemonism imposed on it and accuse the right of thinking the United States does not deserve having the world's problems imposed on it. Those critics have a valid point, but there is room for both viewpoints within US non-interventionism and it can be the basis for a new consensus about US military disengagement.

128 pages 2002
0 7146 5098 6 cloth
0 7146 8140 7 paper

FRANK CASS PUBLISHERS
Crown House, 47 Chase Side, Southgate, London N14 5BP
Tel: +44 (0)20 8920 2100 Fax: +44 (0)20 8447 8548 E-mail: info@frankcass.com
NORTH AMERICA
5824 NE Hassalo Street, Portland, OR 97213 3644, USA
Tel: 800 944 6190 Fax: 503 280 8832 E-mail: cass@isbs.com
Website: www.frankcass.com

NATO Enters the 21st Century

Ted Galen Carpenter, *Cato Institute* (Ed)

NATO's military intervention in Yugoslavia highlights the choices and problems confronting the alliance as it enters the new century. An alliance created to keep Western Europe out of the Soviet orbit during the Cold War has sought to reinvent itself as a 'crisis-management' organisation to suppress conflicts on Europe's periphery – and perhaps beyond.

Is NATO suited to playing such a role, or is the alliance a Cold War anachronism? How will Russia react to an enlarged NATO focused on out-of-area peacekeeping and conflict-prevention missions? Are there alternative security institutions that might better address Europe's security needs in the post-Cold War era?

Alan Tonelson, Christopher Layne, Alton Frye, Kori Schake, Amos Perlmutter and Richard Rupp address these and other important issues.

200 pages 2000
0 7146 5058 7 cloth
0 7146 8109 1 paper
A special issue of the Journal of Strategic Studies

FRANK CASS PUBLISHERS
Crown House, 47 Chase Side, Southgate, London N14 5BP
Tel: +44 (0)20 8920 2100 Fax: +44 (0)20 8447 8548 E-mail: info@frankcass.com
NORTH AMERICA
5824 NE Hassalo Street, Portland, OR 97213 3644, USA
Tel: 800 944 6190 Fax: 503 280 8832 E-mail: cass@isbs.com
Website: www.frankcass.com

Explaining NATO Enlargement

Robert W Rauchhaus, *University of California at Berkeley* (Ed)

Advocates of NATO's enlargement believe this policy will have far-reaching positive consequences such as helping to consolidate democratic and market reforms in eastern and central Europe. In contrast, critics of the policy believe that NATO expansion will have far-reaching negative consequences. For example, they worry that enlargement will undermine Russia's willingness to co-operate with the West, and believe that new members will drag NATO into a region that is historically a tinderbox. NATO's decision to offer membership to three of its former Cold War adversaries – Poland, Hungary and the Czech Republic – raises important questions. What are the likely consequences of enlargement? Why did NATO decide to expand eastward? Which countries should be admitted in the future?

The contributors to this volume evaluate the pros and cons of NATO enlargement, explain why the alliance was expanded eastward, and make recommendations about which countries, if any, should be offered membership in the future.

232 pages 2001
0 7146 5127 3 cloth
0 7146 8153 9 paper
A special issue of the journal Contemporary Security Policy

FRANK CASS PUBLISHERS
Crown House, 47 Chase Side, Southgate, London N14 5BP
Tel: +44 (0)20 8920 2100 Fax: +44 (0)20 8447 8548 E-mail: info@frankcass.com
NORTH AMERICA
5824 NE Hassalo Street, Portland, OR 97213 3644, USA
Tel: 800 944 6190 Fax: 503 280 8832 E-mail: cass@isbs.com
Website: www.frankcass.com